COMMON CORE

ELA EXEMPLAR RESOURCE

Instruction with Performance Assessment

Grades 4–5

Printed in the U.S.A.

ISBN 978-0-544-02517-2

   8 9 10   0982   21 20 19 18 17 16 15 14 13

4500421206   A B C D E F G

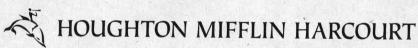

HOUGHTON MIFFLIN HARCOURT

Table of Contents

About the Common Core ELA Exemplar Resource

4–5 TEXT EXEMPLARS

Poetry

Informational Text

Student Selection Copy Masters

Academic Vocabulary

Performance Task Student Checklists and Rubric

Bibliography

Internet Resources

Overview

The *Common Core ELA Exemplar Resource* was developed to provide instruction for the Grades 4–5 text exemplars listed in Appendix B of the *Common Core State Standards for English Language Arts*.

Use this guide to complement the reading instruction of exemplars within your main reading program, or use it separately to provide students with questions and activities that deepen their comprehension of text exemplars selected for independent reading or group discussion.

Text Exemplars

The list of text exemplars provided in Appendix B of the *Common Core State Standards for English Language Arts* was compiled based on the texts' quantitative and qualitative complexity, quality, and range.

The text exemplars are presented in bands of two grade levels each (K–1, 2–3, and 4–5) and are meant to suggest "the breadth of texts that students should encounter in the text types required by the Standards." The works listed were never intended to serve as a partial or complete reading list but rather as a guide to the types of reading materials that will help students successfully meet the Standards.

Organization of This Guide

This guide is organized into three parts.

CONTENTS WITH SUGGESTED PACING
The table of contents lists all the exemplars in the order given in Appendix B, along with the page references for where to find each exemplar in this resource. You will need to select and obtain the texts separately. This section also includes suggested pacing for reading each exemplar and teaching its lesson.

EXEMPLAR LESSONS Most lessons for stories and informational texts are four pages, while most lessons for poetry are two pages. See **Lesson Setup** on p. vii for more information.

ENDMATTER RESOURCES

- **Copying Masters** In the back of this guide, you will find copying masters for several public-domain text exemplars, provided for your convenience.

- **Student Performance Checklists** These checklists will help students assess their writing and speaking and listening.

- **Academic Vocabulary** This compilation lists all the academic vocabulary, or Tier 2 words, introduced and defined in each lesson.

- **Bibliography and Exemplar Websites** These sections include the bibliographic information for each exemplar included in this guide, as well as a list of useful websites that offer additional information for teaching the exemplars and implementing the Standards.

Lesson Setup

Here is the basic setup of a four-page lesson.

PAGE 1 The first part of each lesson provides background information about the text and guidance for introducing the lesson to the class. The following features are included:

- Objectives
- Suggested Instructional Segments
- Options for Reading
- Summary
- About the Author
- Discuss Genre and Set Purpose
- Text Complexity Rubric
- Common Core State Standards met

PAGES 2–4 Each lesson includes two sets of questions that correspond to a "First Read" and a "Second Read" of the text.

- **First-Read Questions** Use these questions during and after an initial reading of the text to help students think through the text and learn to cite text evidence in their responses.

- **Second-Read Questions** Use these questions to guide students through a deeper analysis of the text. These questions give students opportunities for close reading and ask them to make deeper connections between ideas. Here, too, students must cite text evidence to support their ideas.

PERFORMANCE TASK Each lesson culminates in a performance task in which students are asked to demonstrate understanding of the exemplar text. Within each task, students are expected to complete a short writing assignment as well as engage in a speaking and listening activity. Where applicable, the performance task matches the performance-task suggestion provided in Appendix B.

Additional Lesson Features

TEXT COMPLEXITY RUBRIC To help you assess text complexity at a glance, a rubric is provided in every lesson. It identifies the overall complexity as Accessible, Complex, or More Complex. The rubric also includes quantitative measures for the Lexile and the Guided Reading Level and shows qualitative measures on a four-point continuum with text-specific rationales.

DOMAIN SPECIFIC VOCABULARY These content-area, Tier 3 words are included only for texts with heavy discipline-specific content. Students are likely to use these words only within a specific discipline, such as *life cycle* in science.

INDEPENDENT/SELF-SELECTED READING This feature, included on the last page of every lesson, suggests two on-level developmentally and age appropriate books students might use for independent reading and additional application of the Standards addressed in the lesson.

RESPOND TO SEGMENT—Classroom Collaboration These activities are aimed to help students wrap-up each segment of text. Students summarize what they've already learned and address any questions they have before moving on.

Tips for Getting Started

- **Review the list of text exemplars for your grade span.** The exemplars include a variety of classic and contemporary complex texts. Many of the texts will likely relate to cross-curricular topics already present in your current curriculum and can be used as supplementary material to further discuss a given topic.

- **Consider the needs and the reading levels of the students in your classroom.** Each list of exemplars covers a two-grade span, so some titles may not be at the right level for your class at a given point in the year. Use the text complexity rubric to help you select the exemplars that best suit your students' reading or listening comprehension abilities throughout the school year.

- **Work with your school librarian.** Your librarian can help you find copies of the exemplar texts, online magazine articles, and any poems and stories that are in the public domain.

- **Preview the exemplars.** As you prepare for a lesson, make notes to help you consider additional connections that students can make to the text and how you might best prepare them for reading and discussion.

Literature Discussion Groups

The *Common Core ELA Exemplar Instructional Resource* can be effectively implemented with literature discussion groups. You can support students in collaborative discussion to further explore the text exemplars in ways that can foster higher-level thinking and the use of comprehension strategies, vocabulary acquisition, and speaking and listening skills—all essential for meeting the Common Core State Standards for English Language Arts. Use the following tips.

Before Reading

Divide students into small, mixed-proficiency groups, and schedule a time for the groups to meet each day. Assign roles to students, or allow them to choose their own. Possible roles include the following:

- **Discussion Director** moderates the discussion by asking questions provided by the teacher or by creating original questions to pose to the group.

- **Passage Finder** chooses passages that are particularly interesting, revealing, or challenging for the group to focus on.

- **Vocabulary Detective** identifies and records unknown words for the group to look up and discuss.

- **Connector** makes connections between the text and other texts and aspects of real-life, either in general terms or in relation to the students' experiences.

- **Summarizer** summarizes the segment of text read by the group or the teacher prior to the group's discussion and describes major characters, settings, and events or main ideas and details.

Discuss Genre and Set Purpose As groups begin to discuss the text, encourage them to

- identify elements of the text's genre and name other texts in that genre.

- consider the author's purpose in writing.

- review their purpose for reading.

First Read

Have groups read a segment of the text.

- Ask students to take notes or flag sections of the text to later discuss and cite as text evidence.

- Have each group's Summarizer offer a summary of what was read. Others can add missing information as needed.

- Provide Discussion Directors with questions from the lesson, or have them make up their own questions.

- Guide students to use the context of the text to understand academic vocabulary.

- Monitor discussions to ensure groups stay focused and cite text evidence to support responses.

Second Read

Have each group reread portions of the text to further analyze ideas and concepts.

- Guide groups to connect a segment to previous segments. Ensure they understand how the segments and ideas build throughout the text.

- Help groups focus on figurative language and literary elements, such as theme.

- Have groups support their responses with evidence from the text.

- Wrap up the discussion by having students summarize what they've learned.

OBJECTIVES

- Identify how illustrations reflect descriptions in the text
- Identify figurative language
- Identify problem and solution
- Analyze text using text evidence

Alice's Adventures in Wonderland is broken into three instructional segments.

SEGMENTS

Options for Reading

Independent Students read the story independently or with a partner and then answer questions posed by the teacher.

Supported Students read a segment and answer questions with teacher support.

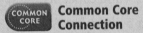 **Common Core Connection**

RL.4.1 refer to details and examples when explaining what the text says explicitly and when drawing inferences; **RL.4.3** describe a character, setting or event, drawing on details; **RL.4.4** determine the meaning of words and phrases, including those that allude to characters in mythology; **RL.4.7** make connections between the text and a visual or oral presentation of it

RL.5.4 determine the meaning of words and phrases, including figurative language; **RL.5.7** analyze how visual and multimedia elements contribute to the meaning, tone, or beauty of a text; **RL.5.10** read and comprehend literature

Alice's Adventures in Wonderland

by Lewis Carroll

SUMMARY When Alice falls down a rabbit hole, she enters a fantastic world full of bizarre characters and creatures. During her adventures in Wonderland, she encounters numerous unusual characters and unique settings. She returns to her real life when she awakens under a tree.

ABOUT THE AUTHOR Lewis Carroll was the pen name for Charles Lutwidge Dodgson, who was born in England in 1832. Carroll experimented with word play and fantasy in his most famous works, *Alice's Adventures in Wonderland* and *Through the Looking-Glass*. By the time Carroll died in 1898, *Alice's Adventures in Wonderland* had become the most popular children's book in England.

Discuss Genre and Set Purpose

FANTASY Have students look at the book and its illustrations and guide them to recognize elements of fantasy, such as unusual characters and settings.

SET PURPOSE Help students set a purpose for reading, such as to discover the adventures Alice goes on in Wonderland.

▲ TEXT COMPLEXITY RUBRIC		*Alice's Adventures in Wonderland* FANTASY
Overall Text Complexity		COMPLEX
Quantitative Measures	Lexile	860L
	Guided Reading Level	V
Qualitative Measures	Text Structure	complex, unfamiliar story concepts
	Language Conventionality and Clarity	increased academic language
	Knowledge Demands	distinctly unfamiliar experience
	Purpose/Levels of Meaning	multiple levels of meaning

Academic Vocabulary

Read each word with students and discuss its meaning.

ignorant (p. 5) • without knowledge; not aware

hoarse (p. 20) • harsh or rough in sound

quiver (p. 25) • shake

pity (p. 38) • shame or misfortune

executed (p. 41) • put to death

coaxing (p. 54) • persuasive

FIRST READ **Think Through the Text**

Have students use text evidence and draw inferences to answer questions.

pp. 1–14 • *How does the illustration on page 1 relate to the events in Chapter 1?* It shows the white rabbit that Alice follows down into the hole. *How do other illustrations in Chapter 1 help the reader visualize events in the story?* Sample answer: *The illustration on page 8 shows Alice finding the little door behind the curtain.* **RL.4.7, RL.5.7**

pp. 15–28 • *Where did the water come from that Alice swims in?* It is from her tears. **RL.4.1, RL.5.10**

pp. 29–58 • *What happens to Alice at the White Rabbit's house?* She gets stuck in the White Rabbit's house because she is too big. *How does Alice solve this problem?* Pebbles are thrown at her. The pebbles turn into cakes. Alice eats a cake and gets small enough to escape. **RI.4.3**

SECOND READ **Analyze the Text**

- *What is Alice's problem after she drinks from the bottle that says DRINK ME? How does she try to solve it?* She becomes small and can't reach the key on top of the table. Then she eats a whole cake that says EAT ME but becomes too big. **RI.4.3**

- Reread pages 30–33 with students. Ask: *How are humor and word play used to describe how the Mouse tries to dry the others?* The Mouse tries to dry the others by telling them a dry story. The author uses two different meanings for dry as humor. **RL.4.4, RL.5.4**

- *What do you think will happen if Alice eats the mushroom she finds at the end of Chapter 4?* Sample answer: *She will get bigger or smaller if she eats it because that's what happens every time she eats or drinks something.* **RL.4.1, RL.5.10**

 ENGLISH LANGUAGE LEARNERS

Use Paraphrasing and Visuals

Ask students yes/no questions about events shown in the illustrations. For example, have them look at the illustrations on pp. 8–9. Ask: *Does Alice get small?* yes *Is she able to follow the White Rabbit?* no *Does the door close?* yes *Is the key still on the table?* yes Then guide students to complete sentence frames such as the following: *Alice watches the white rabbit and then grows _____.* smaller *She cries because _____.* she cannot reach the key that is on the table.

RESPOND TO SEGMENT 1

 Classroom Collaboration

Have partners work together to discuss the events in the first segment. Encourage them to ask questions about things they still don't understand.

ENGLISH LANGUAGE LEARNERS

Use Paraphrasing and Visuals

Ask students to look at the illustrations in this segment. Gauge their comprehension of the details with yes/no questions. Then have students give oral sentences about the illustrations.

RESPOND TO SEGMENT 2

 Classroom Collaboration

Have small groups work together to summarize the events of segment two. Have them ask questions about what they don't understand.

 COMMON CORE **Common Core Connection**

RL.4.1 refer to details and examples when explaining what the text says explicitly and when drawing inferences; **RL.4.3** describe a character, setting or event, drawing on details; **RL.4.7** make connections between the text and a visual or oral presentation of it; **RL.4.10** read and comprehend literature; **W.4.5** develop and strengthen writing by planning, revising, and editing; **W.4.9** draw evidence from literary or informational texts to support analysis, reflection, and research; **SL.4.4** report on a topic or text, tell a story, or recount an experience/speak clearly at an understandable pace

RL.5.1 quote accurately when explaining what the text says explicitly and when drawing inferences; **RL.5.7** analyze how visual and multimedia elements contribute to the meaning, tone, or beauty of a text; **RL.5.10** read and comprehend literature; **W.5.5** develop and strengthen writing by planning, revising, editing, rewriting, or trying a new approach; **W.5.9** draw evidence from literary or informational texts to support analysis, reflection, and research; **SL.5.4** report on a topic or text, tell a story, or recount an experience/ speak clearly at an understandable pace

Academic Vocabulary

Read each word with students and discuss its meaning.

languid (p. 59) • having little or no energy

melancholy (p. 62) • sad; depressed

livery (p. 76) • a uniform

indignantly (p. 96) • angrily

treacle (p. 106) • a sugary syrup

impertinent (p. 125) • disrespectful; impolite

FIRST READ # Think Through the Text

Have students use text evidence and draw inferences to answer questions.

pp. 76–94 • *What upsets Alice most about the actions of the creatures she has met? It upsets her that they all argue so much. On page 80, she says, "'It's really dreadful the way all the creatures argue. It's enough to drive one crazy!'"* **RL.4.1, RL.5.1**

pp. 96–97 • *How does the illustration on page 97 reflect the description in the text? It shows Alice sitting in a large armchair at a table, which is described in the text.* **RL.4.7, RL.5.7**

pp. 112–129 • *How do the subjects feel about the Queen? They are all afraid of her because she threatens to have everyone's head cut off.* **RL.4.1, RL.5.1**

SECOND READ # Analyze the Text

- Discuss with students that personification is a form of figurative language that gives human traits to inanimate objects. Ask: *How does the author use personification in Chapter 7?* Sample answer: *The Hatter tells Alice that Time is a "him," not an "it."* **RL.4.4, RL.5.4**

- Have students look back on 112–119. *How does the illustration on page 113 add to the description of the characters and setting? The text doesn't say that the gardeners are cards. The illustration helps the reader realize what the gardeners are. It also shows that they are painting the roses on the Queen's rose-tree.* **RL.4.7, RL.5.7**

- Review pages 124–128. Ask: *How does the illustration on page 128 help the reader understand the plot events? It shows what the Cheshire Cat looks like and why the characters are arguing about whether or not its head can be cut off.* **RL.4.7, RL.5.7**

Academic Vocabulary

Read each word with students and discuss its meaning.

hastily (p. 148) • quickly

blacking (p. 154) • black shoe polish

spectacles (p. 164) • eyeglasses

diligently (p. 178) • with care and effort

FIRST READ ## Think Through the Text

Have students use text evidence and draw inferences to answer questions.

p. 138 • *How does the text rely on the illustration?* The text says, "If you don't know what a Gryphon is, look at the picture." ◾ **RL.4.1, RL.5.1**

pp. 142–145 • *How are humor and word play used?* The Mock Turtle says that he and the Gryphon called their school master, who was a Turtle, Tortoise. The Mock Turtle says, "We called him Tortoise because he taught us." Lessons got their name because they lessen from day to day. ◾ **RL.4.4, RL.5.4**

p. 177 • *What does the illustration show?* It shows how big Alice grew and how big she is compared to the others. ◾ **RL.4.7, RL.5.7**

SECOND READ ## Analyze the Text

- *How does the illustration on page 141 relate to the book's genre—fantasy?* It shows the Mock Turtle, which is not real. It helps the reader picture the Mock Turtle. ◾ **RL.4.7, RL.5.7**

- Have students reread pages 162–187. Ask: *Why is the Knave of Hearts on trial at court?* The Knave of Hearts is accused of stealing tarts. *How does the trial end?* The King asks for a verdict based on White Rabbit's nonsensical poem. There is no verdict, but the tarts are found on the table. The King says, "Nothing can be clearer than that." ◾ **RL.4.1, RL.5.1**

- *At the end of the story, Alice grows back to her normal size. What does that symbolize?* Alice is growing up. *What does she realize about Wonderland?* She realizes that Wonderland was just a dream full of nonsense and fantasy. ◾ **RL.4.3, RL.5.3**

Independent/Self-Selected Reading

Have students reread *Alice's Adventures in Wonderland* independently to practice analyzing the text on their own, or have them practice the skills using another story. Suggested titles:

- *Charlie and the Chocolate Factory* by Roald Dahl

- *Through the Looking-Glass* by Lewis Carroll ◾ **RL.4.10, RL.5.10**

WRITE & PRESENT

1. Have small groups discuss how the illustrations reflect specific descriptions of Alice in the text. ◾ **RL.4.7, RL.5.7**

2. Have individual students write paragraphs telling how the illustrations connect to descriptions in the text and helped them better understand the characters and settings in the book. ◾ **W.4.9, W.5.9**

3. Have students share their paragraphs in small groups, and work together to edit and revise their writing. ◾ **W.4.5, W.5.5**

4. Encourage individual students to present their final paragraphs to classmates. ◾ **SL.4.4, SL.5.4**

5. Have individual students turn in their final drafts to the teacher.

See Copying Masters, pp. 144–147.

STUDENT CHECKLIST

Writing

- ✔ Write about illustrations.

- ✔ Make connections between illustrations and text.

- ✔ Use correct language conventions.

Speaking & Listening

- ✔ Engage effectively in collaborative conversations.

- ✔ Respond appropriately to questions and comments.

- ✔ Make comments that contribute positively to a discussion.

OBJECTIVES

- Describe characters and settings
- Make inferences based on text evidence
- Interpret information presented visually
- Analyze text using text evidence

The Secret Garden is broken into three instructional segments.

SEGMENTS

Options for Reading

Independent Students read the story independently or with a partner and then answer questions posed by the teacher.

Supported Students read a segment and answer questions with teacher support.

COMMON CORE **Common Core Connection**

RL.4.1 refer to details and examples when explaining what the text says explicitly and when drawing inferences; **RL.4.3** describe a character, setting, or event, drawing on details; **RL.4.7** make connections between the text and a visual or oral presentation of it

RL.5.1 quote accurately when explaining what the text says explicitly and when drawing inferences; **RL.5.3** compare and contrast characters, settings, or events, drawing on details; **RL.5.7** analyze how visual and multimedia elements contribute to the meaning, tone, or beauty of a text

The Secret Garden
by Frances Hodgson Burnett

SUMMARY Orphaned Mary Lennox is sent to live in the English manor of her uncle. Spoiled and sickly, Mary meets people there who help her to become kinder and stronger. As Mary discovers the garden and develops a compassion for those around her, she transforms into a loving young woman.

ABOUT THE AUTHOR Frances Hodgson Burnett was born in England but lived most of her life in America. She began publishing short pieces in American magazines to support her family after her mother died. Frances Hodgson Burnett wrote more than 40 books and became a well-known children's author.

Discuss Genre and Set Purpose

FICTION Have students briefly page through the book to examine the text, sketches, and colorful illustrations. Discuss with students how they can tell that this book is fiction.

SET PURPOSE Help students set a purpose for reading, such as to find out how Mary changes after she discovers the secret garden.

▲ TEXT COMPLEXITY RUBRIC

Overall Text Complexity		*The Secret Garden* FICTION MORE COMPLEX
Quantitative Measures	Lexile	970L
	Guided Reading Level	U
Qualitative Measures	Text Structure	somewhat complex story structure elements
	Language Conventionality and Clarity	figurative, less accessible language
	Knowledge Demands	somewhat unfamiliar situation
	Purpose/Levels of Meaning	multiple levels of complex meaning

Academic Vocabulary

Read each word with students and discuss its meaning.

tyrannical (p. 4) • harsh and demanding

contrary (p. 10) • stubborn

fantastically (p. 26) • elegantly; wonderfully

languid (p. 72) • lacking strength or energy

smothering (p. 86) • covering; preventing from living

Domain Specific Vocabulary

cholera (p. 6) • a deadly disease that spreads quickly

moor (p. 20) • an area of land that is open and wet

flower-bed (p. 68) • an area where flowers grow

FIRST READ ## Think Through the Text

Have students use text evidence and draw inferences to answer questions.

pp. 3–5 • *What text details show that Mary is sickly and spoiled?* Mary had always been ill. She stayed indoors with no fresh air. She ordered the servants around. She has a bad temper. RL.4.1, RL.5.1

pp. 6–9 • *Why is Mary alone in her father's bungalow?* Her parents and many servants died from cholera. Other servants left. RL.4.3

pp. 26–35 • *Compare and contrast Martha and Ayah.* Martha and Ayah both work for wealthy people. Ayah did everything for Mary, including dress her. Martha works at the manor; she wants Mary to do more on her own. Martha is not afraid to scold Mary. RL.4.3, RL.5.3

pp. 74–77 • *Use adjectives to describe Martha's mother.* kind, thoughtful, generous, sensible *What does Martha's mother do for Mary?* Martha's mother buys Mary a skipping-rope so Mary can exercise and get stronger. RL.4.1

SECOND READ ## Analyze the Text

- Have students reread page 42. Ask: *Why does Ben think that he and Mary are alike?* Ben thinks they are both unattractive, have unpleasant personalities, and nasty tempers. Neither has friends. RL.4.3, RL.5.3

- Review pages 82–86 with students. Ask: *What is Mary's plan for the secret garden? How does she carry out her plan?* Mary wants the garden to come alive again. She digs and weeds. *What impact does the garden have on Mary?* The plants make her smile, and the exercise makes her hungry. She gets red cheeks and bright eyes outdoors.
 RL.4.3, RL.5.3

- Have students look back on pages 101–104. Ask: *How does the illustration provide additional information about Dickon, who is described in the text?* Sample answer: Rabbits, a squirrel, and a pheasant are listening closely to Dickon. He has garden tools and a packet of seeds for Mary. His simple outfit differs from Mary's fancy outfit.
 RL.4.7, RL.5.7

ELL ## ENGLISH LANGUAGE LEARNERS

Use Illustrations and Simple Sentences

Have students use the sketches that appear at the beginning of each chapter to describe the characters orally. Then have them state simple sentences about each sketch. For example: *Mary rides on a train. The robin finds a key. Martha cleans. Dickon smiles.* Provide sentence frames for students who need additional support.

RESPOND TO SEGMENT 1

Classroom Collaboration

Have small groups summarize this segment of the story. Tell them to ask questions about anything they don't understand.

Domain Specific Vocabulary

wrapper (p. 132) • a robe worn over a nightgown

footstool (p. 134) • a low bench or seat

 ENGLISH LANGUAGE LEARNERS

Use Illustrations and Gestures

Read aloud the text on pages 164–165 and display the illustration that appears on page 167. Use the illustrations and gestures to show Mary's behavior when she sees the spring flowers. Have students complete sentence frames: *Mary ___ the flowers. She is _____.* *kisses; happy*

RESPOND TO SEGMENT 2

 Classroom Collaboration

Have small groups work together to summarize the story segment. Have students raise questions about what is unclear.

 Common Core Connection

RL.4.10 read and comprehend literature; **W.4.2** write informative/explanatory texts to examine a topic and convey ideas and information clearly; **W.4.5** develop and strengthen writing by planning, revising, and editing; **SL.4.4** report on a topic or text, tell a story, or recount an experience/speak clearly at an understandable pace

RL.5.10 read and comprehend literature; **W.5.2** write informative/explanatory texts to examine a topic and convey ideas and information clearly; **W.5.5** develop and strengthen writing by planning, revising, editing, rewriting, or trying a new approach; **SL.5.4** report on a topic or text, tell a story, or recount an experience/speak clearly at an understandable pace

Academic Vocabulary

Read each word with students and discuss its meaning.

crooked (p. 122) • not straight; bent

inquiringly (p. 171) • curiously

ferociously (p. 177) • harshly; fiercely

indignantly (p. 198) • angrily

shrewd (p. 204) • good at making decisions

FIRST READ Think Through the Text

Have students use text evidence and draw inferences to answer questions.

pp. 122–127 • *What is Mary's reaction after meeting her uncle for the first time? What details does the author provide?* Mary thinks her uncle has a miserable face and looks as if he does not know what in the world to do with her. Mary is happy that her uncle gives her freedom and her own garden. ▬ RL.4.1, RL.5.1

pp. 132–136 • *Describe Colin and his strange situation.* He is Mary's cousin. He stays in his room because others say he may be a hunchback like his father and will die young. ▬ RL.4.1, RL.5.1

pp. 183–187 • *How does Mary change Colin's temper?* She fiercely tells Colin that most of his fears of death and of illness are created by himself. *What does Mary say will help Colin live longer?* learning to control his temper and getting fresh air ▬ RL.4.1

SECOND READ Analyze the Text

- Have students reread page 125. Ask: *How does Mr. Craven feel when Mary asks for a bit of earth?* At first, he is surprised; then he is touched and pleased. *What text evidence supports this inference?* Mr. Craven's eyes looked soft and kind. He tells Mary that she can have as much earth as she wants. ▬ RL.4.1, RL.5.1

- Review pages 138–139 with students. *Why does Mary want Colin to keep the garden a secret?* Mary thinks Dickon wouldn't come back if people came to the garden. She says that it will never be a secret again. ▬ RL.4.1, RL.5.1

- Guide students to look back at pages 162–167. Ask: *How has the garden changed from winter to spring?* Sample answer: *Plants and flowers are growing, and buds cover branches. Birds are building nests. How has Mary changed?* Mary notices all that is happening outdoors. She kisses flowers and sniffs the earth. ▬ RL.4.7, RL.5.7

Academic Vocabulary

Read each word with students and discuss its meaning.

cautious (p. 230) • careful to avoid danger

gnarled (p. 233) • rough, twisted

persevered (p. 240) • continued doing something even when it was difficult

concealed (p. 249) • hidden

triumphant (p. 256) • having achieved a great success

peering (p. 260) • looking closely

FIRST READ # Think Through the Text

Have students use text evidence and draw inferences to answer questions.

pp. 221–223 • *What effect does entering into the secret garden have on Colin? It makes Colin believe that he will get well.* RL.4.1

pp. 233–235 • *What causes Colin to stand upright for the first time? Ben Weatherstaff says Colin is a "poor cripple." Colin wants to prove Ben wrong, so he forces himself to stand.* RL.4.3, RL.5.1

pp. 260–261 • *Why does Colin pretend to still be ill? He doesn't want anyone to know he is not ill before he can surprise his father.*
RL.4.3, RL.5.3

SECOND READ # Analyze the Text

• Guide students to look back at page 282. Ask: *What does Colin say to show that he believes that thinking good thoughts along with doing something to change will help him get strong and well? He says that the Magic works best when you yourself do work* RL.4.1, RL.5.1

• Have students reread pages 294–298. Ask: *What healing effects does the outdoors have on Mary, Colin, and Mr. Craven?* Sample answer: *Mary and Colin replace disagreeable thoughts with thoughts of the garden's animals and plants. Their work in the garden helps them heal from a lonely childhood. The time Mr. Craven spends outdoors helps him heal from the loss of his wife.* RL.4.3, RL.5.3

Independent/Self-Selected Reading

Have students reread *The Secret Garden* independently to practice analyzing the text on their own, or have them practice the skills using another book. Suggested titles:

• *A Little Princess* by Frances Hodgson Burnett

• *Anne of Green Gables* by L. M. Montgomery RL.4.10, RL.5.10

WRITE & PRESENT

1. Guide partners to discuss the selfish behavior of Mary. Have students also discuss the impact of the cholera outbreak in India.
   RL.4.3, RL.5.3

2. Have individual students write to explain how Mary's behavior impacts a major story event. Encourage them to use text details to make inferences.
   W.4.2, W.5.2

3. Have small groups share their explanations. Have students edit and revise their writing.
   W.4.5, W.5.5

4. Have individual students present their writing to classmates.
   SL.4.4, SL.5.4

5. Have individual students turn in their final drafts to the teacher.

See Copying Masters, pp. 144–147.

STUDENT CHECKLIST

Writing

☑ Write in complete sentences.

☑ Write an explanation including inferences based on text details.

☑ Use correct language conventions.

Speaking & Listening

☑ Engage effectively in collaborative discussion.

☑ Logically connect details in the text to a character's behavior and the impact of the behavior.

☑ Analyze details that demonstrate the impact of a character's behavior on a story event.

OBJECTIVES

- Discuss the narrator's point of view and its influence on story events and the reader
- Compare and contrast characters
- Identify themes
- Analyze text using text evidence

The Black Stallion is broken into three instructional segments.

SEGMENTS

Options for Reading

Independent Students read the book independently or with a partner and then answer questions posed by the teacher.

Supported Students read a segment and answer questions with teacher support.

 Common Core Connection

RL.4.1 refer to details and examples when explaining what the text says explicitly and when drawing inferences; **RL.4.2** determine theme from details/summarize; **RL.4.3** describe a character, setting, or event, drawing on details

RL.5.1 quote accurately when explaining what the text says explicitly and when drawing inferences; **RL.5.2** determine theme from details/summarize; **RL.5.3** compare and contrast characters, settings, or events, drawing on details; **RL.5.6** describe how a narrator's or speaker's point of view influences how events are described

The Black Stallion
by Walter Farley

SUMMARY This story tells about the friendship between a wild stallion and a boy, Alec Ramsay, who together survive a shipwreck and many days stranded on a deserted island. Once home, Alex and a local horse trainer work with the Black Stallion to prove that he truly is the fastest of all horses. The stallion rewards Alex's love and loyalty by making the boy's fondest dreams come true.

ABOUT THE AUTHOR Walter Farley began writing *The Black Stallion* in high school having learned about horses from his uncle. The response of readers led him to write over 30 books about horses, some of which were made into films. His son continued the series after Walter died.

Discuss Genre and Set Purpose

FICTION Have students look at the title and table of contents and identify elements of fiction such as characters, setting, and events.

SET PURPOSE Have students set a purpose for reading, such as to find out about the main character in the book and his relationship to the Black Stallion.

TEXT COMPLEXITY RUBRIC

Overall Text Complexity		*The Black Stallion* FICTION
		COMPLEX
Quantitative Measures	Lexile	680L
	Guided Reading Level	T
Qualitative Measures	Text Structure	somewhat complex story concepts
	Language Conventionality and Clarity	less straightforward sentence structure
	Knowledge Demands	distinctly unfamiliar experience
	Purpose/Levels of Meaning	multiple levels of meaning

Academic Vocabulary

Read each word with students and discuss its meaning.

surveyed (p. 4) • looked at

inert (p. 7) • still, not moving

crest (p. 17) • top of

incredulous (p. 35) • unable to believe

query (p. 41) • question

Domain Specific Vocabulary

gangplank (p. 5) • a ramp that people walk over to get onto and off of a ship

---

FIRST READ ▶ ## Think Through the Text

Have students use text evidence and draw inferences to answer questions.

p. 4 • *What is the first hint the author gives that Alec loves horses?* He says that Uncle Ralph had taught him how to ride—the one thing in the world he had always wanted to do. RL.4.1, RL.5.1

p. 31 • *How do you know from the text that the Black is a fast horse?* It says on page 31, after Alec rides him for the first time, that he never dreamed a horse could run so fast. RL.4.1, RL.5.1

pp. 51–53 • *How do you know from the Black's behavior that he behaves differently with Alec than with others?* He is wild around other people and horses, but after the fight with the chestnut, Alec is able to calm him down. RL.4.3, RL.5.3

SECOND READ ## Analyze the Text

- *Describe how Alec acts and feels when he starts his voyage.* He isn't looking forward to the trip. He says it is going to be a long trip. He is bored. *How does he feel after the Black gets on board? Why?* He is excited because he is interested in the horse. RL.4.3, RL.5.3

- Ask: *What does the narrator think about Alec's behavior during the storm and on the island?* Sample answer: The narrator sees Alec as sensible, brave, and kind. *What examples from the text support your ideas?* Sample answer: He survives a shipwreck, remembers to use his pocketknife to cut himself free of the rope, finds food and shelter on the island, and cares for the horse. RL.5.6

- Ask: *What do you think is a major theme of this segment?* Sample answer: survival *What examples from the text support your ideas?* Sample answer: Alec survives the storm and then survives living on the island. RL.4.2, RL.5.2

ELL ENGLISH LANGUAGE LEARNERS

Use Gestures

Guide students in acting out parts of the story to help them understand key events. For instance, a small group can pretend to be trying to control a horse or to be Alec when he visits the Black at his stall on the ship. Encourage them to use words and phrases to tell what they are acting out, if possible.

RESPOND TO SEGMENT 1

Classroom Collaboration

Have partners work together to create and present a summary, as well as raise questions that might be answered in the next segment.

Domain Specific Vocabulary

paddock (p. 179) • a fenced area where horses eat or exercise

post (p. 181) • starting point of a horse race

 ENGLISH LANGUAGE LEARNERS

Use Comprehensible Input

Help students identify Alec's qualities by asking yes/no questions, such as: *Is he lazy? Is he a good friend?* Then ask students to suggest words to describe Alec.

RESPOND TO SEGMENT 2

 Classroom Collaboration

Have groups summarize what they have learned and ask questions about what they don't understand.

 Common Core Connection

RL.4.3 describe a character, setting, or event, drawing on details; **RL.4.10** read and comprehend literature; **W.4.2** write informative/explanatory texts to examine a topic and convey ideas and information clearly; **W.4.5** develop and strengthen writing by revising and editing; **SL.4.4** report on a topic or text, tell a story, or recount an experience/speak clearly at an understandable pace

RL.5.5 explain how chapters, scenes, or stanzas fit together to provide the overall structure; **RL.5.6** describe how a narrator's or speaker's point of view influences how events are described; **RL.5.10** read and comprehend literature; **W.5.2** write informative/explanatory texts to examine a topic and convey ideas and information clearly; **W.5.5** develop and strengthen writing by planning, revising, editing, rewriting, or trying a new approach; **SL.5.4** report on a topic or text, tell a story, or recount an experience/speak clearly at an understandable pace

Academic Vocabulary

Read each word with students and discuss its meaning.

lurched (p. 92) • jerked forward

tutelage (p. 107) • instruction

contrary (p. 116) • being disagreeable

jarred (p. 118) • shaken

clamored (p. 133) • made a loud noise

FIRST READ ▶ ## Think Through the Text

Have students use text evidence and draw inferences to answer questions.

p. 72 • *How do you know from the text that Henry knows about horses?* *When he sees the Black for the first time, he says that the Black has a good head, wide chest, and strong legs.* ▬ **RL.4.1, RL.5.1**

p. 83 • *How do you know from the text that the Black and Napolean are very different?* *It says on page 83 that it seemed child's play to handle the gentle old gray horse after the spirited stallion.* ▬ **RL.4.3, RL.5.3**

p. 125 • *How do you know that Jake agrees with Henry about the Black?* *Jake says that Henry was right about the Black and he calls the Black "a real horse."* ▬ **RL.4.3, RL.5.3**

SECOND READ ## Analyze the Text

• Discuss with students how the narrator's point of view influences the way events are described. Ask: *What does the narrator think about horses and horse racing?* *He thinks horses are beautiful and that horse racing is fun and exciting.* ***How do you know?*** *He describes the Black as savage and beautiful, and all of the characters in the book like horses or are involved in horse racing.* ***How does this influence the way the narrator describes events?*** *He thinks the events are exciting so he describes them that way.* ▬ **RL.4.3, RL.5.6**

• Guide students in a discussion about the relationship between Alec and Henry. Ask: *What have you learned about Henry that helps you to understand why he is working with Alec?* *Henry is a former racehorse trainer who still loves horses. He understands Alec's passion and love for riding.* ***In what other ways are they similar?*** *Sample answer: Both are good riders, risk-takers, and determined.* ▬ **RL.4.3, RL.5.3**

• Ask: *What is a major theme of these chapters?* *Sample answer: determination* ***Why do you think so?*** *Sample answer: because Alec is determined to keep the Black and determined to have him race; Henry is also determined to help him succeed* ▬ **RL.4.2, RL.5.2**

Academic Vocabulary

Read each word with students and discuss its meaning.

slackened (p. 135) • lessened

skeptical (p. 143) • unsure; questioning

brusquely (p. 150) • abruptly; a little rudely

temperamental (p. 176) • easily upset or excited

FIRST READ ## Think Through the Text

Have students use text evidence and draw inferences to answer questions.

p. 158 • *How do you know from the text that Alec is nervous about talking to his father about riding the Black in the race?* The text says that he couldn't keep his voice from faltering. **RL.4.1, RL.5.1**

p. 187 • *How do you know Alec plans to race the Black again?* He says that people are going to hear a lot more about the Black. **RL.4.1**

SECOND READ ## Analyze the Text

• Ask: *What is the problem in the third segment?* The Black doesn't have a pedigree so he cannot race. *How does Joe Russo's return to the story help solve the problem?* He finds a way that the Black can race. **RL.4.3, RL.5.5**

• Guide students to discuss the way the narrator describes different events and how it might influence how readers think about characters such as Alec. Ask: *How do you feel about Alec and his experiences? Why?* Sample answer: *Alec seems like the kind of person I would like to meet. He has exciting and interesting experiences.* **RL.5.6**

• Ask: *What do you think is the theme of the whole book? Why?* Sample answer: *Persistence—Alec persists to survive, he persists to keep the Black, and he persists to have the Black in a race.* **RL.4.2, RL.5.2**

Independent/Self-Selected Reading

Have students reread *The Black Stallion* independently to practice analyzing the text on their own, or have them practice the skills using another book. Suggested titles:

• *The Horse Charmer* by Terri Farley

• *Misty of Chincoteague* by Marguerite Henry **RL.4.10, RL.5.10**

Performance Task

WRITE & PRESENT

1. Have small groups discuss how readers form opinions of characters because of the way the narrator tells the story. Have students identify Alec's traits and what the narrator says about Alec's experiences. **RL.4.3, RL.5.6**

2. Ask students to write a paragraph that explains the narrator's point of view about Alec. Tell them to support their explanation with details from the story. **W.4.2, W.5.2**

3. Have students share their work with their groups and then edit it. **W.4.5, W.5.5**

4. Students present and discuss their final writing. **SL.4.4, SL.5.4**

5. Individual students turn in their final writing to the teacher.

See Copying Masters, pp. 144–147.

STUDENT CHECKLIST

Writing

☑ Write in complete sentences.

☑ Identify the narrator's point of view.

☑ Support ideas with text evidence.

☑ Use correct language conventions.

Speaking & Listening

☑ Present ideas in a meaningful way.

☑ Engage effectively in collaborative discussion.

OBJECTIVES

- Explain the key events in a story
- Describe characters and their challenges
- Identify the theme of a story
- Analyze text using text evidence

The Little Prince is broken into three instructional segments.

SEGMENTS

Options for Reading

Independent Students read the book independently and then answer questions posed by the teacher.

Supported Students read a segment independently or with a partner, and then answer questions with teacher support.

 Common Core Connection

RL.4.1 refer to details and examples when explaining what the text says explicitly and when drawing inferences; **RL.4.2** determine theme from details/summarize; **RL.4.4** determine the meaning of words and phrases, including those that allude to characters in mythology; **RL.4.6** compare and contrast the point of view from which stories are narrated

RL.5.1 quote accurately when explaining what the text says explicitly and when drawing inferences; **RL.5.2** determine theme from details/summarize; **RL.5.4** determine the meaning of words and phrases, including figurative language; **RL.5.6** describe how a narrator's or speaker's point of view influences how events are described

The Little Prince
by Antoine de Saint-Exupéry

SUMMARY This story tells of a pilot stranded in the desert after a plane crash. He encounters an unusual character, the little prince, and learns about the prince's adventures on other planets. Together, the pilot and prince explore the meaning of life and friendship.

ABOUT THE AUTHOR Antoine de Saint-Exupéry was born in France in 1900. He developed a passion for flying and had the dangerous job of flying airmail over the Sahara Desert, which inspired him to write *The Little Prince*. He was also a pilot during World War II. When his plane went down in 1944, he was never found.

Discuss Genre and Set Purpose

FANTASY Display the book, and read the title. Discuss the character illustrated on the cover, and help students think about challenges the character might face. Encourage students to make predictions about the story's plot.

SET PURPOSE Help students set a purpose for reading, such as to discover the challenges the characters face and identify the story's theme, or message.

TEXT COMPLEXITY RUBRIC

Overall Text Complexity		*The Little Prince* FANTASY
		MORE COMPLEX
Quantitative Measures	Lexile	710L
	Guided Reading Level	X
Qualitative Measures	Text Structure	unconventional story structure
	Language Conventionality and Clarity	increased unfamiliar language
	Knowledge Demands	multiple perspectives
	Purpose/Levels of Meaning	multiple levels of meaning

Academic Vocabulary

Read each word with students and discuss its meaning.

boa constrictor (p. 7) • a large snake that kills its prey by squeezing it to death

encounters (p. 8) • brief or unexpected meetings

isolated (p. 9) • apart from other people or places; alone

asteroid (p. 15) • a rock that orbits around the Sun

baobab (p. 20) • a large African tree with a very thick trunk

moralist (p. 22) • a person who teaches about right and wrong

FIRST READ ## Think Through the Text

Have students use text evidence and draw inferences to answer questions.

p. 9 • *What is the pilot's problem?* He crashes in the desert. There's no one to help him. 🔹 RL.4.1, RL.5.1

pp. 9–10 • *The author describes the pilot's reaction to the little prince as "completely thunderstruck." What does he mean by this?* He says the pilot jumped to his feet, completely thunderstruck. The pilot is so surprised that he jumps as if something shocked him. 🔹 RL.4.4, RL.5.4

pp. 19–22 • *What does the prince ask the pilot to draw?* a planet covered with huge baobabs 🔹 RL.4.1

SECOND READ ## Analyze the Text

• *Who is telling the story?* the pilot *What is his viewpoint about himself?* Sample answer: *He believes he sees things differently from others. He thinks he sees things more like a child than an adult.* **How does this view affect how the story is told?** Sample answer: *The pilot tells about the things that he thinks are important, such as the prince being delightful and laughing, rather than only telling facts about him.*
🔹 RL.4.6, RL.5.6

• Have students summarize these chapters. Be sure they discuss the characters, central problem, and events. Then ask: *What is a theme of this part of the story? Explain.* Sample answer: *self-reflection and thoughtfulness about what is important; The pilot thinks about knowing facts about a person or a person's feelings; The pilot treasures his own child-like appreciation of his art.* 🔹 RL.4.2, RL.5.2

 ENGLISH LANGUAGE LEARNERS

Use Visuals

Help students follow the story line with a sequence chain. Either make a class chain or have pairs make their own series of sketches to show what happens in this part of the story. Have students use words and phrases to tell about the major events in the sequence chain.

RESPOND TO SEGMENT 1

 Classroom Collaboration

Have partners work together to review and discuss their summary. Encourage students to raise questions about the plot and characters that might be answered in the next segment.

RESPOND TO SEGMENT 2

Classroom Collaboration

Have small groups review the plot events, discuss their summaries, and ask questions about what they don't understand.

Academic Vocabulary

Read each word with students and discuss its meaning.

abashed (p. 30) • embarrassed

dejection (p. 32) • depression or disappointment

monarch (p. 35) • someone who rules a place; a king or queen

monotony (p. 42) • lack of variety or change; repetitiveness

essential (p. 70) • very important

FIRST READ   ## Think Through the Text

Have students use text evidence and draw inferences to answer questions.

pp. 29–30 • *Is the setting of this segment the same as the setting of the first segment? Explain.* No, the first setting is a desert on Earth. This segment starts on the prince's planet. ▬ RL.4.3, RL.5.3

pp. 29–32 • *Describe the flower. Compare her to the prince.* Sample answer: *The flower is demanding. She wants the prince to get food for her and protect her. The prince is helpful and patient. He judges her words instead of her actions.* ▬ RL.4.3, RL.5.3

p. 30 • *What does the flower call her thorns?* claws *Why does the flower make that comparison?* She calls her thorns claws because she uses her thorns for defense, like tigers use their claws. ▬ RL.4.4, RL.5.4

SECOND READ   ## Analyze the Text

- Direct students' attention to the picture on page 33. Ask: *How does this picture help you understand the story?* Sample answer: *It shows how tiny the planet and the things on it are.* ▬ RL.4.7, RL.5.7

- *How might this segment connect to the first segment?* Sample answer: *This part explains why the prince is on Earth—he is exploring other planets.* ▬ RL.4.1, RL.5.5

- Have students summarize the places the prince visits and describe the characters he meets. Then say: *Each character has a different viewpoint about what is important. What are some of the characters' views?* Sample answer: *The king thinks having his commands obeyed is key. The vain man thinks impressing people is key.* ▬ RL.4.6, RL.5.6

- Tell students to think about the theme. Then ask: *What does the prince learn from the fox?* Sample answer: *He learns about the importance of friendship and the responsibilities of being a friend.* ▬ RL.4.2, RL.5.2

Academic Vocabulary

Read each word with students and discuss its meaning.

fragile (p. 76) • easily broken or hurt

muzzle (p. 79) • something put on an animal to keep it from biting

abyss (p. 84) • a crack in the earth that seems to have no bottom

resolute (p. 86) • having or showing determination

naïve (p. 88) • lacking knowledge or experience

FIRST READ ## Think Through the Text

Have students use text evidence and draw inferences to answer questions.

p. 74 • *Where does Chapter XXIV take place?* the desert *What text evidence tells us about the setting?* The pilot says that it was now the eighth day since he had had his accident in the desert. ● RL.4.1, RL.5.1

pp. 74–79 • *What challenges does the pilot face?* The pilot has no more water. The prince falls asleep so the pilot carries him. *What does the pilot say about the well water?* He says that the water is a different thing from ordinary nourishment and is like a present. ● RL.4.1, RL.5.1

SECOND READ ## Analyze the Text

- Guide students to discuss the sequence of events and the structure of the story. Ask: *How is the story's plot divided among the three segments?* In the first segment, the little prince and the pilot meet in the desert. In the second, the prince tells of his life before he met the pilot. The events in the third segment start where the first segment ended, with the pilot and the little prince in the desert. ● RL.4.1, RL.5.5

- Point out that the author lets the reader decide what happens to the prince at the end. Then ask: *What do you think happens to the prince? Use text details and quotes to explain your answer.* Answers will vary. ● RL.4.1, RL.5.1

- Tell students to think about the different characters and themes in the story. Then say: *Choose a theme for the story. Give details from the text to support it.* Sample answer: curiosity and exploration; The prince learns about the world, people, and relationships by exploring other planets. ● RL.4.2, RL.5.2

Independent/Self-Selected Reading

Have students reread *The Little Prince* independently to practice analyzing the text, or practice skills using another book. Suggested titles:

- *The Wonderful Flight to the Mushroom Planet* by Eleanor Cameron

- *Where the Mountain Meets the Moon* by Grace Lin ● RL.4.10, RL.5.10

Performance Task

WRITE & PRESENT

1. Have small groups discuss the plot events and themes of each segment of the story. ● RL.4.2, RL.5.2

2. Ask students to think about the main themes of the entire story. Have students write about one or more themes of *The Little Prince* and defend their ideas with text evidence and quotes from the story. ● W.4.2, W.5.2

3. Have students share their work with partners. Ask them to revise and edit their writing based on their partner's suggestions. ● W.4.5, W.5.5

4. Have students present their final writing to their classmates. Ask students to respond to the themes and ideas from each student's writing. ● SL.4.4, SL.5.4

See Copying Masters, pp. 144–147.

STUDENT CHECKLIST

Writing

- ☑ State one or more themes of the story.

- ☑ Explain the themes with text evidence and quotes from the story.

- ☑ Use complete sentences and developed paragraphs to structure writing.

- ☑ Use correct language conventions.

Speaking & Listening

- ☑ Read writing aloud with a clear, audible voice.

- ☑ Ask and answer questions to clarify what a speaker says.

▶ **OBJECTIVES**
- Describe settings
- Describe major story events and characters
- Analyze text using text evidence

Tuck Everlasting is broken into three instructional segments.

Options for Reading

Independent Students read the story independently or with a partner and then answer questions posed by the teacher.

Supported Students read a segment and answer questions with teacher support.

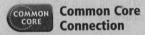

Common Core Connection

RL.4.1 refer to details and examples when explaining what the text says explicitly and when drawing inferences; **RL.4.3** describe a character, setting, or event, drawing on details

RL.5.1 quote accurately when explaining what the text says explicitly and when drawing inferences; **RL.5.3** compare and contrast characters, settings, or events, drawing on details

Tuck Everlasting
by Natalie Babbitt

SUMMARY Ten-year-old Winnie Foster meets the Tuck family in the forest near her house. She soon discovers their secret—that because the family drank from a magical spring, they will live forever. The Tuck family explains the pitfalls of living forever to Winnie and tries to hide from a mysterious stranger who seeks the magical spring so he can sell the magical water to others.

ABOUT THE AUTHOR Natalie Babbitt is an author and illustrator of children's books and has written several stories with magical elements. Her book *Tuck Everlasting* was adapted into a major motion picture.

Discuss Genre and Set Purpose

FANTASY Display the book and read the title. Tell students that one setting in the book is a forest with a magical spring. Guide students to consider this setting to discuss why this book is classified as a fantasy.

SET PURPOSE Help students set a purpose for reading, such as to find out how the setting affects the events of the plot and the conflict between characters.

▲ TEXT COMPLEXITY RUBRIC		*Tuck Everlasting* FANTASY
Overall Text Complexity		COMPLEX
Quantitative Measures	Lexile	770L
	Guided Reading Level	V
Qualitative Measures	Text Structure	somewhat complex story concepts
	Language Conventionality and Clarity	some unfamiliar language
	Knowledge Demands	distinctly unfamiliar experience
	Purpose/Levels of Meaning	multiple levels of meaning

Academic Vocabulary

Read each word with students and discuss its meaning.

gallows (p. 6) • wooden frame used for hanging criminals

brooch (p. 11) • a jeweled pin worn on clothes

cross (p. 13) • angry

resentful (p. 26) • feeling angry or bitter about something

bridle (p. 31) • a harness on a horse's head

dismay (p. 34) • a sudden, helpless fear

FIRST READ ## Think Through the Text

Have students use text evidence and draw inferences to answer questions.

pp. 14–16 • *Why does Winnie want to run away from home?* Winnie wants more freedom. *What text evidence supports this response?* On page 14, Winnie says that she is tired of being looked at and wants to be by herself.
RL.4.1, RL.5.1

pp. 31–34 • *What stops Winnie from drinking from the spring in the wood?* The Tuck family quickly swings her onto a horse and takes her away with them. RL.4.1

pp. 37–41 • *What is the Tuck family's strange story?* Eighty-seven years ago, they all drank from a spring in the wood. In the years after drinking from the spring, they noticed they weren't aging at all. They realized that drinking from the spring had given them the ability to live forever.
RL.4.1

p. 45 • *How would you describe the stranger in the yellow suit?* Sample answer: sneaky, nosy, mysterious RL.4.3

SECOND READ ## Analyze the Text

• Reread page 3. Then ask: *What is the first week of August like?* It is the hottest, driest time of the year. People act strangely during this time. *What details does the author give to describe the setting?* It is motionless and hot with blank white dawns and lightning at night. People do things they regret. RL.4.3

• *Describe the setting in which Winnie discovers the spring.* thick roots, pebbles, low spurt of water *How does the setting influence the conflict between Winnie and Jesse Tuck?* Winnie sees Jesse drink the water. She is thirsty and wants some. He doesn't let her drink from the spring because he knows it causes everlasting life. RL.4.3, RL.5.3

• Revisit page 41. *Why does Mae tell Winnie that it would be bad if everyone knew about the spring?* She wants Winnie to realize that it is important for her to keep the spring a secret. RL.4.1, RL.5.1

 ENGLISH LANGUAGE LEARNERS

Use Sentence Frames

Read aloud the description of the forest setting that appears on page 24. Have students name parts of the setting, such as *flowers, tree trunk, birds*. Then have students use sentence frames, such as the following, to describe the setting.

• _____ grow in the wood. *Vines*

• _____ live in the wood. *Ants*

RESPOND TO SEGMENT 1

 Classroom Collaboration

Have partners work together to create and present a summary of the chapters they have read. Ask them to predict what will happen next.

Use Comprehensible Input

Read aloud the description of the Tucks' house on pages 50–52. Have students name objects in the setting such as *table*, *mouse*, *doll*, and *spoon*. Then guide students to write sentences about the setting of the Tucks' house.

RESPOND TO SEGMENT 2

Classroom Collaboration

Have small groups work together to summarize this segment of the story. Encourage students to ask questions about what they still don't understand.

COMMON CORE Common Core Connection

RL.4.1 refer to details and examples when explaining what the text says explicitly and when drawing inferences; **RL.4.3** describe a character, setting, or event, drawing on details; **RL.4.10** read and comprehend literature; **W.4.2** write informative/explanatory texts to examine a topic and convey ideas and information clearly; **W.4.5** develop and strengthen writing by planning, revising, and editing; **SL.4.4** report on a topic or text, tell a story, or recount an experience/speak clearly at an understandable pace

RL.5.1 quote accurately when explaining what the text says explicitly and when drawing inferences; **RL.5.3** compare and contrast characters, settings, or events, drawing on details; **RL.5.10** read and comprehend literature; **W.5.2** write informative/explanatory texts to examine a topic and convey ideas and information clearly; **W.5.5** develop and strengthen writing by planning, revising, editing, rewriting, or trying a new approach; **SL.5.4** report on a topic or text, tell a story, or recount an experience/speak clearly at an understandable pace

---

Academic Vocabulary

Read each word with students and discuss its meaning.

melancholy (p. 48) • sad

blacksmith (p. 53) • a craftsmen who uses iron

flapjacks (p. 56) • pancakes

constable (p. 75) • a police officer

ordeal (p. 75) • an unpleasant experience

FIRST READ # Think Through the Text

Have students use text evidence and draw inferences to answer questions.

pp. 53–55 • *How does Mae feel about her everlasting life?* Sample answer: *She treats it as something ordinary. On page 54, she says that life has got to be lived, no matter how long or short. In her view, her family lives like everybody else, one day at a time.* ▬ RL.4.1, RL.5.1

p. 64 • *Does Tuck want Winnie to tell others about the spring?* no *Why?* *People would drink the water, and then the world would be crowded with people who do not love life.* ▬ RL.4.1

pp. 71–72 *How does Jesse agree with what Tuck told Winnie?* He agrees *that Winnie needs to keep the spring a secret.* **How does Jesse's plan differ from what his parents want for Winnie?** *Jesse's parents do not want Winnie to drink from the spring, but Jessie suggests that Winnie can drink from it when she is seventeen like him. Then they can get married and travel the world.* ▬ RL.4.3, RL.5.3

SECOND READ # Analyze the Text

- Review pages 50–52. Ask: *How is the Tucks' house different from Winnie's house?* Sample answer: *Winnie's cottage is always clean. The Tucks' house is messy.* ▬ RL.4.3, RL.5.3

- Have students revisit pages 53–54. Ask: *How are Miles and Jesse's lifestyles different?* *Miles is a carpenter and a blacksmith. Jesse takes odd jobs like working in the fields or in a saloon.* **Although they are different, do they care about each other?** yes *Explain.* *Every ten years the brothers meet at the spring during the first week of August and go home together.* ▬ RL.4.3, RL.5.3

- Review pages 61–64. Ask: *What does Tuck compare life to? Use text evidence to support your response.* Sample answer: *Tuck compares life to a wheel that keeps on turning without ever stopping.* **How does his view of his family fit into this comparison?** *He says they have dropped off the wheel. They are left behind as everything around them keeps moving and changing.* ▬ RL.4.1, RL.5.1

Academic Vocabulary

Read each word with students and discuss its meaning.

haunted (p. 96) • appeared frequently

marionette (p. 102) • a puppet that is moved by strings

soothing (p. 106) • comforting

mingled (p. 113) • combined

pry (p. 123) • to loosen or remove

FIRST READ ## Think Through the Text

Have students use text evidence and draw inferences to answer questions.

pp. 97–99 • *What is the man in the yellow suit's plan for the spring?* *The man plans to sell the water to people who he thinks deserve it, such as those who are wealthy and smart.* ◼ RL.4.1

p. 105 • *Why is Mae's punishment a problem?* *Mae will not die if she is hung on the gallows. The Tucks' secret will be revealed.* ◼ RL.4.1

pp. 114–115 • *Why does Winnie want to risk helping the Tucks free Mae?* *The Tucks are Winnie's friends. She also wants to do something that will make a difference in the world.* ◼ RL.4.3

SECOND READ ## Analyze the Text

• Reread pages 102–103. Then ask: *How does the author describe Tuck's view of the motionless stranger on the ground?* Sample answer: *The text says that he was entranced and envious.* *Why does she describe him this way?* *to show that he envies someone who can die because he is tired of living forever and wants his everlasting life to end* ◼ RL.4.1, RL.5.1

• Have students revisit the Epilogue. *What does the Epilogue tell you about Winnie? How do you know she agreed with Tuck's view of the spring water?* Sample answer: *Winnie never drank the water. She decided to be a part of life's wheel—moving, growing, and changing. She got married, had children, and died.* ◼ RL.4.3, RL.5.3

Independent/Self-Selected Reading

Have students reread *Tuck Everlasting* independently to practice analyzing the text on their own, or have them practice the skills using another book. Suggested titles:

• *Kneeknock Rise* by Natalie Babbitt

• *Goody Hall* by Natalie Babbitt ◼ RL.4.10, RL.5.10

Performance Task

WRITE & PRESENT

1. Guide partners to describe the idyllic setting of the spring, drawing on specific details in the text. Encourage students to look for supporting details, such as the color of the sky and the sounds of the water in the spring. ◼ RL.4.3, RL.5.1

2. Have individual students write a paragraph about the spring, the forest, and the Tucks' home. Remind them to use details from the text and adjectives to strengthen their writing. ◼ W.4.2, W.5.2

3. Have partners reconvene to share their descriptions of the setting. Have students use their partner's suggestions to revise and edit their writing. ◼ W.4.5, W.5.5

4. Ask individual students to present their final work. ◼ SL.4.4, SL.5.4

5. Have individual students turn in their final work to the teacher.

See Copying Masters, pp. 144–147.

STUDENT CHECKLIST

Writing

☑ Write in complete sentences.

☑ Write a detailed description of a story setting.

☑ Use correct language conventions.

Speaking & Listening

☑ Engage effectively in collaborative discussion.

☑ Logically connect details in the text to a story setting.

☑ Describe details in their own writing that demonstrate an understanding of a story setting.

- Describe story events
- Describe characters and settings
- Analyze text using text evidence

"Zlateh the Goat" is broken into three instructional segments.

SEGMENTS

Options for Reading

Independent Students read the story independently or with a partner and then answer questions posed by the teacher.

Supported Students read a segment and answer questions with teacher support.

COMMON CORE **Common Core Connection**

RL.4.1 refer to details and examples when explaining what the text says explicitly and when drawing inferences; **RL.4.3** describe a character, setting, or event, drawing on details; **RL.4.7** make connections between the text and a visual or oral presentation of it

RL.5.1 quote accurately when explaining what the text says explicitly and when drawing inferences; **RL.5.3** compare and contrast characters, settings, or events, drawing on details; **RL.5.7** analyze how visual and multimedia elements contribute to the meaning, tone, or beauty of a text

"Zlateh the Goat"
by Isaac Bashevis Singer

SUMMARY Reuven decides he must sell his family's goat so his family will have money for a celebration of Hanukkah. Reuven's son Aaron leads Zlateh the goat from the village to the butcher in town. A huge blizzard forces Aaron and Zlateh to depend on each other for survival. Aaron decides he can't part with Zlateh and leads the goat back home.

ABOUT THE AUTHOR Isaac Bashevis Singer wrote many short stories. In 1967, his first book for children, *Zlateh the Goat and Other Stories*, was named a Newbery Honor Book. Later, in 1978, he received the Nobel Prize for Literature.

Discuss Genre and Set Purpose

FOLKTALE Tell students that this story is a folktale. Explain that a folktale is an old story that has been passed down over the course of many years. A folktale often has a lesson or message and includes ideas from the culture it came from. Then have students page through the book and predict what this folktale might be about.

SET PURPOSE Help students set a purpose for reading, such as to find out how characters overcome conflicts in the story.

TEXT COMPLEXITY RUBRIC

Overall Text Complexity		"Zlateh the Goat" FOLKTALE ACCESSIBLE
Quantitative Measures	Lexile	850L
	Guided Reading Level	U
Qualitative Measures	Text Structure	conventional story structure
	Language Conventionality and Clarity	some unfamiliar language
	Knowledge Demands	some cultural and literary knowledge useful
	Purpose/Levels of Meaning	single level of simple meaning

Academic Vocabulary

Read each word with students and discuss its meaning.

astonished (p. 80) • amazed

penetrated (p. 81) • passed through

imp (p. 81) • a little demon

bored (p. 82) • made a hole by digging

chaos (p. 85) • confusion or disorder

exuded (p. 85) • produced

Domain Specific Vocabulary

Hanukkah (p. 79) • a Jewish festival in December

peasants (p. 79) • poor farmers

furrier (p. 79) • a person who sells furs

gulden (p. 79) • money used in the Netherlands

eddies (p. 81) • circular patterns of blowing snow

FIRST READ ## Think Through the Text

Have students use text evidence and draw inferences to answer questions.

pp. 79–80 • *Why does Reuven hesitate before he decides to sell Zlateh to the butcher?* *Zlateh is special to Reuven's family.* ⬛RL.4.1

p. 80 • *How does the rest of the family feel about Reuven's decision to sell Zlateh?* *The family is unhappy. Aaron agrees to take Zlateh to the butcher in town only because he wants to obey his father. Aaron's mother sheds tears and his sisters cry loudly when they say good-bye to Zlateh.* ⬛RL.4.3, RL.5.3

pp. 80–81 • *What changes occur after Aaron leaves the village?* *At first, the sun is shining. Then the weather changes, and it begins to hail and then snow. It snows so hard that Aaron cannot see where he is going.* ⬛RL.4.3, RL.5.3

SECOND READ ## Analyze the Text

- Review pages 78–79. Ask: *How does the illustration help you understand the setting?* Sample answer: *The illustration shows what the land looks like without snow in the winter. It provides visuals of the village, the peasants' houses, and the boy's clothing, which show that this story takes place long ago.* ⬛RL.4.7, RL.5.7

- Review page 80. Then ask: *How do you know that Zlateh is trusting but confused at this time? Use text evidence to support your response.* Sample answer: *The text says that Zlateh trusted human beings and knew that they always fed her and never did her any harm. But she seems confused when Aaron starts to lead her to town because she has never been in that direction before.* ⬛RL.4.1, RL.5.1

- Reread page 81. Then ask: *Why does Zlateh stop walking?* *She can't move through the fallen snow.* *What details does the author provide?* *Her legs keep sinking deeper into the snow. Her beard has icicles on it. Her horns are covered with frost. The author says that she bleated as if pleading to be taken home.* ⬛RL.4.1, RL.5.1

ELL ENGLISH LANGUAGE LEARNERS

Use Gestures and Sentence Frames

Read aloud the text on page 80 that tells how the family reacts to losing Zlateh. Have students use gestures to portray the reactions. Then have them orally complete sentence frames, such as the following:

- Leah _____ when she heard the news. *cried*

- Aaron _____ his father. *obeyed*

RESPOND TO SEGMENT 1

 Classroom Collaboration

Have partners create a summary of the plot events in this segment. Then have students predict what might happen next in the story.

Domain Specific Vocabulary

dreidel (p. 90) • a game with a four-sided top that is played at Hanukkah

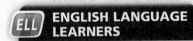

ENGLISH LANGUAGE LEARNERS

Use Gestures and Complete Sentences

Use phrases and gestures to show what Aaron does when he finds the haystack on page 82. Have students repeat after you. Then have students summarize Aaron's actions using complete sentences.

RESPOND TO SEGMENT 2

Classroom Collaboration

Have small groups work together to summarize this story segment. Encourage students to ask questions about anything they still don't understand.

Common Core Connection

W.4.2 write informative/explanatory texts to examine a topic and convey ideas and information clearly; **W.4.5** develop and strengthen writing by planning, revising, and editing; **SL.4.4** report on a topic or text, tell a story, or recount an experience/speak clearly at an understandable pace
RL.5.4 determine the meaning of words and phrases, including figurative language; **W.5.2** write informative/explanatory texts to examine a topic and convey ideas and information clearly; **W.5.5** develop and strengthen writing by planning, revising, editing, rewriting, or trying a new approach; **SL.5.4** report on a topic or text, tell a story, or recount an experience/speak clearly at an understandable pace

FIRST READ | # Think Through the Text

Have students use text evidence and draw inferences to answer questions.

p. 82 • *Why is it good that Aaron is a village boy?* He knows how to use the haystack to help himself and Zlateh. *Why is the haystack so important?* The haystack will give shelter from the blizzard. Zlateh can eat the hay. ▄ RL.4.3

pp. 82–86 • *How does Aaron need Zlateh?* Aaron needs Zlateh's milk and her warmth. He also needs Zlateh to listen to him when he talks. *How does Zlateh need Aaron?* Zlateh needs Aaron to take care of the haystack that provides warmth and food for her. ▄ RL.4.3, RL.5.3

SECOND READ | ## Analyze the Text

• Reread pages 81–82. Then ask: *What key details in the text describe Aaron's situation?* Sample answer: The text says that the snowfall had reached his knees. His hands were numb, and he could no longer feel his toes. It also says he chokes when breathing and his nose feels like wood. He hears Zlateh's cries and starts to pray. *Why does the author include these details?* He wants to show how serious the situation is. ▄ RL.4.1, RL.5.1

• Review page 86. Then ask: *How does the author use figurative language to create a vivid description of the wind?* The author gives the wind human characteristics. The wind wails and sometimes has the sound of devilish laughter. ▄ RL.4.1, RL.5.4

• Guide students to use pages 85–86 to answer the question: *Why does Aaron talk to Zlateh even though Zlateh cannot answer him with anything besides "Maaaa"?* Sample answer: Aaron is alone. He is separated from his family and he wants to talk. Aaron imagines how Zlateh would respond if she could talk. ▄ RL.4.3

FIRST READ ## Think Through the Text

Have students use text evidence and draw inferences to answer questions.

p. 89 • *What does Aaron dream about while in the haystack?* *Aaron dreams about warm weather. He pictures green fields, trees covered with blossoms, clear brooks, and singing birds.* **RL.4.1, RL.5.1**

p. 89 • *Why does the peasant point the way to the village rather than to the town?* *Aaron made the decision that he can never part with Zlateh so he is not going to the butcher in town. Aaron is taking Zlateh home to the village.* **RL.4.3**

p. 90 • *Why is the family so grateful to Zlateh?* *Her milk and warmth saved Aaron's life.* **How do the family members show their appreciation to Zlateh?** *The sisters give Zlateh a special treat. When Aaron's mom makes pancakes for Hanukkah, Zlateh is given some too. And Zlateh is always allowed in the kitchen.* **RL.4.1**

SECOND READ ## Analyze the Text

• Reread page 89. Then ask: *Why does Aaron start to think of himself as a snow child?* Sample answer: *Aaron has been inside the haystack so long that he starts to think that the snow has been falling forever; that he has no parents, but was "born of the snow."* **RL.4.1, RL.5.1**

• Guide students to look back at the text on page 89. Then ask: *What does Aaron's family do during the storm?* *Aaron's family and neighbors search for Aaron and Zlateh, but cannot find them.* **How do the family members react to this situation? What evidence in the text supports this?** *The text says that Aaron's mother and sisters cried for him; his father remained silent and gloomy.* **RL.4.1, RL.5.1**

• Review page 90. Then ask: *How has the family's situation changed since the beginning of the story?* Sample answer: *At the beginning of the story, business is bad for Reuven because the winter has been mild. Reuven decides to sell Zlateh to have money for Hanukkah, and the family is sad to lose Zlateh. At the end of the story, the family is full of joy because Aaron and Zlateh are still alive after being stuck in the storm. Reuven has more business since the storm brought cold weather. The family can enjoy Hanukkah.* **RL.4.3, RL.5.3**

Independent/Self-Selected Reading

Have students reread "Zlateh the Goat" independently to practice analyzing the text on their own, or have them practice the skills using another book. Suggested titles:

• *A Day of Pleasure: Stories of a Boy Growing Up in Warsaw* by Isaac Bashevis Singer

• *Stories for Children* by Isaac Bashevis Singer **RL.4.10, RL.5.10**

Performance Task

WRITE & PRESENT

1. Guide partners to refer to the text to discuss key events from the story, such as when the family says good-bye to Zlateh. Encourage students to draw on specific details from the text as they ask and answer questions about the events. **RL.4.3, RL.5.3**

2. Have individual students choose one major story event. Ask them to write a paragraph describing the event, drawing on specific details from the text. Encourage them to include details about what caused the event and what happened as a result of the event. **W.4.2, W.5.2**

3. Have partners reconvene to share their descriptions and edit their writing. **W.4.5, W.5.5**

4. Have individual students present their final work to classmates. **SL.4.4, SL.5.4**

5. Individual students turn in their final paragraphs to the teacher.

See Copying Masters, pp. 144–147.

STUDENT CHECKLIST

Writing

☑ Write in complete sentences.

☑ Write a detailed description of a major story event.

☑ Use correct language conventions.

Speaking & Listening

☑ Engage effectively in collaborative discussion.

☑ Logically connect details in the text to a major event.

☑ Cite text evidence about a major story event.

- Describe a character, setting, or event
- Ask and answer questions about details in a text
- Use information from a text to demonstrate understanding
- Analyze text using text evidence

M. C. Higgins, the Great is broken into three instructional segments.

Options for Reading

Independent Students read the book independently or with a partner and then answer questions posed by the teacher.

Supported Students read a segment and answer questions with teacher support.

Common Core Connection

RL.4.1 refer to details and examples when explaining what the text says explicitly and when drawing inferences; **RL.4.3** describe a character, setting, or event, drawing on details; **RL.4.4** determine the meaning of words and phrases, including those that allude to characters in mythology

RL.5.1 quote accurately when explaining what the text says explicitly and when drawing inferences; **RL.5.3** compare and contrast characters, settings, or events, drawing on details; **RL.5.4** determine the meaning of words and phrases, including figurative language

M. C. Higgins, the Great

by Virginia Hamilton

SUMMARY This novel is the story of Mayo Cornelius (M. C.) Higgins, a young boy who lives with his family in the mountains in Ohio. M. C. has to decide whether to encourage his family to move to avoid probable disaster from a nearby mine or to stay in the mountains they love.

ABOUT THE AUTHOR Virginia Hamilton grew up in southwestern Ohio, where her descendants had settled after escaping slavery through the Underground Railroad. She wrote 41 books and won many major literary awards for her works. *M. C. Higgins, the Great* won the Newbery Medal, the National Book Award, and the Boston Globe-Horn Book Award.

Discuss Genre and Set Purpose

FICTION Remind students that a work of fiction includes characters, a setting, and events. Point out that although this work of fiction is made up, some of the characters, settings, and events may be based upon the author's own experiences.

SET PURPOSE Help students set a purpose for reading, such as to find out what happens to M. C. Higgins and other characters in the story.

▲ TEXT COMPLEXITY RUBRIC		*M. C. Higgins, the Great* FICTION
Overall Text Complexity		**ACCESSIBLE**
Quantitative Measures	Lexile	620L
	Guided Reading Level	X
Qualitative Measures	Text Structure	less familiar story concepts
	Language Conventionality and Clarity	increased, clearly-assigned dialogue
	Knowledge Demands	somewhat unfamiliar perspective
	Purpose/Levels of Meaning	multiple levels of meaning

Academic Vocabulary

Read each word with students and discuss its meaning.

furtively (p. 1) • in a secretive or sly way

ravine (p. 5) • a deep, narrow area between two mountains or hills

sensation (p. 25) • feeling

contact (p. 45) • meeting; communication

intense (p. 77) • very strong

strutting (p. 88) • walking in a proud or bold way

 ENGLISH LANGUAGE LEARNERS

Use Sentence Frames

Guide students to generate adjectives that could describe M. C. Higgins and the other characters. Then have them orally complete sentence frames such as the following. *M. C. is _____. worried Jones is _____. powerful Lewis is _____. friendly*

FIRST READ ## Think Through the Text

Have students use text evidence and draw inferences to answer questions.

pp. 1–4 • *What is M. C.'s plan to get his family off the mountain?* He will have the man with the tape recorder make his mother a singing star. *How do you know?* It says on pages 3–4 that M. C. thinks that Dude is going to make Mama a star singer like Sister Baby on the radio. **RL.4.1, RL.5.1**

pp. 25–30 • *How do you know from the text what M. C. does with the pole?* He climbs it. The text says that he was forty feet up and higher than everything on the outcropping. **RL.4.1, RL.5.1**

pp. 40–45 • *How does M. C. feel when Lewis tells him that the spoil is absorbing rain and will slide down the mountain?* He is frightened. *How do you know?* It says on page 41 that it was his nightmare come to life. **RL.4.1, RL.5.1**

RESPOND TO SEGMENT 1
 Classroom Collaboration

Have partners work together to create and present a summary, as well as raise questions that might be answered in the next segment.

SECOND READ ## Analyze the Text

• Review pages 28–43. Ask: *How do M. C. and James K. Lewis treat each other when they meet for the first time?* Give specific examples from the text. *M. C. is helpful. He watches out for Lewis and takes him a walking stick. Lewis is friendly and polite. He lets M. C. look at the tape recorder.* **RL.4.3, RL.5.3**

• Have students reread page 52. Ask: *What does the word* yodel *mean?* a song that changes quickly between high and low sounds *What are some clues to the meaning of* yodel? *M. C. calls with the sounds "Yad'dlo! Yo'dlay-dio! D'lay-dio!" The text says he made his voice high and loud.* **RL.4.4, RL.5.4**

• Have students reread pages 55–67. Say: *Summarize the relationship between M. C. and his father.* Sample answer: *Jones loves his son, but sometimes has a rough way of showing it. M. C. loves and respects his father, but sometimes seems a little afraid of him.* **RL.4.3, RL.5.3**

ENGLISH LANGUAGE LEARNERS

Use Cognates

Point out the English/Spanish cognates to aid students' comprehension: *mountain/ montaña, family/familia, radio/radio, tunnel/túnel, ancient/anciano.* Then have students use the words in sentences related to the text.

RESPOND TO SEGMENT 2

Classroom Collaboration

Have small groups work together to summarize what they have learned. Have them ask questions about what they don't understand.

COMMON CORE Connection

RL.4.1 refer to details and examples when explaining what the text says explicitly and when drawing inferences; **RL.4.3** describe a character, setting, or event, drawing on details; **RL.4.10** read and comprehend literature; **W.4.2** write informative/explanatory texts to examine a topic and convey ideas and information clearly; **W.4.5** develop and strengthen writing by planning, revising, and editing; **SL.4.4** report on a topic or text, tell a story, or recount an experience/speak clearly at an understandable pace

RL.5.1 quote accurately when explaining what the text says explicitly and when drawing inferences; **RL.5.3** compare and contrast characters, settings, or events, drawing on details; **RL.5.10** read and comprehend literature; **W.5.2** write informative/explanatory texts to examine a topic and convey ideas and information clearly; **W.5.5** develop and strengthen writing by planning, revising, editing, rewriting, or trying a new approach; **SL.5.4** report on a topic or text, tell a story, or recount an experience/speak clearly at an understandable pace

---

Academic Vocabulary

Read each word with students and discuss its meaning.

lured (p. 98) • attracted, tempted

anxious (p. 100) • nervous; worried

altered (p. 119) • changed

dread (p. 122) • terror, fear

FIRST READ ## Think Through the Text

Have students use text evidence and draw inferences to answer questions.

pp. 104–107 • *What does the text say is the reason that the family will never leave the mountain?* Banina says that the pole is the marker for all of the dead. Jones will never leave the pole or the mountain.
▬ RL.4.1, RL.5.1

pp. 114–124 • *How do you know that Lewis was impressed with Banina's singing?* After listening to her sing, he says on page 123 that she swept him off his feet ▬ RL.4.1, RL.5.1

pp. 148–152 • *What does the girl who M. C. meets think about land?* She thinks land is treasured by people. She says on page 149 that land is the basis of all power and that people hold on to their land. She also says that she would like to have some land someday. ▬ RL.4.1, RL.5.1

SECOND READ ## Analyze the Text

• Have students reread pages 108–124 and discuss the conversation between M. C., Lewis, and Jones. Ask: *Why is M. C. confused?* Lewis tells them he thinks the spoil heap will slide down. M. C. does not realize that his father knows about the spoil heap sliding down until Jones says they will let the spoil get hard, then rope it and drag it away. Lewis disagrees with this approach, so M. C. is not sure who to believe. ▬ RL.4.3, RL.5.3

• Guide students to review pages 137–176 and compare and contrast M. C. and the girl. Ask: *What do their responses and actions tell about their characters?* Sample answer: *The girl is tough and competitive when she insists on holding her breath and swimming through the tunnel. She is dishonest when she tricks M. C. and doesn't tell him she can't swim. M. C. is cautious and thoughtful by trying to make sure the girl is prepared for the tunnel; when he realizes she can't swim, he feels responsible to save her.* ▬ RL.4.3, RL.5.3

> ### Academic Vocabulary
>
> Read each word with students and discuss its meaning.
>
> **predicament** (p. 255) • difficult situation
>
> **festering** (p. 271) • becoming rotten
>
> **ripple** (p. 274) • a small movement
>
> **urgent** (p. 278) • needing immediate attention

FIRST READ ▶ Think Through the Text

Have students use text evidence and draw inferences to answer questions.

pp. 208–217 • *How does M. C. feel about going to Ben's house?* He doesn't want to go; he is frightened. *How does Lurhetta feel?* She is curious and excited. 🔲 **RL.4.3, RL.5.3**

pp. 259–268 • *How do you know from the text that Lurhetta left?* She and the tent are gone. *What does the text say she leaves for M. C.?* her knife 🔲 **RL.4.3**

pp. 276–277 • *Why does Jones give Great-grandmother Sarah's gravestone to M. C.?* to add to the wall *How do you know?* On page 277, when asked about the purpose of the stone, M. C. says his father brought it to make the wall strong. 🔲 **RL.4.1, RL.5.1**

SECOND READ ▶ Analyze the Text

• Have students reread pages 190–199. Say: *At the end of page 199, M. C. knows he will never be the same because Lurhetta has seen the difference. What does this mean?* Sample answer: She has seen how M. C. and his family treated her kindly, but are unkind to the Killburns, their neighbors who are different than they are. 🔲 **RL.4.3, RL.5.3**

• Guide students to review pages 273–278. Ask: *What do M. C.'s actions tell about how he has changed by the end of the story?* Sample answer: He realizes that he wants to be friends with Ben, and he defies his father to do so. He wants to stay on the mountain, so he begins to build a wall to keep back the spoil. 🔲 **RL.4.3, RL.5.3**

Independent/Self-Selected Reading

Have students reread *M. C. Higgins, the Great* independently to practice analyzing the text on their own, or have them practice the skills using another book. Suggested titles:

• *Zeely* by Virginia Hamilton

• *The People Could Fly: American Black Folktales* by Virginia Hamilton 🔲 **RL.4.10, RL.5.10**

WRITE & PRESENT

1. Have small groups refer to the text to explain the way the main character, M. C. Higgins, interacts with other characters. Have them use a graphic organizer to record their observations. 🔲 **RL.4.3, RL.5.3**

2. Have individual students choose one of the supporting characters and write a paragraph that describes the ways that the character and M. C. interact. Remind them to cite information from the text that supports their ideas. 🔲 **W.4.2, W.5.2**

3. Students share their paragraphs with partners and edit their writing. 🔲 **W.4.5, W.5.5**

4. Students present their final paragraphs to classmates. 🔲 **SL.4.4, SL.5.4**

5. Students turn in their final paragraphs to the teacher.

See Copying Masters, pp. 144–147.

STUDENT CHECKLIST

Writing

☑ Explain how the main character interacts with supporting characters.

☑ Use a graphic organizer to record details and ideas.

☑ Provide reasons supported by facts and details from the text.

☑ Use correct language conventions.

Speaking & Listening

☑ Engage effectively in collaborative conversations.

☑ Logically present claims and findings.

- Summarize themes using text details
- Compare and contrast the treatment of themes and topics
- Ask and answer questions about details in a text
- Analyze text using text evidence

The Birchbark House is broken into three instructional segments.

SEGMENTS

Options for Reading

Independent Students read the book independently or with a partner and then answer questions posed by the teacher.

Supported Students read a segment and answer questions with teacher support.

COMMON CORE **Common Core Connection**

RL.4.1 refer to details and examples when explaining what the text says explicitly and when drawing inferences; **RL.4.2** determine theme from details/summarize; **RL.4.3** describe a character, setting, or event, drawing on details

RL.5.1 quote accurately when explaining what the text says explicitly and when drawing inferences; **RL.5.2** determine theme from details/summarize; **RL.5.3** compare and contrast characters, settings, or events, drawing on details

The Birchbark House
by Louise Erdrich

SUMMARY This book shares the customs and traditions of the Ojibwa tribe through the story of Omakayas, a young Ojibwa girl who lives on an island in Lake Superior in the 1840s. When a white visitor comes to the island, the lives of Omakayas and her family change forever.

ABOUT THE AUTHOR Louise Erdrich explores her American Indian and German heritage in her novels and poems. She has written nonfiction, poems, short stories, and novels for children and adults. Her books for children include *Grandmother's Pigeon, The Game of Silence,* and *The Porcupine Year*.

Discuss Genre and Set Purpose

HISTORICAL FICTION Tell students that this story is about an American Indian girl who lives with her family on an island in the 1840s. Have them page through the book and look at the illustrations. Then discuss with students elements of historical fiction, such as realistic characters, settings, and events that reflect a specific time period in history.

SET PURPOSE Help students set a purpose for reading, such as to find out what happens to the girl and her family.

◢ TEXT COMPLEXITY RUBRIC

Overall Text Complexity		*The Birchbark House* HISTORICAL FICTION
		ACCESSIBLE
Quantitative Measures	Lexile	970L
	Guided Reading Level	T
Qualitative Measures	Text Structure	less familiar story concepts
	Language Conventionality and Clarity	some unfamiliar language
	Knowledge Demands	somewhat unfamilar experience
	Purpose/Levels of Meaning	multiple levels of meaning

Academic Vocabulary

Read each word with students and discuss its meaning.

nimble (p. 5) • able to move quickly and easily

isolated (p. 19) • separated

haughty (p. 25) • proud; arrogant

envy (p. 25) • feel jealous of

ferocious (p. 57) • fierce; violent

dismay (p. 69) • disappointment

FIRST READ ## Think Through the Text

Have students use text evidence and draw inferences to answer questions.

pp. 5–7 • *What do you know from the text about Omakayas?* She is seven years old, has shining brown hair, and is missing her two top front teeth. She lives on an island in Lake Superior. RL.4.1, RL.5.1

pp. 26–32 • *How does Omakayas treat the bear cubs and their mother?* She gives the cubs berries and thinks about taking them home with her. She stays still while the mother bear smells her. RL.4.3

pp. 68–70 • *How do you know that Omakayas understands the reason behind her father's gift?* It says on page 69 that she took Deydey's gift with an understanding of how he liked to give the presents but rarely offered praise. RL.4.1, RL.5.1

SECOND READ ## Analyze the Text

• Have students reread pp. 1–18. Ask: *How does Omakayas feel about her family?* She loves her parents, her grandmother, and especially Baby Neewo. She thinks her older sister is perfect and hopes to be like her. She does not like Little Pinch very much because he is greedy and too loud. RL.4.3, RL.5.3

• Guide students to review pages 33–40. Ask: *How do you know from the text that Omakayas changes after her encounter with the bear?* She is quiet and thoughtful. She is kinder to her sister. She has dizzy feelings and thinks that she feels the presence of the mother bear. RL.4.3, RL.5.3

• Have students think about what has happened to Omakayas so far. Then ask: *What is the theme of the story?* growing up; learning to get along with family members *What are some examples from the text to support your ideas?* Sample answer: *The author describes how Omakayas compares herself to her sister. Omakayas talks about her family responsibilities such as playing with Little Pinch.* RL.4.2, RL.5.2

 ENGLISH LANGUAGE LEARNERS

Use Peer Supported Learning

Organize students into mixed-proficiency small groups. Tell students to ask questions about the characters and story events. Then have students take turns saying sentences that tell the events that have happened in the story.

RESPOND TO SEGMENT 1
Classroom Collaboration

Have partners work together to create and present a summary, as well as raise questions that might be answered in the next segment.

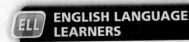

ENGLISH LANGUAGE LEARNERS

Use Cognates

Point out the English/Spanish cognates to aid students' comprehension: *island/isla; ferocity/ferocidad; treaty/ tradado; violence/violencia; indignation/indignación; affection/afecto; envy/envidio.* Have students use the words in complete sentences related to the text.

RESPOND TO SEGMENT 2

 Classroom Collaboration

Have small groups work together to summarize what they have learned. Have them ask questions about what they don't understand.

 Common Core Connection

RL.4.1 refer to details and examples when explaining what the text says explicitly and when drawing inferences; **RL.4.2** determine theme from details/summarize; **RL.4.3** describe a character, setting or event, drawing on details; **RL.4.9** compare and contrast the treatment of similar themes and topics; **RL.4.10** read and comprehend literature; **W.4.2** write informative/ explanatory texts to examine a topic and convey ideas and information clearly; **W.4.5** develop and strengthen writing by planning, revising, and editing; **SL.4.4** report on a topic or text, tell a story, or recount an experience/speak clearly at an understandable pace

RL.5.2 determine theme from details/ summarize; **RL.5.10** read and comprehend literature; **RL.5.9** compare and contrast stories in the same genre on their approaches to themes and topics; **RL.5.10** read and comprehend literature; **W.5.2** write informative/ explanatory texts to examine a topic and convey ideas and information clearly; **W.5.5** develop and strengthen writing by planning, revising, editing, rewriting, or trying a new approach; **SL.5.4** report on a topic or text, tell a story, or recount an experience/speak clearly at an understandable pace

Academic Vocabulary

Read each word with students and discuss its meaning.

indignation (p. 76) • anger; annoyance

betrayed (p. 87) • deceived

ferocity (p. 106) • intensity

treaties (p. 112) • agreements, contracts

smallpox (p. 142) • a disease that spreads easily and causes a high fever, rash, and blisters

---

FIRST READ ## Think Through the Text

Have students use text evidence and draw inferences to answer questions.

pp. 102–104 • *How do you know from the text that Omakayas is interested in her grandmother's bundles and packets of medicine?* It says on the top of page 103 that Omakayas noticed all of these bundles, how cleverly they were tied. Then, she and her grandmother talk about them.
RL.4.1, RL.5.1

pp. 142–144 • *What reason does the text give to explain how the visitor to the dance changes the lives of the people forever?* He died of smallpox. He exposed the people to "the scratching sickness."
RL.4.1, RL.5.1

pp. 182–185 • *How is the family saved from starvation?* Grandmother has a dream that the buck will wait for Deydey. She sends Deydey out to hunt and he kills the animal. The family shares the meat with others.
RL.4.3

SECOND READ ## Analyze the Text

- Review pages 95–98 with students. Ask: *How do the events at the rice gathering change Omakayas?* Sample answer: *She joins Two Strike Girl in dancing the rice. She enjoys the task, and the two girls become good friends.* **RL.4.3, RL.5.3**

- Have students reread pages 146–158. Ask: *What decision does Omakayas make?* She decides to go into the family house even though she is not sick. *How does her decision affect her and her family?* She nurses most of the family members back to health. She is there to hold Neewo when he dies. **RL.4.3**

- Have students look back at the first two segments. Ask: *What is the theme of the book?* growing up *How do you know?* The book tells about what happens to Omakayas as she grows up and learns to make decisions for herself. For example, she helps heal her family when they are sick. **RL.4.2, RL.5.2**

Academic Vocabulary

Read each word with students and discuss its meaning.

surge (p. 189) • rush or flow

admonished (p. 223) • cautioned or scolded

bewilderment (p. 225) • confusion

FIRST READ Think Through the Text

Have students use text evidence and draw inferences to answer questions.

pp. 194–199 • *Why is collecting maple sap so important to the family?*
*The sap flowing signals that winter is over and spring is coming. They
can move past the terrible things that happened in winter.* ⬛ RL.4.3

pp. 230–234 • *What does Old Tallow tell Omakayas about Omakayas's past?*
*Omakayas lived on an island called Spirit Island. She was the toughest
one and the only one on the island to survive a smallpox outbreak. Then
Old Tallow rescued her, and Deydey and his wife took her as their
daughter.* ⬛ RL.4.1, RL.5.1

p. 235 • *What does Old Tallow say is the reason that Omakayas was sent
to their island? She tells Omakayas that she was sent to save the others.*
⬛ RL.4.1, RL.5.1

SECOND READ Analyze the Text

• Have students discuss Omakayas's relationship with Pinch. Ask: *How
did their relationship change as they got older? Use specific examples
from the text.* Sample answer: *At the beginning of the book,
Omakayas does not like her brother, and they are mean to each other.
At the end of the book, Omakayas heals his burns, and Pinch is nice to
her when he lets Andeg crawl onto her shoulders.* ⬛ RL.4.3, RL.5.3

• Have students think about *The Birchbark House* and another coming-
of-age novel they have recently read, such as *Bud, Not Buddy*. Guide
them to use text evidence to compare and contrast the themes of the
two novels. ⬛ RL.4.9, RL.5.9

Independent/Self-Selected Reading

Have students reread *The Birchback House* independently or practice
analyzing text using another book. Suggested titles:

• *The Porcupine Year* by Louise Erdrich

• *The Game of Silence* by Louise Erdrich ⬛ RL.4.10, RL.5.10

Performance Task

WRITE & PRESENT

1. Have small groups discuss the
   theme of the story. Then have
   them compare the approach to the
   topic of growing up with the
   approach in another story, such as
   Bud, Not Buddy. Suggest that they
   create a T-chart or Venn diagram
   to record details from the text.
   ⬛ RL.4.9, RL.5.9

2. Have students write a paragraph
   that compares and contrasts how
   the two stories approach the
   theme of growing up. Have them
   cite specific information from the
   text that supports their ideas.
   ⬛ W.4.2, W.5.2

3. Students reconvene to share their
   paragraphs and edit their writing.
   ⬛ W.4.5, W.5.5

4. Students present their final
   paragraphs to classmates.
   ⬛ SL.4.4, SL.5.4

5. Students turn in their final
   paragraphs to the teacher.

See Copying Masters, pp. 144–147.

STUDENT CHECKLIST

Writing

☑ Compare and contrast how two
texts approach the same theme.

☑ Use a graphic organizer to record
details and ideas.

☑ Provide reasons supported by
facts and details from the text.

Speaking & Listening

☑ Engage effectively in
collaborative conversations.

☑ Logically present claims and
findings.

☑ Cite text evidence to support ideas.

Bud, Not Buddy is broken into three instructional segments.

Options for Reading

Independent Students read the book independently or with a partner and then answer questions posed by the teacher.

Supported Students read a segment and answer questions with teacher support.

Common Core Connection

RL.4.1 refer to details and examples when explaining what the text says explicitly and when drawing inferences; **RL.4.2** determine theme from details/summarize; **RL.4.3** describe a character, setting or event, drawing on details

RL.5.1 quote accurately when explaining what the text says explicitly and when drawing inferences; **RL.5.2** determine theme from details/summarize

Bud, Not Buddy
by Christopher Paul Curtis

SUMMARY Set against the backdrop of the Depression, this novel tells the story of ten-year-old Bud Caldwell. After being mistreated by a foster family, Bud sets out to find the man who he believes is his father, bandleader Herman E. Calloway. During his adventures, Bud learns much about life and ultimately finds a home and a family.

ABOUT THE AUTHOR **Christopher Paul Curtis**, an African-American writer, was born in 1953 and grew up in Flint, Michigan, the setting for *Bud, Not Buddy*. He also wrote *The Watsons Go to Birmingham—1963*. Both novels have been awarded the Newbery Honor.

Discuss Genre and Set Purpose

HISTORICAL FICTION Tell students that *Bud, Not Buddy* is an example of historical fiction. Explain that the novel takes place during a historical time period, specifically the Depression of the 1930s, and has a realistic plot. Discuss how the characters, settings, and events all reflect what that time period was like, but the story is made up.

SET PURPOSE Help students set a purpose for reading, such as to find out who Bud is and what happens to him in the story.

TEXT COMPLEXITY RUBRIC

Overall Text Complexity		*Bud, Not Buddy* HISTORICAL FICTION
Quantitative Measures	Lexile	MORE COMPLEX — 950L
	Guided Reading Level	T
Qualitative Measures	Text Structure	complex, unfamiliar story concepts
	Language Conventionality and Clarity	more complex sentence structure
	Knowledge Demands	cultural and literary knowledge useful
	Purpose/Levels of Meaning	multiple levels of meaning

Academic Vocabulary

Read each word with students and discuss its meaning.

commence (p. 5) • start

provoked (p. 11) • caused to happen in a bad way

lavatory (p. 11) • bathroom

conscience (p. 15) • the inside feeling of right or wrong

stricken (p. 56) • looking upset or distressed

 ENGLISH LANGUAGE LEARNERS

Use Sentence Frames

Have students fill in sentence frames to review what has happened so far:
First, Bud is in an _____.
orphanage
Next, he is put in a _____.
foster home
Then, he decides to _____.
run away

FIRST READ ▶ Think Through the Text

Have students use text evidence and draw inferences to answer questions.

pp. 1–2 • *Who is telling the story?* Bud Caldwell, a ten-year-old boy *How do you know?* Sample answer: *On page 2, the narrator responds to the name Buddy Caldwell by saying that it's Bud, not Buddy. The text says that the boy in the home Bud is being sent to is twelve and two years older than Bud.* ▬ RL.4.1, RL.5.1

pp. 2–4 • *What good news does the woman have for Bud?* He is leaving the Home to live with another family. *Does Bud think it is good news?* no *How do you know?* He says that he is the one who's going to have problems. ▬ RL.4.1, RL.5.1

pp. 41–42 • *Why won't Bud let people call him Buddy?* His mother named him and told him that Buddy was a dog's name, but Bud was like a flower waiting to open and be seen by the world. ▬ RL.4.3

SECOND READ ▶ Analyze the Text

- Remind students that Bud says that people are grown up at the age of six. Ask: *What are the three things mentioned in the text that make Bud think people are adults at the age of six?* Adults beat him; his teeth start falling out; his mother died. ▬ RL.4.1

- Discuss the relationship Bud had with his mother. Then ask: *What clues in the text show that Bud and his mother loved each other?* Sample answer: *The text says that they read together, her things are his special treasures, and she told him she loved him.* ▬ RL.4.3

- Have students review the segment. Ask: *What is the author's approach to the topic of growing up?* Sample answer: *The author shows that growing up can be difficult, especially with the kinds of challenges Bud faces, but that kind and helpful people do exist.* *What are some examples that support your ideas?* Bud's experience at the Home and his time with the Amoses show the challenges he faces; the family that helps him get breakfast and the librarian show him that there are kind people in the world. ▬ RL.4.2, RL.5.2

RESPOND TO SEGMENT 1

 Classroom Collaboration

Have partners work together to summarize what they have learned and ask questions about anything they don't understand.

Use Visuals

Help students identify the different objects that Bud has in his suitcase by drawing or displaying actual objects such as a paper flyer, a rock, a blanket, and a photograph. Have students draw and name the objects or say sentences that describe each object.

RESPOND TO SEGMENT 2

Classroom Collaboration

Have small groups work together to present a short summary as well as raise questions that might be answered in the next segment.

Common Core Connection

RL.4.1 refer to details and examples when explaining what the text says explicitly and when drawing inferences; **RL.4.3** describe a character, setting or event, drawing on details; **RL.4.9** compare and contrast the treatment of similar themes and topics; **RL.4.10** read and comprehend literature; **W.4.4** produce writing in which development and organization are appropriate to task, purpose, and audience; **W.4.5** develop and strengthen writing by planning, revising, and editing; **SL.4.4** report on a topic or text, tell a story, or recount an experience/speak clearly at an understandable pace

RL.5.1 quote accurately when explaining what the text says explicitly and when drawing inferences; **RL.5.3** compare and contrast characters, settings, or events, drawing on details; **RL.5.9** compare and contrast stories in the same genre on their approaches to themes and topics; **RL.5.10** read and comprehend literature; **W.5.4** produce writing in which development and organization are appropriate to task, purpose, and audience; **W.5.5** develop and strengthen writing by planning, revising, editing, rewriting, or trying a new approach; **SL.5.4** report on a topic or text, tell a story, or recount an experience/speak clearly at an understandable pace

Academic Vocabulary

Read each word with students and discuss its meaning.

devoured (p. 91) • greatly enjoyed

paltry (p. 117) • very small

resourceful (p. 132) • using what is available to solve problems

dignity (p. 139) • feeling good about oneself

FIRST READ # Think Through the Text

Have students use text evidence and draw inferences to answer questions.

pp. 60–62 • *Who is Bugs? another boy from the Home who runs away What do Bugs and Bud decide to do? jump the train and go west to look for work Are they successful? Bugs gets on the train, but Bud misses it.* ▬ RL.4.3, RL.5.3

pp. 89–95 • *Why does Bud want to find Herman E. Calloway? He thinks Herman is his father. How do you know? It says on page 94 that his daddy plays a giant fiddle and his name is Herman E. Calloway.* ▬ RL.4.1, RL.5.1

p. 141 • *How does Bud get to meet Herman E. Calloway? Lefty Lewis takes him to a place where Calloway's band is playing. How do you know from the text? The sign on the building says that Herman E. Calloway is playing there.* ▬ RL.4.1

SECOND READ # Analyze the Text

- Ask: *What does Deza Malone help Bud understand about families?* Sample answer: *Families are important; they need to be there for each other; even when separated they can be carried inside the heart. How does what Deza says affect Bud? Bud was thinking of going to California, but decides to stay in Michigan and look for his own family.* ▬ RL.4.3

- Guide students to discuss Lefty Lewis and his family. Ask: *How do Lefty Lewis, his daughter, and his grandchildren treat each other? They like to joke around, but you can tell that they really love each other. How do they treat Bud? They tease Bud, but treat him nicely. Why is this important? They remind Bud what it means to have a loving family.* ▬ RL.4.3, RL.5.3

- Have students refer to the first two segments to summarize the theme of the novel. Ask: *What do you think the theme is?* Sample answer: *As you grow up, you realize how important family is. What examples from the text show this?* Sample answer: *Bud thinks about his own family a lot. Bud learns about family from Deza and Lefty Lewis's family.* ▬ RL.4.2, RL.5.2

Academic Vocabulary

Read each word with students and discuss its meaning.

festering (p. 155) • growing irritation

shunned (p. 156) • ignored, rejected

bawling (p. 173) • crying

suspicious (p. 181) • not trusting

insinuating (p. 216) • hinting about something in an unpleasant way

FIRST READ ▶ Think Through the Text

Have students use text evidence and draw inferences to answer questions.

pp. 150–152 • *What happens when Bud says that Herman E. Calloway is his father?* The band members say it cannot be true. *What happens next? They decide to take Bud to a restaurant for dinner. What must Bud do after they eat?* tell them the truth ▭ RL.4.3

pp. 175–182 • *Where does Bud sleep in Grand Calloway Station?* in a girl's room *How do you know?* On page 177, Bud asks about the closets in the room, and Miss Thomas says that there's nothing in there but girl's clothes and toys. ▭ RL.4.1, RL.5.1

pp. 210–221 • *How does Bud finally prove that he is related to Herman E. Calloway?* He shows the picture of his mother. ▭ RL.4.1, RL.5.1

SECOND READ ▶ Analyze the Text

• Have students review the events that happen at the Sweet Pea restaurant. Ask: *Why does Bud cry?* He feels like he is home. *How do you know from the text how he feels?* He says that this was where he was supposed to be. ▭ RL.4.1, RL.5.1

• Have students think about the theme of *The Birchbark House* or another coming-of-age novel they have read recently. Then guide them to compare and contrast the novel to *Bud, Not Buddy* using text evidence to explain how they are alike and different. ▭ RL.4.9, RL.5.9

Independent/Self-Selected Reading

Have students reread *Bud, Not, Buddy* independently to practice analyzing the text on their own or have them practice the skills using another book, such as:

• *The Watsons Go to Birmingham—1963* by Christopher Paul Curtis

• *Holes* by Louis Sachar ▭ RL.4.10, RL.5.10

Performance Task

WRITE & PRESENT

1. Have small groups compare and contrast the theme of growing up in *The Birchbark House*, or another coming-of-age novel, with the same theme in *Bud, Not Buddy*. Ask students to record their ideas in a Venn diagram. ▭ RL.4.9, RL.5.9

2. Have students write a paragraph that compares and contrasts the two novels' approaches to the theme of growing up. Have them use information from their Venn diagram. Encourage them to cite text evidence. ▭ W.4.4, W.5.4

3. Have students exchange paragraphs and offer suggestions for revising and editing. Students edit their writing based on these suggestions. ▭ W.4.5, W.5.5

4. Students present their paragraphs to the class and then submit them to the teacher. ▭ SL.4.4, SL.5.4

See Copying Masters, pp. 144–147.

STUDENT CHECKLIST

Writing

☑ Write a paragraph comparing and contrasting stories.

☑ Identify story themes.

☑ Use correct language conventions.

Speaking & Listening

☑ Participate effectively in a collaborative discussion.

☑ Ask and answer questions about text details.

☑ Demonstrate an understanding of the text.

▶ OBJECTIVES

- Describe characters, settings, and events
- Determine theme
- Explain how chapters and scenes fit together
- Analyze text using text evidence

Where the Mountain Meets the Moon is broken into three instructional segments.

SEGMENTS

Options for Reading

Independent Students read the selection independently or with a partner and then answer questions posed by the teacher.

Supported Students read a segment and answer questions with teacher support.

![COMMON CORE] Common Core Connection

RL.4.1 refer to details and examples when explaining what the text says explicitly and when drawing inferences; **RL.4.2** determine theme from details/summarize; **RL.4.3** describe a character, setting or event, drawing on details

RL.5.1 quote accurately when explaining what the text says explicitly and when drawing inferences; **RL.5.2** determine theme from details/summarize; **RI.5.3** compare and contrast characters, settings, or events, drawing on details; **RL.5.5** explain how chapters, scenes, or stanzas fit together to provide the overall structure

Where the Mountain Meets the Moon
by Grace Lin

SUMMARY During the day, Minli and her parents work hard in a rice field in the Valley of the Fruitless Mountain. At night, Minli's father tells her tales about the Jade Dragon who keeps the fields barren and the Old Man of the Moon who has the power to change destinies. Hoping to change her family's fortune, Minli embarks on a journey to find the Old Man of the Moon.

ABOUT THE AUTHOR Grace Lin won fourth place in a book contest when she was in seventh grade. After that, she continued to write stories and decided she wanted to be an author and illustrator when she grew up. She has written many books for children that reflect her Asian heritage. *Where the Mountain Meets the Moon* won a Newbery Honor in 2010.

Discuss Genre and Set Purpose

FICTION Have students page through the book to examine the illustrations and the text. Discuss with students how they can tell that this story is fiction and has made-up characters and events.

SET PURPOSE Help students set a purpose for reading, such as to find out if Minli finds the Old Man of the Moon.

▲ TEXT COMPLEXITY RUBRIC

Overall Text Complexity		Where the Mountain Meets the Moon FICTION
		MORE COMPLEX
Quantitative Measures	Lexile	820L
	Guided Reading Level	V
Qualitative Measures	Text Structure	somewhat complex story concepts
	Language Conventionality and Clarity	figurative, symbolic language
	Knowledge Demands	cultural and literary knowledge useful
	Purpose/Levels of Meaning	multiple levels of meaning

Academic Vocabulary

Read each word with students and discuss its meaning.

impulsive (p. 2) • acting on a sudden urge to do something

manipulation (p. 19) • the act of controlling someone or something for personal gain

subdued (p. 52) • quiet and thoughtful

engrossed (p. 65) • having all of one's attention

 ENGLISH LANGUAGE LEARNERS

Use Sentence Frames
Guide students to generate words that could describe Minli, such as *impulsive, clever, thoughtful, kind,* and *helpful*. Then have them orally complete sentence frames, such as *Minli is ____ because ____.*

FIRST READ **Think Through the Text**

Have students use text evidence and draw inferences to answer questions.

pp. 2–3 • *What does the text say about Minli?* She has glossy black hair with pink cheeks, shining eyes always eager for adventure, and a fast smile that flashed from her face. She is lively and impulsive. **How is she different from the other villagers?** She is not brown and dull like the rest of the village. ▭ RL.4.3, RL.5.1

pp. 30–31 • *How do you know from the text that Minli decides to change her family's fortune?* Minli writes a note to her parents saying that she will go to Never-Ending Mountain to ask the Old Man of the Moon how she can change her family's fortune. ▭ RL.4.1, RL.5.1

pp. 46–49 • *Who does Minli meet in the forest?* the dragon **How is he different from what Minli thought he would be like?** She thought he would be wise, powerful, and grand, but he is crying. ▭ RL.4.3, RL.5.3

RESPOND TO SEGMENT 1

Classroom Collaboration

Have small groups summarize what they have read. Have them ask questions about what they don't understand.

SECOND READ **Analyze the Text**

- Discuss how the stories told by different characters help to explain what is happening in the main story. Have students reread "The Story of Fruitless Mountain" on pages 4–8. Ask: *How does this story connect with what we have learned about Fruitless Mountain?* It explains why nothing lives or grows on Fruitless Mountain. ▭ RL.5.5

- Tell students that the characters' words and actions often provide clues to the theme of the story. Reread the dialogue between Pa, Ma, and the goldfish man on pages 67–68. Ask: *What does the goldfish man tell Ma?* Even fates written in the Book of Fortunes can be changed. *How can anything be impossible?* **What might a possible theme for this story be?** It's not impossible to change your life. RL.4.2, RL.5.2

- Reread "The Story of the Paper of Happiness" on pages 80–87. Ask: *How does the text describe the message of Ba's story?* It says on page 87 that, like the secret word and the paper of happiness, Minli is not meant to be found. ▭ RL.4.1, RL.5.1

RESPOND TO SEGMENT 2

Classroom Collaboration

Have partners work together to create and present a summary of what has happened so far, as well as make predictions about what might happen in the next segment.

Common Core Connection

RL.4.1 refer to details and examples when explaining what the text says explicitly and when drawing inferences; **RL.4.2** determine theme from details/summarize; **RL.4.9** compare and contrast the treatment of similar themes and topics; **RL.4.10** read and comprehend literature; **W.4.2** write informative/explanatory texts to examine a topic and convey ideas and information clearly; **W.4.5** develop and strengthen writing by planning, revising, and editing; **SL.4.4** report on a topic or text, tell a story, or recount an experience/speak clearly at an understandable pace

RL.4.1 refer to details and examples when explaining what the text says explicitly and when drawing inferences; **RL.4.2** determine theme from details/summarize; **RL.5.9** compare and contrast stories in the same genre on their approaches to themes and topics; **RL.5.10** read and comprehend literature; **W.5.2** write informative/explanatory texts to examine a topic and convey ideas and information clearly; **W.5.5** develop and strengthen writing by planning, revising, editing, rewriting, or trying a new approach; **SL.5.4** report on a topic or text, tell a story, or recount an experience/speak clearly at an understandable pace

---

Academic Vocabulary

Read each word with students and discuss its meaning.

daunting (p. 99) • difficult

vaguely (p. 110) • unclearly; without specifics

intricate (p. 128) • complicated; having many small details

implored (p. 161) • begged; pleaded

malevolence (p. 163) • the wish to harm others

FIRST READ ▸ ## Think Through the Text

Have students use text evidence and draw inferences to answer questions.

pp. 120–125 • *Who does the beggar turn out to be?* the king *What detail in the text shows how Minli knows?* He wore a gold bracelet in the shape of a dragon. The buffalo boy had told her that only kings are allowed to wear the golden dragon. ▪ RL.4.1, RL.5.1

pp. 136–156 • *What does Minli get from the king and Dragon?* The king gives her a piece of paper that was torn from the Book of Fortune and passed down through many generations. The dragon gets a red string of destiny from the lion and gives it to Minli. *Why is Minli not sure which is the real borrowed line?* Because a line can be a sentence from a book or a poem, or it can be a piece of string or thread, so either could be the real one. ▪ RL.4.3

pp. 162–166 • *What happens to Dragon?* He is badly wounded by the Green Tiger. *How do you know?* It says on page 165 that the ugly wounds had turned black, and evil-looking liquid was starting to seep. ▪ RL.4.1, RL.5.1

SECOND READ ▸ ## Analyze the Text

- Reread page 114. Then ask: *What is Minli starting to learn?* Possessions and riches don't make people happy. Happy people are satisfied with what they have. ▪ RL.4.2, RL.5.2

- Reread pages 150–152 with students. Ask: *How has the relationship between Ba and Ma changed since the beginning of the story? Support your answer with story details.* At the beginning of the story, Ma thinks Ba is foolish. She thinks his stories are ridiculous. Now they are growing closer, and she is starting to understand him. On page 152, she tells him he may be right, and puts her hand in his. *Why might Ba think that* faith *might be the word written over and over on the paper of happiness?* Sample answer: *He believes that faith will bring Minli home.* ▪ RL.4.3, RL.5.3

Academic Vocabulary

Read each word with students and discuss its meaning.

hospitality (p. 204) • friendly greeting and treatment of guests

chagrined (p. 218) • disappointed and embarrassed

immortals (p. 228) • those that live or last forever

flourished (p. 239) • grew well; thrived

FIRST READ ## Think Through the Text

Have students use text evidence and draw inferences to answer questions.

pp. 218–219 • *How does Minli solve the problem of the tall mountain?* *She makes a kite of the two borrowed lines to get the attention of the Old Man of the Moon.* **RL.4.1, RL.5.1**

pp. 248–250 • *Which question does Minli choose?* She chooses to ask Dragon's question. *How do you know she makes the right choice?* It says that Minli knew clearly what question to ask. **RL.4.1, RL.5.1**

pp. 271–273 • *How has the Fruitless Mountain changed?* It was a black mountain that cast a gloom upon the village. Now it is a green mountain that sits in harmony with the blue sky. *How did this change happen?* After Minli and her family gave the Dragon Pearl to the king, the king gave the village seeds and farming equipment. **RL.4.3, RL.5.3**

SECOND READ ## Analyze the Text

• Reread page 250 with students. Ask: *What word is written on the page Minli borrowed from the king?* thankfulness *What do you think the theme of this story is?* Happiness comes from being thankful for what you have. **RL.4.2, RL.5.2**

• Reread "The Story That Ma Told" on pages 252–254. Ask: *How is this story similar to "The Story of Wu Kang"?* Both stories are about people who are not satisfied with what they have. *Unlike Wu Kang, how does Ma show that she has learned her lesson?* She realizes her daughter's laughter and love could not be improved by having riches, but instead joy had been a gift waiting to be opened. **RL.4.9, RL.5.9**

Independent/Self-Selected Reading

Have students reread *Where the Mountain Meets the Moon* independently, or have them practice the skills using another book. Suggested titles:

• *Charlie and the Chocolate Factory* by Roald Dahl

• *The Magician's Elephant* by Kate DiCamillo **RL.4.10, RL.5.10**

Performance Task

WRITE & PRESENT

1. Have small groups refer to the text to discuss ways the author uses story details and the traditional tales within the story to reveal the theme. **RL.4.2, RL.5.2**

2. Individual students write a paragraph that explains how the story reveals the theme. Tell them to include details from their small group discussions and use details from the story and the tradtional tales. **W.4.2, W.5.2**

3. Have partners reconvene to share and edit their writing. **W.4.5, W.5.5**

4. Partners present their final explanations to their classmates. **SL.4.4, SL.5.4**

5. Individual students turn in their final drafts to the teacher.

See Copying Masters, pp. 144–147.

STUDENT CHECKLIST

Writing

☑ Write in complete sentences.

☑ Give specific details and examples from the tales that show how the author reveals the theme.

☑ Use correct language conventions.

Speaking & Listening

☑ Participate effectively in a collaborative discussion.

☑ Provide reasons and details to support points.

☑ Speak clearly at an understandable pace.

- Explain the meaning of poetry texts
- Examine rhyme and figurative and archaic language in poetry
- Analyze text using text evidence

Options for Reading

Independent Students read the poem independently or with a partner and then answer questions posed by the teacher.

Supported Students read a segment and answer questions with teacher support.

Common Core Connection

RL.4.1 refer to details and examples when explaining what the text says explicitly and when drawing inferences; **RL.4.5** explain major differences between poems, drama, and prose/refer to their structural elements; **RL.4.10** read and comprehend literature; **RF.4.4b** read orally with accuracy, appropriate rate, and expression; **W.4.2** write informative/explanatory texts to examine a topic and convey ideas and information clearly; **W.4.5** develop and strengthen writing by planning, revising, and editing; **SL.4.4** report on a topic or text, tell a story, or recount an experience/speak clearly at an understandable pace

RL.5.1 quote accurately when explaining what the text says explicitly and when drawing inferences; **RL.5.4** determine the meaning of words and phrases, including figurative language; **RL.5.5** explain how chapters, scenes, or stanzas fit together to provide the overall structure; **RL.5.10** read and comprehend literature; **RF.5.4b** read orally with accuracy, appropriate rate, and expression; **W.5.2** write informative/explanatory texts to examine a topic and convey ideas and information clearly; **W.5.5** develop and strengthen writing by planning, revising, editing, rewriting, or trying a new approach; **SL.5.4** report on a topic or text, tell a story, or recount an experience/speak clearly

"The Echoing Green"
by William Blake

SUMMARY This poem takes a joyful tone as it describes the sounds and images of children playing on a grassy area on a spring day. The poem includes rhyme, visual imagery, and similes.

ABOUT THE POET **William Blake**, born in London in 1757, was both a poet and an artist. He made his living as an engraver and illustrator for books and magazines and wrote and published poetry on the side.

Discuss Genre and Set Purpose

POETRY Look at the poem with students. Guide them to distinguish it from prose. Help them note that the poem is written in lines organized into stanzas, rather than into paragraphs as prose is.

TEXT FOCUS: Rhyme Help students identify the poem's regular rhyming pattern in which every pair of lines rhyme. These pairs are called rhyming couplets. Also explain that "The Echoing Green" was written more than 200 years ago and uses some old-fashioned words, such as *green* in the title, that may be difficult to understand.

SET PURPOSE Help students set a purpose for reading, such as to find out what is happening in the poem, or to enjoy the rhyming pattern.

▲ TEXT COMPLEXITY RUBRIC		"The Echoing Green" POETRY
Overall Text Complexity		MORE COMPLEX
Quantitative Measures	Lexile	N/A
	Guided Reading Level	N/A
Qualitative Measures	Text Structure	somewhat complex poetic structure
	Language Conventionality and Clarity	archaic, unfamiliar language
	Knowledge Demands	somewhat unfamiliar situation
	Purpose/Levels of Meaning	multiple levels of meaning

Academic Vocabulary

Read each word with students and discuss its meaning.

sports (line 9) • play, something done for recreation

echoing (line 10) • the repeating of sound

green (line 10) • a large lawn; a grassy area

FIRST READ **Think Through the Text**

Have students use text evidence and draw inferences to answer questions.

• *What is happening in the first stanza?* *The sun comes up, and children are playing.* *How do you know?* *The poem says that the sun does arise and that sports shall be seen.* ▪RL.4.1, RL.5.1

• *What words rhyme in lines 1–4?* arise/skies; ring/Spring ▪RL.4.1, RL.5.1

SECOND READ **Analyze the Text**

• Explain that *green* is an old-fashioned word for a grassy area. *Why does the poet say that the green is "echoing"?* Sample answer: *It is echoing from the sounds of the bells, birds, and children.* Encourage students to ask and answer questions about other old-fashioned words or poetic language to clarify meaning. ▪RL.4.1, RL.5.4

• Recall that a simile uses *like* or *as* to compare. Ask: *What is the simile in the last stanza?* *The tired children going back to their mothers' laps are compared to birds returning to their nests to sleep.* ▪RL.4.1, RL.5.4

• Review Carl Sandburg's "Fog." Ask: *What does Sandburg compare fog to?* a cat *How is this different from the simile in "The Echoing Green"?* *Sandburg uses a metaphor and says the fog is a cat. He does not use the word* like *to make a comparison.* ▪RL.4.1, RL.5.4

☑ Practice Fluency

EMPHASIZE RATE Remind students that when they read poetry aloud, they should adjust their rate to match what happens in each stanza. Read aloud the first stanza at a fast rate to reflect what happens on the green in the morning. Discuss what happens in each subsequent stanza and how that stanza should be read. Then read the poem chorally with the class using an appropriate rate. ▪RF.4.4b, RF.5.4b

Independent/Self-Selected Reading

If students have already demonstrated comprehension of "The Echoing Green," have them practice skills using another poem. Suggested titles:

• *Poetry for Young People: William Blake* edited by John Maynard

• *Color Me a Rhyme* by Jane Yolen ▪RL.4.10, RL.5.10

WRITE & PRESENT

1. Have small groups discuss what happens in each stanza of the poem, how the stanzas build, and how they have to "translate" the rhymes and old-fashioned language to understand it better. Encourage them to ask and answer questions about old-fashioned and poetic language to clarify meaning. ▪RL.4.5, RL.5.5

2. Have each student choose a stanza and rewrite it as a paragraph in contemporary prose, citing details and quoting accurately to support their "translations." ▪W.4.2, W.5.2

3. Students work with their small groups to share and edit their work. ▪W.4.5, W.5.5

4. Have students share their paragraphs with the class. Tell students to read the stanza selected from the poem first and then read their prose. ▪SL.4.4, SL.5.4

See Copying Masters, pp. 144–147.

STUDENT CHECKLIST

Writing

☑ "Translate" and rewrite a stanza of the poem as a paragraph in prose.

☑ Cite details and quote accurately to support "translations."

☑ Use correct language conventions.

Speaking & Listening

☑ Participate effectively in a collaborative discussion.

☑ Ask and answer questions about old-fashioned and poetic language to clarify meaning.

☑ Present the work to the class, reading fluidly at an understandable pace.

"The New Colossus"
by Emma Lazarus

SUMMARY This poem was written to commemorate the gift of the Statue of Liberty from France to the United States. It contrasts the American statue with the ancient Colossus of Rhodes, a gigantic Greek statue built at the harbor of Rhodes. This poem helped the Statue of Liberty become a symbol of freedom and welcome to all.

ABOUT THE POET Emma Lazarus was born in 1849 in New York. She wrote "The New Colossus" in 1883 as a donation for a fundraiser. It was forgotten until over 20 years after Lazarus's death when it was inscribed on a plaque on the pedestal of the statue.

Discuss Genre and Set Purpose

POETRY Share the summary above. Explain that this poem is a sonnet, a poem with 14 lines, each of which has 10 syllables.

TEXT FOCUS: Allusion Explain to students that a poem may refer, or allude, to other people, stories, or events. A reader has to be familiar with the allusion to understand what the poet means. Point out that students may even have to do a little research to figure out an allusion.

SET PURPOSE Help students set a purpose for reading, such as to identify the allusions in the poem and figure out what they mean.

◮ TEXT COMPLEXITY RUBRIC		"The New Colossus" POETRY
Overall Text Complexity		MORE COMPLEX
Quantitative Measures	Lexile	N/A
	Guided Reading Level	N/A
Qualitative Measures	Text Structure	complex, unfamiliar poetic structure
	Language Conventionality and Clarity	figurative, symbolic language
	Knowledge Demands	cultural and literary knowledge useful
	Purpose/Levels of Meaning	multiple levels of complex meaning

FIRST READ **Think Through the Text**

Have students use text evidence and draw inferences to answer questions.

- *What is the New Colossus?* the Statue of Liberty 🔲RL.4.4, RL.5.4

- *What is the Statue of Liberty holding?* a torch 🔲RL.4.1, RL.5.1

SECOND READ **Analyze the Text**

- Encourage students to ask and answer questions about any unknown words and phrases to clarify meaning. Then ask: *What does* colossus *allude to?* the Colossus of Rhodes, a huge statue that stood in Rhodes harbor in ancient Greece 🔲RL.4.4, RL.5.4

- Explain that Lazarus uses the Colossus of Rhodes to represent Europe and the "Old World." Ask: *What represents the United States and the "New World"?* the Statue of Liberty 🔲RL.4.4, RL.5.4

- Point out that Lazarus contrasts the old and new colossuses in order to contrast the Old and New Worlds. *What does Lazurus mean when she tells the Old World to keep their ancient lands, their storied pomp?* She wants the Old World to keep their fancy ways, things, and people. *What does Lazarus ask to be sent to the New World instead of the pomp?* the tired, poor, huddled masses; the wretched refuse; the homeless, tempest-tossed 🔲RL.4.4, RL.5.4

- Remind students that the theme of a poem is the message or idea that the poet wants to convey to readers. Ask: *What is the theme of this poem?* Sample answer: *The theme is freedom, hope, and welcome to all, no matter who you are.* 🔲RL.4.2, RL.5.2

☑ Practice Fluency

EMPHASIZE EXPRESSION Point out that lines 1–8 describe the Statue of Liberty and lines 9–14 are a quote that the poet attributes to the statue. Discuss how the expression might differ when reading the two sections. Then have students echo-read the poem with you using appropriate expression. 🔲RF.4.4b, RF.5.4b

Independent/Self-Selected Reading

If students have demonstrated comprehension of "The New Colossus," have them practice skills using another poem. Suggested titles:

- *Hand in Hand: An American History Through Poetry* selected by Lee Bennett Hopkins

- *A Revolutionary Field Trip: Poems of Colonial America* by Susan Katz
  🔲RL.4.10, RL.5.10

WRITE & PRESENT

1. Have small groups discuss the theme of "The New Colussus" and how understanding the allusions, symbols, and other figurative language helps them figure out the theme. 🔲RL.4.2, RL.5.2

2. Individual students write an opinion paragraph that identifies the theme of the poem and how they used the allusions, symbols, and other figurative language to figure it out. 🔲W.4.1, W.5.1

3. Students work with partners to share and edit their work. 🔲W.4.5, W.5.5

4. Have students present their work to the class. 🔲SL.4.4, SL.5.4

See Copying Masters, pp. 144–147.

STUDENT CHECKLIST

Writing

☑ Write an opinion paragraph that identifies the theme of the poem.

☑ Include an explanation of how students used the allusions, symbols, and other figurative language to figure out the theme.

☑ Use correct language conventions.

Speaking & Listening

☑ Participate effectively in a collaborative discussion.

☑ Ask and answer questions about details in a poem.

☑ Speak clearly to report on a text.

OBJECTIVES

- Identify the characteristics of a narrative poem
- Examine the differences in the structural elements between poems and prose
- Analyze text using text evidence

Options for Reading

Independent Students read the poem independently or with a partner and then answer questions posed by the teacher.

Supported Students read several stanzas and answer questions with teacher support.

Common Core Connection

RL.4.1 refer to details and examples when explaining what the text says explicitly and when drawing inferences; **RL.4.2** determine theme from details/summarize; **RL.4.3** describe a character, setting, or event, drawing on details; **RL.4.5** explain major differences between poems, drama, and prose/refer to their structural elements; **RL.4.10** read and comprehend literature; **RF.4.4b** read orally with accuracy, appropriate rate, and expression; **W.4.1** write opinion pieces on topics or texts, supporting a point of view with reasons and information; **W.4.5** develop and strengthen writing by planning, revising, and editing; **W.4.6** use technology to produce and publish writing as well as to interact and collaborate with others/demonstrate keyboarding skills

RL.5.1 quote accurately when explaining what the text says explicitly and when drawing inferences; **RL.5.2** determine theme from details/summarize; **RL.5.10** read and comprehend literature; **RF.5.4b** read orally with accuracy, appropriate rate, and expression; **W.5.1** write opinion pieces on topics or texts, supporting a point of view with reasons and information; **W.5.5** develop and strengthen writing by planning, revising, editing, rewriting, or trying a new approach; **W.5.6** use technology to produce and publish writing as well as to interact and collaborate with others/demonstrate keyboarding skills; **SL.5.1d** review key ideas expressed and draw conclusions in light of information from the discussions

"Casey at the Bat"
by Ernest L. Thayer

SUMMARY This narrative poem tells the story of how Casey, Mudville's star hitter, strikes out in the last inning of a baseball game.

ABOUT THE POET Ernest L. Thayer, a writer for *The San Francisco Examiner*, wrote this narrative poem about the mythical Mudville team for the newspaper in 1888. "Casey at the Bat" did not become popular until several months later when an actor recited it in a theater attended by professional baseball players. It became an instant success.

Discuss Genre and Set Purpose

POETRY Display the poem and discuss elements that characterize it as a poem. Explain that this text is a narrative poem because it tells a story.

TEXT FOCUS: Structural Elements Guide students to explore the poem's structural elements: A poem is arranged in lines that are grouped into stanzas that build on each other. Many poems have a steady rhythm, where the syllables follow a metered pattern. Poems often rhyme.

SET PURPOSE Have students who play baseball briefly discuss the basics of the game to provide background knowledge prior to reading the poem. Then help students set a purpose for reading, such as to discover what happens when Casey bats.

TEXT COMPLEXITY RUBRIC

Overall Text Complexity		"Casey at the Bat" POETRY
		COMPLEX
Quantitative Measures	Lexile	N/A
	Guided Reading Level	N/A
Qualitative Measures	Text Structure	somewhat complex poetic structure
	Language Conventionality and Clarity	increased unfamiliar language
	Knowledge Demands	situation includes unfamiliar aspects
	Purpose/Levels of Meaning	single level of complex meaning

Academic Vocabulary

Read each word with students and discuss its meaning.

unheeded (line 31) • did not pay attention to

visage (line 37) • the way a person's face looks

tumult (line 38) • extreme noise

FIRST READ ▸ ## Think Through the Text

Have students use text evidence and draw inferences to answer questions.

- *What is the problem in the beginning?* *The home team is behind, and people in the stands think that the team will lose.* ⬤ RL.4.3, RL.5.10

- *How would you summarize this poem?* *The home baseball team is behind in the last inning. Two players are on base when Casey comes up to bat. Casey is over-confident and strikes out, losing the game for his team.* ⬤ RL.4.2, RL.5.2

SECOND READ ▸ ## Analyze the Text

- *What kind of person is Casey? Use details from the poem to support your opinions.* Sample answer: *Casey is over-confident and thinks he will win the game with one hit; he says that the first pitch isn't his style, and he ignores the second pitch.* ⬤ RL.4.1, RL.5.1

- Have students identify specific examples that show "Casey at the Bat" is a poem. Then say: *Suppose Thayer wrote the story as prose. How might it change?* Sample answer: *The poem is humorous and fun to read because of the verses, rhythm, and rhyming words. If it were written in sentences and paragraphs, it might lack the fun and the humorous mood.* ⬤ RL.4.5

☑ Practice Fluency

EMPHASIZE EXPRESSION Explain that readers can use different voices and expression for the different speakers' words in this poem. Have small groups take turns reading the different stanzas aloud. ⬤ RF.4.4b, RF.5.4b

Independent/Self-Selected Reading

If students have already demonstrated comprehension of "Casey at the Bat," have them use another narrative poem to practice skills. Suggested titles:

- *The Fastest Game on Two Feet: And Other Poems About How Sports Began* by Alice Low

- *Way to Go! Sports Poems* by Lillian Morrison ⬤ RL.4.10, RL.5.10

WRITE & PRESENT

1. Have small groups refer to the structural elements, including verse, rhythm, and meter, to analyze the poem. Then ask them to contrast the impact and differences of those elements to a prose summary. ⬤ RL.4.5, SL.5.1d

2. Have each student use a computer to write an opinion paragraph that explains the impact the text has because it is a poem instead of prose. Tell them to cite specific details from the text to support their ideas. ⬤ W.4.1, W.5.1

3. Have students exchange paragraphs with a partner. Ask them to offer suggestions for revising and editing. Suggest partners edit their writing based on these suggestions and correct them on the computer. ⬤ W.4.5, W.5.5

4. Have students print out and submit a copy of their paragraphs to the teacher. ⬤ W.4.6, W.5.6

See Copying Masters, pp. 144–147.

STUDENT CHECKLIST

Writing

☑ Write an opinion paragraph that explains how a poetry genre impacts the text as opposed to prose.

☑ Use technology to write, edit, and publish a paragraph.

☑ Use correct language conventions.

Speaking & Listening

☑ Participate effectively in collaborative discussion.

☑ Review key ideas expressed and draw conclusions in light of information from the discussions.

"A Bird Came Down the Walk"

by Emily Dickinson

Options for Reading

Independent Students read the poem independently or with a partner and then answer questions posed by the teacher.

Supported Students read several lines and answer questions with teacher support.

 Common Core Connection

RL.4.1 refer to details and examples when explaining what the text says explicitly and when drawing inferences; **RL.4.2** determine theme from details/summarize; **RL.4.3** describe a character, setting, or event, drawing on details; **RL.4.10** read and comprehend literature; **RF.4.4b** read orally with accuracy, appropriate rate, and expression; **W.4.2** write informative/explanatory texts to examine a topic and convey ideas and information clearly; **W.4.5** develop and strengthen writing by planning, revising, and editing; **SL.4.1d** review key ideas expressed and explain own ideas and understanding; **SL.4.5** add recordings and visual displays to presentations

RL.5.1 quote accurately when explaining what the text says explicitly and when drawing inferences; **RL.5.2** determine theme from details/summarize; **RL.5.4** determine the meaning of words and phrases, including figurative language; **RL.5.10** read and comprehend literature; **RF.5.4b** read orally with accuracy, appropriate rate, and expression; **W.5.2** write informative/explanatory texts to examine a topic and convey ideas and information clearly; **W.5.5** develop and strengthen writing by planning, revising, editing, rewriting, or trying a new approach; **SL.5.1d** review key ideas expressed and draw conclusions in light of information from the discussions; **SL.5.5** include multimedia components and visual displays in presentations

SUMMARY The poet describes a bird's search for food using vivid words. Then, through figurative language, the poet explains how she frightens the bird and causes it to fly away.

ABOUT THE POET **Emily Dickinson** is a highly acclaimed nineteenth-century American poet. She wrote more than 1,800 poems, but published only ten before her death in 1886.

Discuss Genre and Set Purpose

POETRY As students look at the poem, reiterate that poems use the sounds and meanings of words to express ideas. Then discuss how poets are free to ignore conventions of capitalization and punctuation.

TEXT FOCUS: Visual Imagery Explain that poets use vivid words, as well as figurative language, to aid in image enhancement and increase the enjoyment of the poem.

SET PURPOSE Encourage students to set a purpose for reading the poem, such as to picture the encounter with the bird in their minds.

⚠ TEXT COMPLEXITY RUBRIC			"A Bird Came Down the Walk" POETRY
Overall Text Complexity			ACCESSIBLE
Quantitative Measures	Lexile		N/A
	Guided Reading Level		N/A
Qualitative Measures	Text Structure		less familiar poetic structure
	Language Conventionality and Clarity		some unfamiliar or academic words
	Knowledge Demands		perspective includes unfamiliar aspects
	Purpose/Levels of Meaning		single level of simple meaning

Academic Vocabulary

Read each word with students and discuss its meaning.

angle-worm (line 3) • earthworm

plashless (line 20) • a word invented by Dickinson meaning "without a splash"

FIRST READ Think Through the Text

• Have students use text evidence and draw inferences to answer questions.

- *Summarize the poem. A bird is eating and drinking, but gets scared and flies away when the poet offers it a crumb.* **RL.4.2, RL.5.2**

- *What picture do you see in your mind after reading the first stanza? A bird bites a worm into two pieces and then eats it. Which words help you imagine this picture? Sample answer: The poet uses exact words, including* bit *and* raw. **RL.4.1, RL.5.1**

SECOND READ Analyze the Text

- Reread stanza 3 with students. Ask: *What picture do you get in your mind? The bird is scared because it has noticed the poet. How does the word* glanced *help you understand how the bird feels? Sample answer: Glance means to "look quickly." Things that are scared would look quickly around. How would your image change if the poet had used the word* look? *It wouldn't show that the bird is scared.* **RL.4.3, RL.5.4**

- Guide students to explore the poet's use of figurative language. Point out the simile where she compares herself to someone in danger. Then discuss the metaphor comparing the bird flying away to a person smoothly rowing a boat on the ocean. **RL.4.1, RL.5.4**

☑ Practice Fluency

EMPHASIZE ACCURACY Explain that this poem was written in the nineteenth century, so some words may seem awkward or unfamiliar. Poets also invent words, like *plashless*. Tell students they should underline words that they do not know and practice reading those sentences to ensure accurate reading. **RF.4.4b, RF.5.4b**

Independent/Self-Selected Reading

If students have demonstrated comprehension of "A Bird Came Down the Walk," have them read other poems to practice skills. Suggested titles:

- *Poems for Youth* by Emily Dickinson

- *Song of the Water Boatman and Other Pond Poems* by Joyce Sidman
RL.4.10, RL.5.10

WRITE & PRESENT

1. Have partners discuss how the poem uses vivid words to create visual imagery. Encourage them to explain their own ideas and understanding of the images based on the text. **SL.4.1d, SL.5.1d**

2. Tell students to write a paragraph that describes the actions of an animal they have observed. Challenge them to use vivid words to create an image in readers' minds. **W.4.2, W.5.2**

3. Have students exchange paragraphs and offer suggestions for revising and editing. Have them improve their writing and correct it on the computer. **W.4.5, W.5.5**

4. Have students add an image to publish their paragraphs. Ask students to share their writing in small groups. **SL.4.5, SL.5.5**

See Copying Masters, pp. 144–147.

STUDENT CHECKLIST

Writing

☑ Write a paragraph that describes the actions of an animal that students have observed.

☑ Use precise and specific words to help readers get a clear image of the animal in their minds.

☑ Use correct language conventions.

Speaking & Listening

☑ Participate effectively in collaborative discussion.

☑ Use text evidence to explain ideas and understanding.

☑ Demonstrate a connection between features in the poem and their own writing.

"Fog"
by Carl Sandburg

SUMMARY The poet uses an extended metaphor that compares the arrival of fog along the coast to the movement of a cat.

ABOUT THE POET Carl Sandburg is recognized for his free verse, a more modern form of poetry that uses images and figurative language to describe a topic instead of directly explaining it. Sandburg won a Pulitzer Prize for his book *Complete Poems* in 1950.

Discuss Genre and Set Purpose

POETRY Look at the poem with students. Guide them to compare it to prose. Help them note that the poem is arranged in lines that are organized into stanzas, but prose has sentences organized into paragraphs. Point out that "Fog" is free verse, which is poetry that does not rhyme. RL.4.5, RL.5.5

TEXT FOCUS: Metaphor Explain that a metaphor is a kind of figurative language in which the poet compares two unlike things. Point out that metaphors are different from similes because similes use the comparison words *like* and *as,* but metaphors do not.

SET PURPOSE Help students set a purpose for reading the poem, such as to understand the poet's use of metaphor.

TEXT COMPLEXITY RUBRIC

Overall Text Complexity		"Fog" POETRY
		COMPLEX
Quantitative Measures	Lexile	N/A
	Guided Reading Level	N/A
Qualitative Measures	Text Structure	less familiar poetic structure
	Language Conventionality and Clarity	figurative, less accessible language
	Knowledge Demands	somewhat unfamiliar perspective
	Purpose/Levels of Meaning	single level of complex meaning

> **Academic Vocabulary**
>
> Read each word with students and discuss its meaning.
>
> **harbor** (line 4) • a place along the water where ships can dock
>
> **haunches** (line 5) • the body part that a cat sits on

FIRST READ ## Think Through the Text

Have students use text evidence and draw inferences to answer questions.

- *To what does the poet compare fog?* a cat ▬RL.4.1, RL.5.4

- *What kind of figurative language is this comparison?* a metaphor *How do you know?* It compares two things, but does not use the words like or as. ▬RL.4.1, RL.5.4

SECOND READ ## Analyze the Text

- *What do you think the poet means when he says that the fog comes on cat feet?* Sample answer: *Cats are very quiet when they move, and fog is like that, too. Fog comes in quietly like a cat does.* ▬RL.4.1, RL.5.4

- *What is the fog doing when it is sitting on its haunches?* Sample answer: *The fog seems to quietly settle in one place for a little while, like a cat sitting quietly on its haunches.* ▬RL.4.1, RL.5.4

- Ask students to review William Blake's "Echoing Green." Ask: *What two things are being compared in the last stanza? The tired children going back to their mothers' laps are compared to birds returning to their nests to sleep. How is Blake's comparison different from the one in "Fog"? Blake uses a simile with the word like. In "Fog," Sandburg says the fog is a cat. He does not use the word like.* ▬RL.4.1, RL.5.4

☑ Practice Fluency

EMPHASIZE EXPRESSION Explain that a poet's choice of words can influence expressive reading. In "Fog," the many soft sounds of /f/, /s/, /th/, and /z/ reflect the muffling characteristic of fog and suggest reading with a quiet, calm expression. Echo-read the poem with students using a quiet, calm expression. ▬RF.4.4b, RF.5.4b

Independent/Self-Selected Reading

If students have already demonstrated comprehension of "Fog," have them use another poem to practice skills. Suggested titles:

- *Poetry for Young People: Carl Sandburg* compiled by Frances Schoonmaker Bolin

- *Under the Sunday Tree* by Eloise Greenfield ▬RL.4.10, RL.5.10

Performance Task

WRITE & PRESENT

1. Have small groups discuss the meaning of the metaphor of a cat in "Fog" and then compare and contrast that figurative language to the meaning of the simile in William Blake's "The Echoing Green." ▬RL.5.4

2. Individual students write a paragraph that compares and contrasts the metaphor of a cat in "Fog" with the simile in William Blake's "The Echoing Green." ▬W.4.4, W.5.4

3. Have students share their paragraphs with their group. Ask them to add details and edit their writing based on the group's suggestions. ▬W.4.5, W.5.5

4. Invite students to take turns sharing their writing with the class. ▬SL.4.4, SL.5.4

See Copying Masters, pp. 144–147.

STUDENT CHECKLIST

Writing

- ☑ Write a paragraph that compares and contrasts the metaphor of a cat in "Fog" with the simile in William Blake's "The Echoing Green."

- ☑ Develop and strengthen writing by revising and editing.

- ☑ Use correct language conventions.

Speaking & Listening

- ☑ Participate effectively in collaborative discussion.

- ☑ Report on texts, speaking clearly at an understandable pace.

- ☑ Demonstrate a connection between figurative language in poems and their own writing.

OBJECTIVES

- Identify the structure of poetry
- Understand how stanzas build on each other
- Explore the use of symbolism
- Analyze text using text evidence

"Dust of Snow"
by Robert Frost

SUMMARY Using rhyme and rhythm, the poet describes an encounter with a crow while on a walk in the snow. On a literal level, the dusting of snow that falls on the poet makes him happier; but on closer examination, Frost, known for his use of symbolism, is commenting on other life experiences.

ABOUT THE POET Robert Frost wrote many symbolic poems. These poems often depict nature and relationships that represent important life experiences and emotions.

Discuss Genre and Set Purpose

POETRY Have students look at the poem. Guide them to point out that a poem is arranged in lines, which are grouped into stanzas that build on each other to develop the concept or emotion.

TEXT FOCUS: Symbolism Tell students that some poets use a person, object, or event as a symbol to stand for a concept that is hard to explain. Discuss familiar symbols, such as the American flag or product symbols. Then point out that poets seldom explain their poems, so readers must make inferences about the symbols, which can lead to different interpretations of the poems.

SET PURPOSE Help students set a purpose for reading the poem, such as to enjoy the poem's images or to interpret its symbolism.

Options for Reading

Independent Students read the poem independently or with a partner and then answer questions posed by the teacher.

Supported Students read each stanza separately and answer questions with teacher support.

 COMMON CORE

Common Core Connection

RL.4.1 refer to details and examples when explaining what the text says explicitly and when drawing inferences; **RL.4.2** determine theme from details/summarize; **RL.4.3** describe a character, setting, or event, drawing on details; **RL.4.5** explain major differences between poems, drama, and prose/refer to their structural elements; **RL.4.10** read and comprehend literature; **RF.4.4b** read orally with accuracy, appropriate rate, and expression; **W.4.1** write opinion pieces on topics or texts, supporting a point of view with reasons and information; **W.4.5** develop and strengthen writing by planning, revising, and editing; **W.4.6** use technology to produce and publish writing as well as to interact and collaborate with others/demonstrate keyboarding skills

RL.5.2 determine theme from details/summarize; **RL.5.4** determine the meaning of words and phrases, including figurative language; **RL.5.5** explain how chapters, scenes, or stanzas fit together to provide the overall structure; **RL.5.10** read and comprehend literature; **RF.5.4b** read orally with accuracy, appropriate rate, and expression; **W.5.1** write opinion pieces on topics or texts, supporting a point of view with reasons and information; **W.5.5** develop and strengthen writing by planning, revising, editing, rewriting, or trying a new approach; **W.5.6** use technology to produce and publish writing as well as to interact and collaborate with others/demonstrate keyboarding skills

TEXT COMPLEXITY RUBRIC		"Dust of Snow" POETRY
Overall Text Complexity		**COMPLEX**
Quantitative Measures	Lexile	N/A
	Guided Reading Level	N/A
Qualitative Measures	Text Structure	simple, familiar poetic structure
	Language Conventionality and Clarity	figurative, symbolic language
	Knowledge Demands	experience includes unfamiliar aspects
	Purpose/Levels of Meaning	multiple levels of meaning

Academic Vocabulary

Read each word with students and discuss its meaning.

hemlock (line 4) • a kind of evergreen tree

rued (line 8) • felt sadness or remorse

FIRST READ ## Think Through the Text

Have students use text evidence and draw inferences to answer questions.

- *How do you know the speaker's feelings before the snow falls down?*
Sample answer: *In the second stanza, the speaker is feeling sad. The word* rued *means felt sad.* **RL.4.3, RL.5.4**

- *How does the event in the first stanza affect what happens in the second stanza?* *The snow falling on the poet in the first stanza makes him happier in the second stanza.* **RL.4.5, RL.5.5**

SECOND READ ## Analyze the Text

- Remind students that animals or things in poems can be symbols that have deeper meanings. Say: *Think about the characteristics of a crow. What might the bird symbolize?* Sample answer: *A crow is a symbol something bad might happen.* Continue to examine other symbols, such as snow or winter. **RL.4.1, RL.5.4**

- Remind students that readers may interpret symbols in a poem to better understand the poet's message. Then say: *Use your understanding of the symbols to explain the poet's message.* Sample answer: *A crow can be a bad omen, so it represents the poet's bad mood. When snow first falls, it is clean and pure, as well as cold and refreshing. It represents the happier, refreshing thoughts that come to the poet.* **RL.4.2, RL.5.2**

☑ Practice Fluency

EMPHASIZE RATE Explain to students that it is important to read the words of a poem filled with symbolism at a steady, but slower rate so that readers have time to think about the interpretation. Model how to read a poem at a slower rate. Then have students choral-read the poem with you. **RF.4.4b, RF.5.4b**

Independent/Self-Selected Reading

If students have already demonstrated comprehension of "Dust of Snow," have them use another poem to practice skills. Suggested titles:

- *Stopping by Woods on a Snowy Evening* by Robert Frost

- *Flamingos on the Roof* by Calef Brown **RL.4.10, RL.5.10**

Performance Task

WRITE & PRESENT

1. Have small groups review the symbolism in "Dust of Snow" and discuss their interpretations of the poet's message. Encourage each student to contribute to the discussion. **RL.4.2, RL.5.2**

2. Tell students to write a paragraph on the computer that explains their interpretation of the poet's message in "Dust of Snow." Remind them to support their ideas with details from the poem and their knowledge of symbols. **W.4.1, W.5.1**

3. Have students exchange paragraphs and offer suggestions for revising and editing. Suggest that students improve their writing based on these suggestions and make corrections on the computer. **W.4.5, W.5.5**

4. Have students print their paragraphs and submit them to the teacher. **W.4.6, W.5.6**

See Copying Masters, pp. 144–147.

STUDENT CHECKLIST

Writing

☑ Write a paragraph that interprets the message of "Dust of Snow."

☑ Use details about symbols to support ideas.

☑ Use technology to draft, revise, edit, and publish a paragraph.

☑ Use correct language conventions.

Speaking & Listening

☑ Participate effectively in a collaborative discussion.

☑ Use formal English in the discussion.

- Identify the characteristics of a narrative poem
- Explore rhythm in poetry
- Compare the same text written as a poem and prose
- Analyze text using text evidence

"Little Red Riding Hood and the Wolf"

by Roald Dahl

Options for Reading

Independent Students read the poem independently or with a partner and then answer questions posed by the teacher.

Supported Students read several stanzas and answer questions with teacher support.

 Common Core Connection

RL.4.5 explain major differences between poems, drama, and prose/refer to their structural elements; **RL.4.9** compare and contrast the treatment of similar themes and topics; **RL.4.10** read and comprehend literature; **RF.4.4b** read orally with accuracy, appropriate rate, and expression; **W.4.1** write opinion pieces on topics or texts, supporting a point of view with reasons and information; **W.4.5** develop and strengthen writing by planning, revising, and editing; **SL.4.1c** pose and respond to questions and make comments that contribute to the discussion and link to others' remarks

RL.5.3 compare and contrast characters, settings, or events, drawing on details; **RL.5.5** explain how chapters, scenes, or stanzas fit together to provide the overall structure; **RL.5.10** read and comprehend literature; **RF.5.4b** read orally with accuracy, appropriate rate, and expression; **W.5.1** write opinion pieces on topics or texts, supporting a point of view with reasons and information; **W.5.5** develop and strengthen writing by planning, revising, editing, rewriting, or trying a new approach; **SL.5.1c** pose and respond to questions and make comments that contribute to the discussion and link to others' remarks

SUMMARY Roald Dahl uses rhythm and rhyme to retell the familiar fairy tale *Little Red Riding Hood* with a twist. The girl in red takes matters into her own hands and trades her cloak for a lovely wolfskin coat.

ABOUT THE POET Roald Dahl was a British children's writer whose award-winning novels include *James and the Giant Peach, Charlie and the Chocolate Factory,* and *The BFG*.

Discuss Genre and Set Purpose

NARRATIVE POEM Explain that this text is a narrative poem, a kind of poem that tells a story and includes characters, a setting, and a plot. Lead students in comparing the structures of poetry and prose.

TEXT FOCUS: Rhythm Remind students that many poems have rhythm, where words follow a metered pattern of stressed and unstressed syllables. Discuss how rhythm adds interest and fun to the poetry.

SET PURPOSE Have students set a purpose for reading, such as to discover what happens in this version of *Little Red Riding Hood*.

▲ TEXT COMPLEXITY RUBRIC

Overall Text Complexity		"Little Red Riding Hood and the Wolf" POETRY
		ACCESSIBLE
Quantitative Measures	Lexile	N/A
	Guided Reading Level	N/A
Qualitative Measures	Text Structure	simple, familiar poetic structure
	Language Conventionality and Clarity	some unfamiliar language
	Knowledge Demands	several references or allusions to other texts
	Purpose/Levels of Meaning	single level of simple meaning

Academic Vocabulary

Read each word with students and discuss its meaning.

decent (line 2) • enough to meet a purpose

leer (line 17) • a look that shows extreme interest

knickers (line 45) • the British word for women's underwear

FIRST READ **Think Through the Text**

Have students use text evidence and draw inferences to answer questions.

- *Who are the characters in this narrative poem?* *Red Riding Hood and the wolf* ▪RL.4.10, RL.5.10

- *What is the plot?* *The wolf eats Grandma and dresses in her clothes in an attempt to fool and then eat Red Riding Hood.* ▪RL.4.10, RL.5.10

SECOND READ **Analyze the Text**

- Help students recall the traditional prose folktale of *Little Red Riding Hood*. Then ask: *How is Dahl's version like the original?* *Sample answer: The characters and basic story problem are the same; some dialogue is the same.* ▪RL.4.9, RL.5.3

- *How is Dahl's version different from the prose fairy tale?* *Sample answer: Dahl's version is a poem; Red Riding Hood notices the wolf's coat, not his teeth; she shoots the wolf and doesn't need to be rescued; she wears a wolfskin coat at the end of the story.* ▪RL.4.9, RL.5.3

- Explain that mood is the overall feeling of a text. Ask: *What is the mood of the poem?* *silly, humorous How does the poem's rhythm add to the mood?* *Sample answer: The rhythm is steady and happy, which adds to the humor of the poem.* ▪RL.4.10, RL.5.10

☑ Practice Fluency

EMPHASIZE RATE Discuss how rate can contribute to a listener's enjoyment of a poem as well as to the mood. Ask partners to read one stanza of the poem at both fast and slow rates. Discuss how the faster rate adds to the humor and enjoyment of the poem. ▪RF.4.4b, RF.5.4b

Independent/Self-Selected Reading

If students have demonstrated comprehension of "Little Red Riding Hood and the Wolf," have them practice skills using another poem. Suggested titles:

- *Roald Dahl's Revolting Rhymes* by Roald Dahl

- *Complete Nonsense of Edward Lear* edited by Holbrook Jackson
  ▪RL.4.10, RL.5.10

WRITE & PRESENT

1. Provide students with a prose version of *Little Red Riding Hood*. Then tell them to think about which Red Riding Hood version they like better, Dahl's poem or the prose, and why. Tell students to make notes that support their opinion and be prepared to discuss their ideas. ▪RL.4.9, RL.5.3

2. Invite small groups to share their opinions and ideas. Encourage them to link their comments to the previous remarks and elaborate to fully discuss each opinion. ▪SL.4.1c, SL.5.1c

3. Have students each write a persuasive essay that clearly states their opinion. Tell them to cite specific details from the text to support their opinions. ▪W.4.1, W.5.1

4. Have partners exchange essays and offer suggestions for revising and editing. ▪W.4.5, W.5.5

5. To publish the essay, have students neatly write it and submit it to the teacher.

See Copying Masters, pp. 144–147.

STUDENT CHECKLIST

Writing

☑ Write a persuasive essay.

☑ Include details that support the opinion.

☑ Use words and phrases to link opinions and reasons.

Speaking & Listening

☑ Participate in collaborative discussion.

☑ Link remarks on a topic to facilitate a discussion.

"They Were My People"
by Grace Nichols

SUMMARY This lyrical poem uses repetition, rhythm, and visual imagery to evoke the hard labor of slaves working in sugar cane fields in Guyana and the West Indies.

ABOUT THE POET Grace Nichols was born in a village in Guyana. She published her first collection of poetry *I Is a Long-Memoried Woman* in 1983 and won the Commonwealth Poetry Prize for it.

Discuss Genre and Set Purpose

POETRY Guide students to identify the features that make this a poem: repetition, rhythm, and visual imagery. Point out that the poem is mostly organized in a pattern of couplets.

TEXT FOCUS: Repetition Explain that poets use repetition to create rhythm—words, phrases, and sentences that are repeated to create a musical pattern and draw attention to the meaning. Poets may also use repetition to emphasize a theme or point of view.

SET PURPOSE Help students set a purpose for reading, such as to identify the repetition and rhythm in the poem.

TEXT COMPLEXITY RUBRIC

Overall Text Complexity		"They Were My People" POETRY ACCESSIBLE
Quantitative Measures	Lexile	N/A
	Guided Reading Level	N/A
Qualitative Measures	Text Structure	less familiar poetic structure
	Language Conventionality and Clarity	literal, accessible language
	Knowledge Demands	somewhat unfamiliar situation
	Purpose/Levels of Meaning	single level of complex meaning

FIRST READ ## Think Through the Text

Have students use text evidence and draw inferences to answer questions.

- *What are the people doing in this poem?* working to cut and process sugar cane 🔊 RL.4.1, RL.5.10

- *How are the first six lines of the poem similar?* The lines are nearly identical; phrases are repeated. *How are the pairs of lines different?* The couplets identify three different steps in harvesting and processing sugar cane: cutting, carrying, and crushing. 🔊 RL.4.1, RL.5.10

SECOND READ ## Analyze the Text

- Explain that the poet uses repetition to develop important themes. *Which words describe what the people are doing in lines 7–12?* weeding, carrying babies; working so hard *Why does the poet describe the people this way?* She is emphasizing the hard lives of sugar cane workers. 🔊 RL.4.1, RL.5.1

- *Why does the poet repeat* to the rhythm of the sunbeat? Sample answer: *to show that the sun is constant and harsh, like the people's work* 🔊 RL.4.1, RL.5.10

- *What is the relationship of the poet to the people in the poem?* The poet says that they were her people, so the people must be her ancestors. *Why is this important to understanding the poet's point of view?* Sample answer: *The poet has a strong connection to the people, and she wants others to understand how hard they worked long ago.* 🔊 RL.4.1, RL.5.6

☑ Practice Fluency

EMPHASIZE RHYTHM Remind students that when they read poetry aloud, they may enjoy it more if they emphasize its repetition and rhythm. Read the first line of each couplet and have students respond by reading the second line of the couplet. Discuss how this reading sounds like a song. 🔊 RF.4.4b, RF.5.4b

Independent/Self-Selected Reading

If students have already demonstrated comprehension of "They Were My People," have them practice recognizing repetition and rhythm using another poem. Suggested titles:

- *The Negro Speaks of Rivers* by Langston Hughes

- *The 100 Best African American Poems for Children* by Nikki Giovanni 🔊 RL.4.10, RL.5.10

Performance Task

WRITE & PRESENT

1. Have small groups refer to the text to discuss the repetition and rhythm in the poem. Encourage students to explore the poet's point of view and make inferences about the people's lives. 🔊 SL.4.1c, SL.5.1c

2. Have students each write a paragraph about how the poem's repetition and rhythm help them make inferences about the lives of the people and understand the poet's point of view. Tell them to include details and examples from the poem to support their main idea. 🔊 W.4.2, W.5.2

3. Students work with partners to share and edit their work. 🔊 W.4.5, W.5.5

4. Have students add recordings of parts of the poem to support their writing. Then ask students to present their work to the class. 🔊 SL.4.5, SL.5.5

See Copying Masters, pp. 144–147.

STUDENT CHECKLIST

Writing

☑ Write a paragraph about how the poem's repetition and rhythm help readers make inferences about the people's lives and understand the poet's point of view.

☑ Include details and examples from the poem to support the main idea.

Speaking & Listening

☑ Participate effectively in a collaborative discussion.

☑ Ask and answer questions about details in a poem.

☑ Create a recording of parts of the poem to support the writing.

"Words Free as Confetti"

by Pat Mora

SUMMARY This poem celebrates the power of language by comparing words to nature, people, and even foods. The poem also includes some Spanish words.

ABOUT THE POET Pat Mora was born in El Paso, Texas. She is both a poet and the author of numerous children's books. Mora writes about love, nature, religion, Latino themes, and what she calls "bookjoy."

Discuss Genre and Set Purpose

POETRY Ask students to identify the features that make this a poem: short lines, stanzas, rhythm, and sensory language. Point out that the poem includes words in Spanish as well as English.

TEXT FOCUS: Similes Remind students that poets use figurative language that creates vivid images in the reader's mind. Explain that one kind of figurative language is simile. Help students recall that a simile uses *like* or *as* to compare. Point out that the poem's title is a simile.

SET PURPOSE Help students set a purpose for reading, such as to identify and enjoy the similes in the poem.

TEXT COMPLEXITY RUBRIC

Overall Text Complexity		"Words Free as Confetti" POETRY COMPLEX
Quantitative Measures	Lexile	N/A
	Guided Reading Level	N/A
Qualitative Measures	Text Structure	less familiar poetic structure
	Language Conventionality and Clarity	figurative, less accessible language
	Knowledge Demands	perspective includes unfamiliar aspects
	Purpose/Levels of Meaning	single level of complex meaning

FIRST READ ## Think Through the Text

Have students use text evidence and draw inferences to answer questions.

- *What are words compared to in the title?* confetti ▭RL.4.1, RL.5.4

- *What is being compared in the similes in the first stanza?* *Words are compared to the sweetness of plump plums, the bitterness of old lemons, the warmth of almonds, and the tart of apple-red.* ▭RL.4.1, RL.5.4

SECOND READ ## Analyze the Text

- Remind students that poets use sensory words to paint a word picture. Reread lines 2–5, and then ask: *What sense does Mora appeal to in these lines?* taste *What similes help the reader understand how words taste?* sweet as plump plums, bitter as old lemons ▭RL.4.1, RL.5.4

- Ask students to review the rest of the poem. Ask: *What other senses does Mora appeal to?* *smell in lines 6–7, touch in lines 8–14, hearing in lines 15–18, sight in lines 19–22* Then guide students to identify and discuss the similes for each sense. ▭RL.4.1, RL.5.4

- Point out the Spanish words and read them with students. *Why do you think the poet includes these words?* Sample answer: *to add color to poem; to show that words are free in any language* ▭RL.4.1, RL.5.4

- Reread from line 22 to the end of the poem. *How are words like confetti?* *They fly and dance around and are free.* ▭RL.4.1, RL.5.4

☑ Practice Fluency

EMPHASIZE ACCURACY Explain to students that when they read aloud a text that includes foreign words, they should learn how to pronounce these words accurately. Model accurate pronunciation of the Spanish words from the poem: *abuelita*: ah-bwe-**lee**-tah; *gatitos*: gah-**tee**-tohs; *yo soy libre*: yo soy **lee**-bray. Then echo-read the poem with students, focusing on reading words accurately. ▭RF.4.4b, RF.5.4b

Independent/Self-Selected Reading

If students have already demonstrated comprehension of "Words Free as Confetti," have them practice recognizing similes using another poem. Model selecting a book from the classroom library and choosing one poem from the table of contents. Help students read the title and the poet's name. Suggested titles:

- *Color Me a Rhyme* by Jane Yolen

- *Stubborn as a Mule and Other Silly Similes* by Nancy Jean Loewen ▭RL.4.10, RL.5.10

WRITE & PRESENT

1. Have small groups discuss the similes in the poem and the images they create. Encourage students to discuss any similes they particularly like. Have them link their comments to others' remarks. ▭SL.4.1c, SL.5.1c

2. Have students each write an opinion piece that includes a discussion of the poem's use of similes in the poem, the images they create, and details about a favorite simile from the poem and why they like it. ▭W.4.1, W.5.1

3. Students work with partners to share and edit their work. ▭W.4.5, W.5.5

4. Have students share their writing with the class. ▭SL.4.4, SL.5.4

See Copying Masters, pp. 144–147.

STUDENT CHECKLIST

Writing

☑ Write an opinion piece.

☑ Include a discussion of the poem's use of similes in the poem and the images they create.

☑ Include details about a favorite simile from the poem and why they like it.

Speaking & Listening

☑ Participate effectively in a collaborative discussion.

☑ Ask and answer questions about details in a poem.

☑ Present writing to the class, speaking clearly at an understandable pace.

▶ **OBJECTIVES**

- Explain how an author uses reasons and evidence to support points
- Summarize main ideas and supporting details
- Analyze text using text evidence

Discovering Mars is broken into three instructional segments.

Options for Reading

Independent Students read the selection independently or with a partner and then answer questions posed by the teacher.

Supported Students read a segment and answer questions with teacher support.

 Common Core Connection

RI.4.1 refer to details and examples when explaining what the text says explicitly and when drawing inferences; **RI.4.3** explain events/procedures/ideas/concepts in a text; **RI.4.7** interpret information presented visually, orally, or quantitatively; **RI.4.8** explain how an author uses reasons and evidence to support points

RI.5.1 quote accurately when explaining what the text says explicitly and when drawing inferences; **RI.5.3** explain the relationships between individuals/events/ideas/concepts in a text; **RI.5.7** draw on information from print and digital sources to locate answers or solve problems; **RI.5.8** explain how an author uses reasons and evidence to support points

Discovering Mars
The Amazing Story of the Red Planet

by Melvin Berger

SUMMARY Billions of years ago, Mars was formed from bits of dust and gas. This book explores the past, present, and future of the Red Planet. It also shows how technology has helped people learn more about Mars.

ABOUT THE AUTHOR Melvin Berger is the author of more than 200 books for young people. Through his books, he shares his enthusiasm for science and scientific discovery. He has been honored for his work by groups such as the Children's Book Council and the National Science Teacher's Association.

Discuss Genre and Set Purpose

INFORMATIONAL TEXT Have students identify features of informational text in the book, including section headings, maps, diagrams, and photographs and captions.

SET PURPOSE Help students set a purpose for reading, such as to find out information about the planet Mars.

▲ TEXT COMPLEXITY RUBRIC		*Discovering Mars* INFORMATIONAL TEXT
Overall Text Complexity		COMPLEX
Quantitative Measures	Lexile	670L
	Guided Reading Level	O
Qualitative Measures	Text Structure	more than one text structure
	Language Conventionality and Clarity	general academic and domain-specific language
	Knowledge Demands	specialized knowledge required
	Purpose/Levels of Meaning	multiple purposes

Academic Vocabulary

Read each word with students and discuss its meaning.

conquest (p. 13) • the act of conquering

menace (p. 14) • something that is dangerous; a threat

broadcast (p. 14) • a program on the radio or television

Domain Specific Vocabulary

astronomers
(p. 9) • scientists who study stars, planets, and space

FIRST READ Think Through the Text

Have students use text evidence and draw inferences to answer questions.

pp. 6–7 • *What text detail describes how Mars is different from other planets and stars? Mars is deep red in color.* RI.4.1, RI.5.1

pp. 9–11 • *What three things led scientists to believe that Mars had life? the large white areas around the north and south poles, which looked like ice caps; the way the surface of the planet changed from light to dark; and the "canals"* RI.4.3, RI.5.3

p. 14 • *Why were people easily fooled by the made-up news story about Martians? They thought that there were intelligent beings on Mars. Some thought that Martians wanted to attack Earth.* RI.4.1, RI.5.1

SECOND READ Analyze the Text

• Have students look back at the photograph on page 7. Ask: *Why do you think the author chose to include this photograph? It shows Mars's deep red color and illustrates what makes Mars different from other planets.* RI.4.7, RI.5.7

• Reread page 9 with students. Ask: *What reason does the author give to support the idea that the Red Planet frightened early people? Since red sometimes makes people think of blood, some people feared that war and killing were coming.* RI.4.1, RI.5.1

• Guide students to review page 11. Ask: *What details show why people believed what Percival Lowell said about Mars? Sample answer: He was a well-known scientist, people often believe what scientists say.*
RI.4.8, RI.5.8

ENGLISH LANGUAGE LEARNERS

Use Visuals

Point to the photograph of Mars on page 7 and say *Mars*. Have students repeat. Model simple sentences to describe Mars. For example, *Mars is a planet. Mars is red.* Ask students to create sentences to describe the photo orally.

RESPOND TO SEGMENT 1

Classroom Collaboration

Have small groups summarize what they have learned and ask questions about what they still don't understand.

RESPOND TO SEGMENT 2

Classroom Collaboration

Have partners work together to present a summary of what they have learned and raise questions that may be answered in the next segment.

Academic Vocabulary

Read each word with students and discuss its meaning.

mammoth (p. 20) • huge

bombarded (p. 29) • attacked or blasted

FIRST READ Think Through the Text

Have students use text evidence and draw inferences to answer questions.

pp. 15–16 • *How are the moons Phobos and Deimos alike?* They are potato-shaped moons. *How are they different?* Deimos is smaller, and its orbit is farther away. **RI.4.3, RI.5.3**

p. 19 • *What have scientists learned about Mars?* It is very cold and very dry. Its surface is covered with volcanoes and lava. **RI.4.1, RI.5.1**

pp. 28–29 • *What did the Mariner missions accomplish?* They took measurements of temperatures, gases, and radiation and discovered that Mars is being bombarded by cosmic rays and ultraviolet rays that would be deadly to most forms of life. **RI.4.1, RI.5.1**

p. 33 • *What changes Mars's color from light to dark?* Violent dust storms blow the top layer of soil, which is lighter in color. The darker-colored soil underneath is then exposed. **RI.4.3, RI.5.3**

SECOND READ Analyze the Text

- Have students look back at page 18. Ask: *Why are new tools so helpful to astronomers?* The tools help astronomers see many more details on the surface of Mars. They can use the tools to measure the temperature, tell what chemicals are on the surface, and identify different gasses in the atmosphere. **RI.4.1, RI.5.1**

- Show students the visuals on page 21. Explain that authors include illustrations and diagrams to help readers picture important information. Ask: *How do the visuals support the text?* They help readers picture how wide and how tall Mount Olympus is compared to the size of Texas and Mauna Loa. **RI.4.7, RI.5.7**

- Review page 33 with students. Ask: *What reasons and evidence support the point that Martian soil is red?* The author says that Martian soil contains twice as much iron as the soil on Earth and the iron is rusted, which is why it is reddish-brown. **RI.4.8, RI.5.8**

Academic Vocabulary

Read each word with students and discuss its meaning.

immense (p. 36) • very large

fanciful (p. 50) • unrealistic

FIRST READ ## Think Through the Text

Have students use text evidence and draw inferences to answer questions.

p. 38 • *Why did scientists send the* Vikings *to Mars?* *to search for microbes* *What did the samples from the* Vikings *show?* *They showed no sign of microbes or other forms of life.* ◼ RI.4.1, RI.5.1

pp. 40–43 • *What are two possible plans for getting astronauts to Mars?* *One plan will place a space station in orbit around Earth. From the space station, people will launch a cargo ship, with fuel, supplies, and a landing craft, to orbit around Mars. Astronauts on the space station will take another ship to meet with the cargo ship, and then use the landing craft to explore Mars. The second plan would use a super-powerful rocket to carry people and supplies directly to Mars.* ◼ RI.4.3, RI.5.3

pp. 46–49 • *Why is a year on Mars longer than a year on Earth?* *Mars has a longer orbit around the sun and moves slower than Earth.* ◼ RI.4.3, RI.5.3

SECOND READ ## Analyze the Text

• Have students reread pages 43–45. Ask: *What are some of the effects that weak gravity would have on astronauts?* Sample answer: *Astronauts could jump higher and run faster; their muscles would become weak and flabby, and their bones would become thin and brittle.* ◼ RI.4.1, RI.5.1

• Review page 54 with students. Ask: *What reasons does the author give to support the main idea that "the future is very exciting indeed"?* *Astronauts will probably land on Mars in the next century. Mars could be a livable place for plants in 100 to 10,000 years. It might even be livable for humans one day in the very distant future.* ◼ RI.4.8, RI.5.8

Independent/Self-Selected Reading

If students have demonstrated comprehension of *Discovering Mars*, have them practice skills using another book. Suggested titles:

• *Our Solar System* by Seymour Simon

• *You Are the First Kid on Mars* by Patrick O'Brien ◼ RI.4.10, RI.5.10

Performance Task

WRITE & PRESENT

1. Have small groups choose a topographical feature of Mars, such as its soil, volcanoes, or craters, and create a chart that shows how the author supports main ideas about the feature with reasons and evidence. ◼ RI.4.8, RI.5.8

2. Have individual students use their charts to write a paragraph about one of the main ideas from the book and how the author supports it with reasons and evidence. ◼ W.4.2, W.5.2

3. Students return to their groups to share and edit their writing. ◼ W.4.5, W.5.5

4. Students present their final paragraphs to their classmates. ◼ SL.4.4, SL.5.4

5. Have individual students turn in their final descriptions to the teacher.

See Copying Masters, pp. 144–147.

STUDENT CHECKLIST

Writing

☑ Use reasons and evidence to support a particular idea about a topographical feature of Mars.

☑ Write in complete sentences.

☑ Use correct language conventions.

Speaking & Listening

☑ Participate effectively in a collaborative discussion.

☑ Answer any questions posed by listeners.

☑ Use language that is appropriate for the purpose.

OBJECTIVES

- Interpret information presented visually in maps
- Use text evidence when drawing inferences and answering questions
- Explain the relationship between graphics and ideas in the text

Let's Investigate Marvelously Meaningful Maps is broken into three instructional segments.

SEGMENTS

Options for Reading

Independent Students read the selection independently or with the teacher and then answer questions posed by the teacher.

Supported Students read each segment with a partner, and then answer questions with teacher support.

Common Core Connection

RI.4.1 refer to details and examples when explaining what the text says explicitly and when drawing inferences; **RI.4.3** explain events/procedures/ideas/concepts in a text; **RI.4.4** determine the meaning of general academic and domain-specific words and phrases; **RI.4.7** interpret information presented visually, orally, or quantitatively

RI.5.1 quote accurately when explaining what the text says explicitly and when drawing inferences; **RI.5.3** explain the relationship between individuals/events/ideas/concepts in a text; **RI.5.4** determine the meaning of general academic and domain-specific words and phrases; **RI.5.7** draw on information from print and digital sources to locate answers or solve problems

Let's Investigate

Marvelously Meaningful Maps

by Madelyn Wood Carlisle

SUMMARY This book in the Let's Investigate series tells about the kinds of maps that people use to study land, sea, and sky. It includes facts about some of the earliest maps, as well as explanations of how and why cartographers create maps.

ABOUT THE AUTHOR Madelyn Wood Carlisle is an author of children's books who has written several books in the Let's Investigate series, including books about meteorites, snow, and sand.

Discuss Genre and Set Purpose

INFORMATIONAL TEXT Have students look through the book and identify features of informational text, such as photographs, captions, and diagrams.

SET PURPOSE Help students set a purpose for reading, such as to learn information about the kinds of maps and how maps are made.

TEXT COMPLEXITY RUBRIC

Overall Text Complexity		Marvelously Meaningful Maps INFORMATIONAL TEXT
		ACCESSIBLE
Quantitative Measures	Lexile	990L
	Guided Reading Level	S
Qualitative Measures	Text Structure	some sophisticated graphics, may occasionally be essential to understanding the text
	Language Conventionality and Clarity	some unfamiliar or academic words
	Knowledge Demands	some specialized knowledge required
	Purpose/Levels of Meaning	single topic

Academic Vocabulary

Read each word with students and discuss its meaning.

cargoes (p. 4) • goods being transported on a ship, airplane, or vehicle

loot (p. 4) • goods usually taken by stealing or other dishonest means

dimensions (p. 6) • measure of extension in different directions

ancestors (p. 10) • relatives who lived long ago

Domain Specific Vocabulary

constellations (p. 5) • groups of stars that form patterns

atlas (p. 9) • a book of maps

geography (p. 11) • the study of the earth's surface, climate, landforms, and bodies of water

FIRST READ ## Think Through the Text

Have students use text evidence and draw inferences to answer questions.

pp. 4–5 • *What kinds of information can maps give us?* how to get from one place to another; the location of geographic features; details of other planets ⬤ RI.4.1

pp. 6–7 • *What is a relief map?* a three-dimensional map used to show surfaces, such as hills and mountains ⬤ RI.4.4, RI.5.4

pp. 10–11 • *What did Vespucci name the land he visited?* "Mundus Novus, or 'New World'" *Who called the New World* America *instead?* German mapmaker Martin Waldseemuller *Why?* He thought the discovered lands should be named after Vespucci. ⬤ RI.4.1, RI.5.1

SECOND READ ## Analyze the Text

• Reread pages 8–9 with students. Ask: *What does it mean if a map is drawn to scale?* an amount of space on a map represents a certain amount of space on land *Why might maps of different countries in an atlas be drawn to different scales?* Different countries are different sizes. Each country's map has a different scale so it will fit on a page. *What is the scale of the map of China on page 9?* 1 inch = 500 miles ⬤ RI.4.7, RI.5.7

• Revisit the information presented in the text and map on pages 10–11. Say: *Compare and contrast the journeys of Columbus and Vespucci.* Sample answer: They both sailed from Europe to the Americas; Columbus thought he landed somewhere that Europeans had already explored. Vespucci thought he had found a new place. RI.4.3, RI.5.3

ELL ### ENGLISH LANGUAGE LEARNERS

Use Visuals and Sentence Frames

To explain the different reasons people use maps, have students point to various maps throughout the section. Prompt students to use the following sentence frame to explain the purpose of the maps: *People use maps to _____.*

RESPOND TO SEGMENT 1

Classroom Collaboration

Have small groups work together to summarize what they have learned. Encourage them to ask questions about what they don't understand.

Domain Specific Vocabulary

latitude (p. 12) • distance measured in degrees north or south from the equator

longitude (p. 12) • distance measured in degrees east or west from the Prime Meridian

 ENGLISH LANGUAGE LEARNERS

Use Props

Complete the experiment on page 13 using an orange. Then, using the orange as reference, have students explain why countries near the poles appear larger on maps than on globes.

RESPOND TO SEGMENT 2

 Classroom Collaboration

Have partners create a summary and ask questions that might be answered in the next segment.

 Common Core Connection

RI.4.10 read and comprehend informational texts; **W.4.2** write informative/explanatory texts to examine a topic and convey ideas and information clearly; **W.4.5** develop and strengthen writing by planning, revising, and editing; **SL.4.1c** pose and respond to questions and make comments that contribute to the discussion and link to others' remarks

RI.5.10 read and comprehend informational texts; **W.5.2** write informative/explanatory texts to examine a topic and convey ideas and information clearly; **W.5.5** develop and strengthen writing by planning, revising, editing, rewriting, or trying a new approach; **SL.5.1c** pose and respond to questions, make comments that contribute to the discussion, and elaborate on others' remarks

---

Academic Vocabulary

Read each word with students and discuss its meaning.

accurately (p. 12) • correctly

foreign (p. 12) • situated outside of your own country

satellites (p. 16) • spacecrafts that orbit around a planet to gather information

FIRST READ ## Think Through the Text

Have students use text evidence and draw inferences to answer questions.

p. 12 • *Which imaginary line is found at 0 degrees latitude midway between the north and south poles?* the equator *What is the Prime Meridian?* an imaginary line at 0 degrees longitude ◼ RI.4.4, RI.5.4

p. 14 • *Aside from information about roads, what else can road maps tell you?* the location of places such as parks, museums, and other attractions ◼ RI.4.1

p. 16 • *How do scientists get information that they put on weather maps?* Instruments on ships, aircrafts, balloons, and satellites record information, and it is then drawn on maps. ◼ RI.4.3, RI.5.3

SECOND READ ## Analyze the Text

• Reread pages 12–13 with students. Ask: *How is a Mercator projection different from a globe?* It presents a flat map of Earth; the lines of longitude are drawn parallel to each other. On a globe, those lines curve and meet at the poles. *Why do lands closest to the poles look bigger than they really are?* The areas near the poles need to be stretched to make the map look flat. Any land in that area is made larger on the map to take up that space. ◼ RI.4.3, RI.5.3

• Guide students to analyze the symbols map of Michigan on page 15. Ask: *Which highway is the shortest route from Detroit to Flint?* Route 75 *What type of road is Route 53?* other through highway *What is the southern-most state park with camping facilities?* Algonac ◼ RI.4.7, RI.5.7

• Have students compare and contrast the weather maps on pages 20 and 21. Then ask: *What types of information do both maps provide?* temperatures, precipitation, fronts, high and low areas of pressure *How are the two maps different?* The map on page 21 uses color to show temperature ranges. It includes pictures to show sunny and cloudy weather. ◼ RI.4.7, RI.5.7

Academic Vocabulary

Read each word with students and discuss its meaning.

lot (p. 22) • a piece of land

reproduced (p. 23) • copied; reprinted

mule (p. 24) • an animal that is a cross between a horse and a donkey

rival (p. 28) • competing

FIRST READ ## Think Through the Text

Have students use text evidence and draw inferences to answer questions.

pp. 22–23 • *What do surveyors do?* *They measure the land; they help plan new buildings and help create maps of new places.* ◼ **RI.4.4, RI.5.4**

p. 25 • *Why do cartographers still update maps?* *They redraw maps to show both man-made and natural changes to the land.* ◼ **RI.4.3, RI.5.3**

p. 28 • *What are coast charts and harbor charts used for?* *Coast charts guide ships while they are sailing in water close to shore. Harbor charts help ships sail safely into harbors.* ◼ **RI.4.1, RI.5.1**

SECOND READ ## Analyze the Text

• Have students reread pages 24–25. Say: *What is a topographic map?* *a map that shows geographic features* If an area on a topographic map *has lines far apart, what could you conclude about that land?* *It is flat.* *Which text feature tells that?* *the caption on page 25* ◼ **RI.4.7, RI.5.7**

• Guide students to analyze the map and symbols on page 27. Ask: *Where are most of the orchards located?* *west of Route 81* Where are *the majority of homes found?* *along Route 11* Why might the homes *be there?* *to have access to a major road* ◼ **RI.4.7, RI.5.7**

• Revisit pages 30–31. Ask: *How do scientists measure the depths of the ocean?* *They send sound signals to the bottom and measure the time it takes for the sound to bounce back up again.* ◼ **RI.4.3, RI.5.3**

Independent/Self-Selected Reading

If students have demonstrated comprehension of *Marvelously Meaningful Maps*, have them practice skills using another book. Suggested titles:

• *Maps and Globes* by Jack Knowlton

• *National Geographic World Atlas for Young Explorers, Third Edition*
◼ **RI.4.10, RI.5.10**

Performance Task

WRITE & PRESENT

1. Have small groups choose a map from the book and then discuss the information they gained from the map and the supporting text. ◼ **RI.4.7, RI.5.7**

2. Have individual students create their own maps of their home, school, town, or state. Then ask students to write a paragraph that explains the different features of the map and why they decided to include each one. ◼ **W.4.2, W.5.2**

3. Have students share and edit their work in small groups. Encourage students to ask and answer questions to clarify their maps and writing. ◼ **W.4.5, W.5.5**

4. Have students present their maps and writing to the class. Have each presenter ask questions that prompt classmates to interpret information from the map. ◼ **SL.4.1c, SL.5.1c**

See Copying Masters, pp. 144–147.

STUDENT CHECKLIST

Writing

☑ Create a map using a model from the book.

☑ Write a paragraph that gives information about the map and map symbols.

☑ Use correct language conventions.

Speaking & Listening

☑ Engage effectively in collaborative conversations.

☑ Ask and answer questions about classmates' maps and writing.

- Describe the structure of ideas, concepts, or information presented in the text
- Explain the connection between scientific ideas
- Interpret text features

Hurricanes: Earth's Mightiest Storms is broken into three instructional segments.

SEGMENTS

Options for Reading

Independent Students read the selection independently and then answer questions posed by the teacher.

Supported Students read each segment with a partner and answer questions posed by the teacher after each segment.

COMMON CORE **Common Core Connection**

RI.4.1 refer to details and examples when explaining what the text says explicitly and when drawing inferences; **RI.4.4** determine the meaning of general academic and domain-specific words and phrases; **RI.4.5** describe the overall structure of a text or part of a text; **RI.4.7** interpret information presented visually, orally, or quantitatively; **RI.4.8** explain how an author uses reasons and evidence to support points

RI.5.1 quote accurately when explaining what the text says explicitly and when drawing inferences; **RI.5.2** determine two or more main ideas and explain how they are supported by details/ summarize; **RI.5.4** determine the meaning of general academic and domain-specific words and phrases; **RI.5.5** compare and contrast the overall structure in two or more texts; **RI.5.8** explain how an author uses reasons and evidence to support points

Hurricanes
Earth's Mightiest Storms

by Patricia Lauber

SUMMARY This book uses narratives to describe some of the most powerful hurricanes in U.S. history and provides in-depth information about these dangerous storms. The book explains how hurricanes form, the type of damage they can cause, and the instruments people can use to predict their severity.

ABOUT THE AUTHOR Patricia Lauber has written more than 100 books for children. Many of her books are about science and the natural world. In 1987, one of her most famous books, *Volcano: The Eruption and Healing of Mount St. Helens*, was named a Newbery Honor Book.

Discuss Genre and Set Purpose

INFORMATIONAL TEXT Show students the book's cover. Then have them look at the table of contents and predict what types of information will be included in each chapter. Have students browse the images in each chapter to try to confirm their predictions.

SET PURPOSE Help students set a purpose for reading, such as to learn how hurricanes form and discover what damage they cause.

▲ TEXT COMPLEXITY RUBRIC

Overall Text Complexity		*Hurricanes: Earth's Mightiest Storms* **INFORMATIONAL TEXT**
		COMPLEX
Quantitative Measures	Lexile	930L
	Guided Reading Level	T
Qualitative Measures	Text Structure	complex science concepts
	Language Conventionality and Clarity	increased academic language
	Knowledge Demands	specialized knowledge required
	Purpose/Levels of Meaning	multiple purposes

Academic Vocabulary

Read each word with students and discuss its meaning.

mooring (p. 7) • equipment used to secure a ship in place, such as cables

barreling (p. 8) • moving at a high speed

ablaze (p. 11) • on fire

eerie (p. 14) • mysterious and frightening

rotation (p. 20) • the act of turning around a center

bulge (p. 23) • a part that sticks out

Domain Specific Vocabulary

satellites
(p. 7) • spacecraft that orbit a planet

barrier beaches
(p. 8) • narrow strips of beach that protect the mainland from storms

storm surge
(p. 10) • water that is pushed ashore by a hurricane's winds

condense
(p. 19) • to change from gas to liquid

FIRST READ Think Through the Text

Have students use text evidence and draw inferences to answer questions.

pp. 7–17 • *What path did the 1938 hurricane take?* It hit Miami first. Then it hit, in order, New Jersey, Long Island, Connecticut, Rhode Island, Massachusetts, Vermont, and New Hampshire. 🔲RI.4.1, RI.5.2

p. 19 • *What is atmosphere?* the envelope of air that surrounds the earth and presses on its surface *What is the pressure like when hurricanes begin?* low 🔲RI.4.4, RI.5.4

p. 21 • *What is the eye of a storm?* the center of the storm where there is low air pressure *Describe what it is like.* It is calm, usually with blue skies and sunshine. 🔲RI.4.1, RI.5.2

SECOND READ Analyze the Text

• Reread pages 7–18. Ask: *Which kind of text structure is used in the first segment? Explain.* It uses chronology, or time-order. The chapter opens with the start of the hurricane. Then it tells about the events in order. *Compare this to the structure in the opening pages of* Horses *by Seymour Simon or another informational text. How are the structures different?* Sample answer: Horses is more descriptive; it tells information about horses. 🔲RI.4.5, RI.5.5

• Reread pages 18–20. *Using information from the text and the diagrams, explain how hurricanes form.* Warm, moist air rises from the ocean in a low-pressure area. The air cools as it rises and condenses into clouds. Heat is given off, which powers the storm. Rain falls. Warm air travels inside the eye; the air travels in a spiral because the earth is rotating.
🔲RI.4.7, RI.5.7

• Have students look back at pages 22–23. *What are two reasons that explain why the hurricane took a difference path?* The Bermuda High was more north than usual. A band of low pressure was along the coast. 🔲RI.4.8, RI.5.8

ENGLISH LANGUAGE LEARNERS

Use Visuals

Point to the labels on the diagram on page 20. Have students repeat the label names after you. Then have students use sentences to explain what happens when a hurricane is forming.

RESPOND TO SEGMENT 1

 Classroom Collaboration

Have small groups work together to summarize what they have learned so far. Encourage them to ask questions about what they still don't understand.

Domain Specific Vocabulary

altitude (p. 37) • the height above sea level

mangrove (p. 44) • a tropical tree that grows along tidal shores

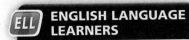

ENGLISH LANGUAGE LEARNERS

Use Visuals and Sentence Frames

Guide students to look at images on page 31 and point to the eye of the storm. Use sentence frames to check comprehension. For example, *The hurricane weakened on _____.*

RESPOND TO SEGMENT 2

Classroom Collaboration

Have partners present a short summary of this segment and suggest questions that may be answered in the next segment.

Common Core Connection

RI.4.2 determine the main idea and explain how it is supported by details/summarize; **RI.4.3** explain events/procedures/ideas/concepts in a text; **W.4.2** write informative/explanatory texts to examine a topic and convey ideas and information clearly; **W.4.5** develop and strengthen writing by planning, revising, and editing; **SL.4.4** report on a topic or text, tell a story, or recount an experience/speak clearly at an understandable pace

RI.5.3 explain the relationships between individuals/events/ideas/concepts in a text; **W.5.2** write informative/explanatory texts to examine a topic and convey ideas and information clearly; **W.5.5** develop and strengthen writing by planning, revising, editing, rewriting, or trying a new approach; **SL.5.4** report on a topic or text, tell a story, or recount an experience/speak clearly at an understandable pace

Academic Vocabulary

Read each word with students and discuss its meaning.

bucked (p. 29) • moved forward with a series of jerks

seized (p. 29) • took hold of in a quick, forceful way

migrant (p. 41) • moving from place to place to find work

wreckage (p. 41) • what is left after something has been destroyed

looters (p. 41) • people who steal, often from abandoned buildings

FIRST READ Think Through the Text

Have students use text evidence and draw inferences to answer questions.

p. 30 • *How do satellites help scientists?* Satellites show the size of hurricanes, their growth, and the size of the eye. They also show where a hurricane is located, its speed, and its track. ▬ **RI.4.3, RI.5.3**

p. 35 • *How are hurricanes named?* Hurricanes are named alphabetically, starting with an A name every hurricane season. The list of names repeats every six years. Different sets of names are used in different parts of the world. ▬ **RI.4.1**

p. 45 • *What types of land exist in South Florida today that did not exist around 1871?* urban areas, water conservation areas, agricultural land ▬ **RI.4.7, RI.5.3**

SECOND READ Analyze the Text

- Have students reread pages 29–30 and look at page 31. Then ask: *In which radar images is the eye clearly defined?* the third, fourth, and fifth *Use this information to tell when the storm started to weaken. It started to weaken on September 21 at 10:01 a.m. You can tell because the eye grew bigger.* ▬ **RI.4.7, RI.5.3**

- Guide students to reread page 32 and study the map on page 33. Then say: *Summarize how computer models help predict hurricanes. Computers compare the hurricane to similar hurricanes in the past. They predict possible paths of the hurricane.* ▬ **RI.4.2, RI.5.2**

- *What type of structure does the text on pages 44–48 follow—chronology, comparison, cause/effect, or problem/solution?* cause/effect *What are some examples of causes and effects the author provides?* Sample answer: *Cause: Land has been drained and cleared; Effect: The natural flow of water has changed.* ▬ **RI.4.5, RI.5.5**

Academic Vocabulary

Read each word with students and discuss its meaning.

trend (p. 54) • a general movement or course over time

suburbs (p. 55) • communities located just outside a city

equator (p. 57) • the imaginary circle around the earth that is halfway between the North Pole and the South Pole

evacuate (p. 59) • to move people out of an area for safety reasons

FIRST READ ## Think Through the Text

Have students use text evidence and draw inferences to answer questions.

pp. 54–55 • *What is a hurricane cycle?* *a 10- to 20-year period that may be "light" when few hurricanes hit or "heavy" when many large storms occur* ▭ **RI.4.4, RI.5.4**

p. 56 • *What did scientists hope would occur after using silver iodide in clouds?* *the eye would expand and weaken the storm* ▭ **RI.4.3, RI.5.3**

p. 59 • *How does a hurricane watch differ from a hurricane warning?* *A watch means a hurricane may hit in the future; a warning means a hurricane is probably going to hit within 24 hours.* ▭ **RI.4.4, RI.5.4**

SECOND READ ## Analyze the Text

• Reread pages 55–56. Ask: *What effect do "light" hurricane cycles have on human behavior?* *More people move to the coastline and build up cities and communities there.* *Why?* *They don't know or remember the damage that hurricanes can cause.* ▭ **RI.4.3, RI.5.3**

• Have students review page 59. Then ask: *Which text structure best fits these paragraphs—chronology, comparison, cause/effect, or problem/solution?* *problem/solution* *What solutions have people devised to be better equipped to deal with hurricanes?* *better forecasts, evacuation plans, building codes, flood walls* Then revisit *Horses* or another informational text students have read recently, and ask them to identify sections of text that follow the problem/solution structure. ▭ **RI.4.5, RI.5.5**

Independent/Self-Selected Reading

If students have already demonstrated comprehension of *Hurricanes*, have them compare and contrast its overall structure of ideas with that of another text. Suggested titles:

• *The Earth's Weather: Changing Patterns and Systems* by Rebecca Harman

• *Storms* by Seymour Simon ▭ **RI.4.5, RI.5.5**

WRITE & PRESENT

1. Have small groups use Venn diagrams as an aid to discussing text structures. Label one circle *Hurricanes* and the other circle *Horses* or the title of another informational text students have read. Label the overlapping area *Both*. Have students record how the structures of the two texts are similar and different. ▭ **RI.4.5, RI.5.5**

2. Have individual students write a paragraph comparing the structures of the two texts. Ask them to use text evidence to compare and contrast the text structures. ▭ **W.4.2, W.5.2**

3. Have students share their writing in small groups and then edit their writing. ▭ **W.4.5, W.5.5**

4. Have students present their Venn diagrams and paragraphs to the class. ▭ **SL.4.4, SL.5.4**

See Copying Masters, pp. 144–147.

STUDENT CHECKLIST

Writing

☑ Complete a Venn diagram comparing the texts' structures.

☑ Include examples that illustrate similarities and differences.

☑ Use correct language conventions.

Speaking & Listening

☑ Engage effectively in collaborative discussion.

☑ Ask questions that assist writing revisions.

▶ **OBJECTIVES**

- Interpret visual graphics to further understanding of the text
- Compare and contrast different concepts about money
- Define domain-specific vocabulary using context and the glossary

The Kid's Guide to Money is broken into three instructional segments.

Options for Reading

Independent Students read the selection independently or with a partner and then answer questions posed by the teacher.

Supported Students read each segment and answer questions with teacher support.

COMMON CORE **Common Core Connection**

RI.4.1 refer to details and examples when explaining what the text says explicitly and when drawing inferences; **RI.4.3** explain events/procedures/ideas/concepts in a text; **RI.4.4** determine the meaning of general academic and domain-specific words and phrases; **RI.4.8** explain how an author uses reasons and evidence to support points

RI.5.3 explain the relationships between individuals/events/ideas/concepts in a text; **RI.5.4** determine the meaning of general academic and domain-specific words and phrases; **RI.5.8** explain how an author uses reasons and evidence to support points

The Kid's Guide to Money
Earning It, Saving It, Spending It, Growing It, Sharing It

by Steve Otfinoski

SUMMARY This how-to book explains the ins and outs of money management for children. It gives ideas for how young people can make and save money. The book also provides guidelines for how to borrow money and donate earnings.

ABOUT THE AUTHOR Steve Otfinoski is the author of more than 100 books for children and young adults. He has written informational texts on numerous topics, including money, computers, koalas, and seahorses.

Discuss Genre and Set Purpose

INFORMATIONAL TEXT Explain to students that a table of contents and an index can help them find specific information in a book. Have students use the table of contents and index to find out what information about money is presented in the book.

SET PURPOSE Help students set a purpose for reading, such as to find out ways that they can earn and save money.

▲ **TEXT COMPLEXITY RUBRIC**

Overall Text Complexity		The Kid's Guide to Money INFORMATIONAL TEXT
		COMPLEX
Quantitative Measures	Lexile	890L
	Guided Reading Level	Q
Qualitative Measures	Text Structure	multiple text structures
	Language Conventionality and Clarity	some unfamiliar language
	Knowledge Demands	some specialized knowledge required
	Purpose/Levels of Meaning	multiple purposes

Academic Vocabulary

Read each word with students and discuss its meaning.

reap (p. 25) • bring about

technique (p. 39) • a method of accomplishing a goal

boutiques (p. 42) • small shops, usually for gifts and accessories

counterfeit (p. 52) • fake; imitation

Domain Specific Vocabulary

CDs (p. 12) • Certifications of Deposit; documents from a bank that tell the amount of interest your money will gain over a certain amount of time

manufacturers (p. 39) • companies that make or produce goods

FIRST READ ▸ # Think Through the Text

Have students use text evidence and draw inferences to answer questions.

pp. 18–19 • *What are some examples of jobs that you might do? shoveling snow, cleaning houses, and baby-sitting What text feature gave you these ideas? the bulleted list and the chart*  RI.4.1

p. 22 • *What is a* profit? *the money you have after you subtract the money you spent from the money you have earned If you spend $12 on lemonade for a lemonade stand and earn $54, what is your profit? $42* RI.4.4, RI.5.4

pp. 31–32 • *What are* taxes? *money that the government collects from people What do people pay taxes on? income, property, things they buy What do taxes help pay for?* Sample answer: *schools, libraries, roads, national parks* RI.4.4, RI.5.4

SECOND READ ▸ # Analyze the Text

- Have students reread the section "Five Tips for Conducting Your Business" on pages 27–29. Ask: *What are some reasons why you should keep accurate records? to see how much money you made; to figure out if you made enough to pay taxes; to remember your customers* RI.4.8, RI.5.8

- Review pages 38–42. Say: *Imagine an advertisement for a breakfast cereal that uses "The Celebrity Endorsement" or the "Image is Everything" advertising technique. Describe what the ad might look like. Answers will vary.* RI.4.3, RI.5.3

- Guide students to review the section "Shopping Through the Mail" on pages 52–55. Explain that many people ordered items through the mail before the Internet was popular. Ask: *How can you apply this advice about shopping through the mail to shopping online?* Sample answer: *You should still look for facts, read the entire ad, and check your order before submitting it. You should only purchase items with a parent's permission.* RI.4.3, RI.5.3

ELL ENGLISH LANGUAGE LEARNERS

Use Comprehensible Input

Discuss the idiom in the first sentence on page 11. Explain that when people have money that they really want to spend right away for no special reason, they can use this expression. Provide an example: *Let's go to the store. I have $10, and it's burning a hole in my pocket. I want to go buy something!* Then ask students to provide their own examples.

RESPOND TO SEGMENT 1

Classroom Collaboration

Have small groups work together to summarize what they have learned. Encourage them to ask questions about what they don't understand.

Academic Vocabulary

Read each word with students and discuss its meaning.

mechanized (p. 74) • equipped to operate without the work of humans

vault (p. 77) • a room for safely keeping money or valuable items

charities (p. 82) • organized groups that help those in need

phony (p. 83) • not real; fake

FIRST READ ## Think Through the Text

Have students use text evidence and draw inferences to answer questions.

p. 64 • *What is a deposit?* money you put into an account *What is a withdrawal?* money you take out of an account ◼ **RI.4.4, RI.5.4**

pp. 69–71 • *Why is it useful to have a checking account if you have a business?* The text says you can take money out to buy things or pay bills by writing a check. *What should you do in your checkbook after you write a check?* You should write down the amount you spent and subtract it from the amount of money in your account. ◼ **RI.4.1, RI.5.1**

pp. 85–88 • *Aside from donating money, how else can you give to those in need?* You can donate items you no longer want or need. You can volunteer your time. ◼ **RI.4.3, RI.5.3**

SECOND READ ## Analyze the Text

- Reread the section about banks on pages 61–62. Ask: *What are some reasons that a bank is a good place to keep your money?* Sample answer: It is a safe place to keep money; banks will give you interest to make your money grow. *What text structure did the author use to write the reasons?* The reasons are given in a numbered list, with a heading for each reason. ◼ **RI.4.8, RI.5.8**

- Have students look back at the image of a deposit slip on p. 64. Ask: *What information do you need to write on a deposit slip?* your name and account number; the date; the amount you are depositing in cash and checks; the total amount you are depositing *How much did Daniel deposit in cash?* $5.50 *How much did he deposit in checks?* $25 ◼ **RI.4.7, RI.5.7**

- Discuss the section "Giving Money" on pages 82–83. Ask: *Why do you think the author listed some excuses people make for not donating money?* because the reader might have these excuses *Why might the author have included explanations after each excuse?* to provide alternate ideas ◼ **RI.4.8, RI.5.8**

Academic Vocabulary

Read each word with students and discuss its meaning.

walloping (p. 96) • exceptionally large

debt (p. 97) • something owed to someone else

privileges (p. 97) • rights given to a person

inventory (p. 101) • a list of goods that you have on hand

matures (p. 103) • becomes fully developed or due

FIRST READ ## Think Through the Text

Have students use text evidence and draw inferences to answer questions.

pp. 91–92 • *What three things do financial institutions often use to check your credit?* income, job history, credit history *Is it easier to get a loan if you have a steady job and good credit?* yes RI.4.3, RI.5.3

p. 94 • *What are ways credit card companies make money?* They charge interest on unpaid balances and many charge their customers annual fees. RI.4.1, RI.5.1

pp. 100–101 • *How can collectible items be an investment?* Items can gain value over time. You can sell them and make a profit. RI.4.1

SECOND READ ## Analyze the Text

• Have students reread pages 90–91. Ask: *What is the difference between borrowing money from a bank and borrowing money from a finance company?* A bank will check to see if you will be able to pay them back. They may ask about your job or make sure you have collateral. A finance company might not check for collateral, but will charge a higher interest rate than a bank. RI.4.3, RI.5.3

• Guide students to look back at the graphic on page 97. Ask: *What is the minimum payment due?* $32 *According to page 96, why should the person pay the full balance of $64?* so that he isn't charged interest and so that his debt won't grow RI.4.7, RI.5.7

Independent/Self-Selected Reading

If students have demonstrated comprehension of *The Kid's Guide to Money*, have them integrate facts they learned with information from other books. Suggested titles:

• *The Story of Money* by Betsy Maestro

• *Growing Money: A Complete Investing Guide for Kids* by Gail Karlitz and Debbie Honig RI.4.9, RI.5.9

Performance Task

WRITE & PRESENT

1. Have partners examine the budget chart on page 37 and create their own personal budgets—either real or imagined. RI.4.7, RI.5.7

2. Have students write an essay explaining their weekly income, their needs, and the money remaining after needs have been met. Ask them to describe what they would spend the remaining money on and explain how much they would save for the future. W.4.2, W.5.2

3. Have partners share their budgets and essays and provide peer feedback. Then have students edit their writing. W.4.5, W.5.5

4. Have students present their work to their classmates. Tell them to explain why budgets are important. SL.4.4, SL.5.4

See Copying Masters, pp. 144–147.

STUDENT CHECKLIST

Writing

☑ Use the budget example in the text to create a personal budget.

☑ Write an essay explaining the budget.

☑ Incorporate domain-specific vocabulary learned from the text.

Speaking & Listening

☑ Present details about why budgets are important.

☑ Ask and answer questions.

☑ Engage effectively in collaborative conversations.

OBJECTIVES

- Identify and explain sequence of events
- Identify and explain cause-and-effect relationships
- Determine how an author structures text
- Interpret information presented visually
- Analyze text using text evidence

Toys! Amazing Stories Behind Some Great Inventions is broken into three instructional segments.

SEGMENTS

Options for Reading

Independent Students read the book independently or with a partner and then answer questions posed by the teacher.

Supported Students read a segment and answer questions with teacher support.

 Common Core Connection

RI.4.1 refer to details and examples when explaining what the text says explicitly and when drawing inferences; **RI.4.3** explain events/procedures/ideas/concepts in a text; **RI.4.5** describe the overall structure of a text or part of a text; **RI.4.8** explain how an author uses reasons and evidence to support points

RI.5.3 explain the relationships between individuals/events/ideas/concepts in a text; **RI.5.8** explain how an author uses reasons and evidence to support points

Toys!
Amazing Stories Behind Some Great Inventions

by Don Wulffson

SUMMARY This book tells the background stories of some of the world's most famous toys. The text explains how and when they were invented, gives some of the reasons they became popular, and offers anecdotal facts.

ABOUT THE AUTHOR Don Wulffson was a teacher before he became a full-time writer in 1994. He has written nonfiction books for children about inventions, toys, sports, and true adventures. Wulffson has received several literary awards including the National Council for the Social Studies/Children's Book Council Award in 2002.

Discuss Genre and Set Purpose

INFORMATIONAL TEXT Look at the selection with students, and help them find and identify characteristics of informational text, including chapter headings, illustrations, and lists of facts about each toy.

SET PURPOSE Help students set a purpose for reading, such as to learn how various toys were invented.

TEXT COMPLEXITY RUBRIC

Overall Text Complexity		**Toys!** INFORMATIONAL TEXT
		COMPLEX
Quantitative Measures	Lexile	1110L
	Guided Reading Level	R
Qualitative Measures	Text Structure	organization of main idea and details is complex but largely explicit
	Language Conventionality and Clarity	less straightforward sentence structure
	Knowledge Demands	moderately complex theme
	Purpose/Levels of Meaning	multiple purposes

Academic Vocabulary

Read each word with students and discuss its meaning.

flop (p. 5) • a failure or mistake

engineer (p. 5) • someone who plans and builds things

devices (p. 6) • pieces of equipment that have specific purposes

standard (p. 9) • usual, average

synthetic (p. 33) • manufactured instead of being found in nature

decay (p. 34) • to rot or break down

ironically (p. 39) • in a way that contradicts

ENGLISH LANGUAGE LEARNERS

Use Visuals

Discuss the way each toy works. Have students point to the corresponding visual in the book and tell about it. Then help them complete sentence frames such as the following:

Tops are toys that _____. spin on one end

When you play checkers, you move the pieces _____ diagonally across the board

FIRST READ ## Think Through the Text

Have students use text evidence and draw inferences to answer questions.

pp. 16–18 • *What does the text say are some of the ways Christiansen and his son improved their toy bricks?* They used plastic instead of wood to lower the cost of making the bricks. They added colors. They added tubes to make it easier to connect the bricks. **RI.4.1**

pp. 23–27 • *Why did Merrill and Henry Hassenfeld offer to buy the rights to Lerner's invention?* They were toy manufacturers, and they wanted to produce the toy themselves. **RI.4.3, RI.5.3**

RESPOND TO SEGMENT 1

Classroom Collaboration

Have partners work together to create and present a summary, as well as raise questions that might be answered in the next segment.

SECOND READ ## Analyze the Text

• Guide students to look back at pages 5–10. Ask: *Which two text structures does the author primarily use to explain how this toy was invented? How do you know?* The author primarily uses sequence, which follows the toy from the first idea through production. He also includes cause-and-effect when he explains how and why the toy was invented. **RI.4.5, RI.5.3**

• Review the first paragraph on page 13. Ask: *Why does the author suggest that readers think about how the seesaw was once used the next time they are on one?* Sample answer: The author wants readers to remember that the Romans used the seesaw in their circuses and compare that to how we use the seesaw today. **RI.4.8, RI.5.8**

• *In the last paragraph on page 39, the author uses the word* ironically. *What is the irony that he refers to?* For years, no one could find a practical use for this product. Then, after it became a popular toy, people found practical uses for it. **RI.4.8, RI.5.8**

**Use Gestures and
Sentence Frames**

Use gestures to describe the
process of creating toys.
Then have students
complete sentence frames
such as the following:

*In 1871, Redgrave added a
_____ and _____ to Bagatelle.*
spring, pins *Then in 1931,
Williams turned pinball into
an _____game.* electronic

RESPOND TO SEGMENT 2

**Classroom
Collaboration**

Have students summarize
what they have learned and
ask questions about the text.

**COMMON
CORE** **Common Core
Connection**

RI.4.1 refer to details and examples when
explaining what the text says explicitly and
when drawing inferences; **RI.4.4** determine
the meaning of general academic and domain-
specific words and phrases; **RI.4.7** interpret
information presented visually, orally, or
quantitatively; **RI.4.10** read and comprehend
informational texts; **W.4.2** write informative/
explanatory texts to examine a topic and convey
ideas and information clearly; **W.4.5** develop
and strengthen writing by planning, revising, and
editing; **SL.4.4** report on a topic or text, tell a
story, or recount an experience/speak clearly at
an understandable pace

RI.5.1 quote accurately when explaining what
the text says explicitly and when drawing
inferences; **RI.5.4** determine the meaning of
general academic and domain-specific words
and phrases; **RI.5.7** draw on information
from print and digital sources to locate
answers or solve problems; **RI.5.10** read and
comprehend informational texts; **W.5.2** write
informative/explanatory texts to examine a
topic and convey ideas and information clearly;
W.5.5 develop and strengthen writing by
planning, revising, editing, rewriting, or trying
a new approach; **SL.5.4** report on a topic or
text, tell a story, or recount an experience/speak
clearly at an understandable pace

Academic Vocabulary

Read each word with students and discuss its meaning.

versions (p. 46) • different forms of something
inspiration (p. 47) • influence or encouragement to do something
evolved (p. 50) • developed from
converted (p. 59) • changed
tokens (p. 80) • game pieces

FIRST READ **Think Through the Text**

Have students use text evidence and draw inferences to answer questions.

pp. 47–48 • *What evidence in the text supports the statement that the
first wheeled hobbyhorses appeared in China?* The author includes that
a fourteenth-century silk wall hanging from China shows children riding
on hobbyhorses with wooden wheels. **RI.4.1, RI.5.1**

pp. 58–62 • *What happened as a result of the flop of Whitehead's military
torpedo?* British toy manufacturers successfully used the idea to create
remote-controlled toy boats. *What happened to military remote-controlled
miniature airplanes after World War II?* They were reconceived as toys.
RI.4.3, RI.5.3

pp. 78–81 • *What evidence in the text supports that it would be hard
to find a game with more surprising origins than Parcheesi?* The author
explains that the game was invented in the 1570s in a weaving factory.
It quickly became the most popular game in India. Members of the
royalty made life-sized games. The game became a board game in
England before it was taken to America. **RI.4.8, RI.5.8**

SECOND READ **Analyze the Text**

- Have students find the idiom *eyes suddenly lit up* on page 63. *What
does this idiom mean?* got excited *What does* put on his thinking cap
on page 73 *mean?* He started to think of ideas. **RI.4.4, RI.5.4**

- Guide students to look at the illustrations on pages 82–85. Ask: *How do
these illustrations relate to the text?* Sample answer: *The illustration on
page 82 is a funny way to show that the pieces are called men. The
illustration on page 83 is a funny way to show that ancient Egyptian
pharaohs were buried with checkers sets. The illustration on page 84
shows that characters from* The Odyssey *played checkers in the story.*
RI.4.7, RI.5.7

- Guide students to reread pages 82–85. Then ask: *How are Twister®
and checkers alike?* They both appeal to adults and children.
RI.4.8, RI.5.8

Academic Vocabulary

Read each word with students and discuss its meaning.

patented (p. 98) • got the rights to protect an idea

strategy (p. 99) • approach or policy

trivial (p. 118) • unimportant

novelty (p. 130) • a small toy

FIRST READ ## Think Through the Text

Have students use text evidence and draw inferences to answer questions.

p. 95 • *Which was built first, real trains or toy trains?* real trains *How do you know?* The text says that the first real train was built in 1550 and toy trains soon followed. ▬ **RI.4.1, RI.5.1**

pp. 109–110 • *Explain how table tennis got a new name.* The Parker Brothers toy company wanted a name for their version of table tennis. One employee noticed that the sounds the ball made when hitting the table and the paddle were *ping* and *pong*. ▬ **RI.4.3, RI.5.3**

pp. 112–114 • *Who helped make pinball more like it is today?* Harry Williams *How do you know?* It says on page 113 that he was the father of the modern pinball. ▬ **RI.4.1, RI.5.1**

SECOND READ ## Analyze the Text

- Guide students to reread pages 102–105. Ask: *Why and how did the uses for this product change?* It started out as a cleaning product but did not sell well. After a teacher began using it like clay, it became popular as a toy. *How did these changes affect the Kutol Chemical Company?* The company changed from manufacturing cleaning products to making this clay-like toy, and became more successful. ▬ **RI.4.3, RI.5.3**

- Review pages 124–129. Then ask: *What does the text include about how the military used kites?* Sample answer: The Chinese and the Europeans used kites as signaling devices. They also used soldiers in kites as spies. The U.S. Army used kites for anti-aircraft training. ▬ **RI.4.1**

Independent/Self-Selected Reading

Have students reread *Toys!* or have them practice skills with another book. Suggested titles:

- *The Kid Who Invented the Popsicle and Other Surprising Inventions* by Don Wulffson

- *A History of Toys* by Antonia Fraser ▬ **RI.4.10, RI.5.10**

Performance Task

WRITE & PRESENT

1. Have small groups refer to the text to discuss how different toys were invented and became popular. Encourage students to take notes and record the relationships between the different ideas of the inventors. ▬ **RI.4.3, RI.5.3**

2. Have students select one toy they read about and write a paragraph that explains the relationship between the different ideas of the inventor of that toy. Then have them include an illustration of the toy. ▬ **W.4.2, W.5.2**

3. Students reconvene to share their summaries in their small groups and then edit their writing. ▬ **W.4.5, W.5.5**

4. Students present their final summaries to classmates. ▬ **SL.4.4, SL.5.4**

5. Individual students turn in their final summaries to the teacher.

See Copying Masters, pp. 144–147.

STUDENT CHECKLIST

Writing

☑ Write in complete sentences.

☑ Describe the relationship between different ideas of toys' inventors.

☑ Use correct language conventions.

Speaking & Listening

☑ Engage effectively in collaborative conversations.

☑ Logically present claims and findings.

☑ Cite text evidence demonstrating sequence and cause-and-effect relationships.

- Identify opinions and supporting reasons
- Identify main idea and supporting details
- Interpret information presented visually
- Compare and contrast information
- Analyze text using text evidence

"Good Pet, Bad Pet" is broken into three instructional segments.

SEGMENTS

Options for Reading

Independent Students read the article independently or with a partner and then answer questions posed by the teacher.

Supported Students read a segment and answer questions with teacher support.

 COMMON CORE Common Core Connection

RI.4.1 refer to details and examples when explaining what the text says explicitly and when drawing inferences; **RI.4.5** describe the overall structure of a text or part of a text; **RI.4.7** interpret information presented visually, orally, or quantitatively; **RI.4.8** explain how an author uses reasons and evidence to support points

RI.5.1 quote accurately when explaining what the text says explicitly and when drawing inferences; **RI.5.7** draw on information from print and digital sources to locate answers or solve problems; **RI.5.8** explain how an author uses reasons and evidence to support points

"Good Pet, Bad Pet"

by Elizabeth Schleichert

SUMMARY This *Ranger Rick* magazine article presents information about what to consider when deciding whether or not to get a pet. The author provides facts and opinions about groups of animals she does and does not recommend.

ABOUT THE AUTHOR Elizabeth Schleichert is a former editor and writer for *Ranger Rick* magazine. She now tutors young people in English and writing.

Discuss Genre and Set Purpose

INFORMATIONAL TEXT Look at the selection with students, and help them find and identify characteristics of informational text, including section headings, subheadings, illustrations, keys, and side notes.

SET PURPOSE Help students set a purpose for reading, such as to find information about which animals make good pets, which do not, and why.

TEXT COMPLEXITY RUBRIC

Overall Text Complexity		Good Pet, Bad Pet INFORMATIONAL TEXT
		ACCESSIBLE
Quantitative Measures	Lexile	660L
	Guided Reading Level	O
Qualitative Measures	Text Structure	explicit compare/contrast text structure
	Language Conventionality and Clarity	clear, direct language
	Knowledge Demands	everyday knowledge required
	Purpose/Levels of Meaning	explicitly stated

Academic Vocabulary

Read each word with students and discuss its meaning.

vet (p. 28) • veterinarian, animal doctor

allergic (p. 28) • having an allergy

sprawl (p. 28) • spread out

affectionate (p. 29) • loving

captivity (p. 29) • not in the wild

unpredictable (p. 30) • not being able to guess what will happen

Domain Specific Vocabulary

spaying (p. 28) • an operation on a female dog that makes it impossible for the dog to have puppies

neutering (p. 28) • an operation on a male dog that makes it impossible for the dog to make puppies

FIRST READ ## Think Through the Text

Have students use text evidence and draw inferences to answer questions.

p. 27 • *What information can you learn from this page? You can learn that his article is about different animals and whether they make good or bad pets.*  RI.4.7, RI.5.7

p. 28 • *What does the text say is the reason you should talk with your parents before getting a pet? A parent is the one in charge of pet care and would have to be willing to help out if necessary.* 🔊 RI.4.1

p. 28 • *What do the symbols* T *and* $ *stand for at the end of each section? How do you know? The number of* T *symbols shows how much time a pet takes; for example,* TTT *means a pet takes a lot of time. The number of* $ *symbols shows how expensive a pet is, such as* $$$ *for a very expensive pet. The key on page 29 shows what the symbols mean.*
🔊 RI.4.7, RI.5.7

SECOND READ ## Analyze the Text

• Discuss with students the difference between fact and opinion. Ask: *What is one fact that supports the idea that dogs make good pets? What is one opinion? Sample answer: Fact: Dogs can live from 8 to 16 years; Opinion: A dog can become a best friend and a playmate.*
🔊 RI.4.1, RI.5.1

• *Which section would you read if you wanted to know how long you need to spend each day with your dog? the section titled* TIME
🔊 RI.4.5, RI.5.7

• Point out the section titled FINAL WORD. Ask: *Whose "final word" is this? the author's Where does the author think the best place is to get a dog as a pet? from a shelter or breed-rescue group How do you know? The author states many benefits of getting a dog from one of these places, such as it costs less and mixed breeds are often healthier than purebreds. She also says to avoid large kennels and pet shops.*
🔊 RI.4.8, RI.5.8

ELL ENGLISH LANGUAGE LEARNERS

Comprehensible Input

Ask students yes/no questions to address their opinions about what they read and their personal opinions, such as: *Do you think a dog is a good pet? Is a dog hard to care for? Is an apartment a good place to live with a dog?* Then ask students to expand on answers by giving supporting reasons.

RESPOND TO SEGMENT 1

Classroom Collaboration

Have partners work together to create and present a summary, as well as raise questions that might be answered in the next segment.

RESPOND TO SEGMENT 2

Classroom Collaboration

Have small groups work together to summarize what they have learned. Have them ask questions about what they don't understand.

COMMON CORE **Common Core Connection**

RI.4.1 refer to details and examples when explaining what the text says explicitly and when drawing inferences; **RI.4.3** explain events procedures/ideas/concepts in a text; **RI.4.8** explain how an author uses reasons and evidence to support points; **RI.4.10** read and comprehend informational texts; **W.4.1** write opinion pieces on topics or texts, supporting a point of view with reasons and information; **W.4.5** develop and strengthen writing by planning, revising, and editing; **SL.4.4** report on a topic or text, tell a story, or recount an experience/speak clearly at an understandable pace

RI.5.1 quote accurately when explaining what the text says explicitly and when drawing inferences; **RI.5.3** explain the relationships between individuals/events/ideas/concepts in a text; **RI.5.8** explain how an author uses reasons and evidence to support points; **RI.5.10** read and comprehend informational texts; **W.5.1** write opinion pieces on topics or texts, supporting a point of view with reasons and information; **W.5.5** develop and strengthen writing by planning, revising, editing, rewriting, or trying a new approach; **SL.5.4** report on a topic or text, tell a story, or recount an experience/speak clearly at an understandable pace

FIRST READ **Think Through the Text**

Have students use text evidence and draw inferences to answer questions.

p. 29 • *How long do cats live?* 14–20 years *How do you know?* In the CATS section under the subhead GOOD, it says that they can live 14–20 years. **RI.4.1, RI.5.1**

p. 29 • *How are the main responsibilities of a cat owner and a parakeet owner the same?* A cat owner must clean out the litter box, feed, and play with the cat each day. A parakeet owner also has to clean the cage, feed, and give attention to the bird each day. **RI.4.3, RI.5.3**

p. 30 • *What evidence does the author provide that fish are inexpensive and easy to care for?* She says that fish cost only $1 to $5 each, and after the aquarium is set up, it costs $25 and up per year to run. She also says that it takes only a half hour every few weeks to clean an aquarium and only a few minutes a day for feeding. **RI.4.8, RI.5.8**

SECOND READ **Analyze the Text**

• Guide students to look back at what they learned about dogs. Ask: *How are cats and dogs alike? How are they different?* Sample answer: *They are alike because most cats and dogs are affectionate, they need some attention during the day, and they can both shed. They are different because dogs can be bigger and need more space; dogs need to be walked or have a place outdoors to play; dogs are more expensive.* **RI.4.3, RI.5.3**

• *What is the author's opinion about getting pets that are taken from the wild? How do you know?* She thinks it is bad. Under the subhead GOOD in the Cockatiels and Parakeets section, she says the cockatiels and parrots are not taken from the wild. This means she must think it is bad if they are. She also says not to buy saltwater fish because they are almost always taken from the wild. **RI.4.8, RI.5.8**

• Point out the headings on page 30. Ask: *Why does the author show the headings* RABBITS *and* OTHER BIRDS *in different colors than the headings* FISH *and* RODENTS? Headings with a black background are for pets that she does not recommend. **RI.4.7, RI.5.7**

FIRST READ ## Think Through the Text

Have students use text evidence and draw inferences to answer questions.

p. 31 • *Where in the text does it say whether an animal can make people sick?* under the subhead BAD in each section ▬RI.4.1, RI.5.1

p. 31 • *What does the author tell readers to do if they catch a cricket or other harmless insect?* She says to let your pet go the next day.
▬RI.4.1, RI.5.1

p. 31 • *What evidence does the author provide to prove that it is bad to keep a monkey for a pet?* She gives the following evidence: They can bite. They are noisy, messy, and expensive. They carry diseases. Many are taken illegally from the wild. ▬RI.4.8, RI.5.8

SECOND READ ## Analyze the Text

• Guide students to look back at the text under the subhead *Cockatoos & Large Parrots. How are cockatoos and other large parrots like the animals the author describes on page 31? How are they different?* Sample answer: They are the same because the author recommends that you do not buy any of the animals. They are different because the cockatoos and parrots are birds, but the other animals on page 31 are mammals, reptiles, amphibians, and insects. ▬RI.4.3, RI.5.3

• Remind students that the author mentions throughout the article that she thinks it is bad to get pets that are taken from the wild. Ask: *What evidence on this page supports the author's opinion?* The side note to Rangers says that taking animals from the wild is often illegal and that some species can become endangered. ▬RI.4.8, RI.5.8

• Point out the subheadings under each animal group on page 31. Ask: *How does the author show that she thinks the worst animals to get as pets are reptiles, amphibians, and monkeys?* She does not tell anything that is good about them. ▬RI.4.8, RI.5.8

Independent/Self-Selected Reading

Have students reread "Good Pet, Bad Pet" independently to practice analyzing the text on their own, or have them practice the skills using another book. Suggested titles:

• *National Geographic Kids 125 True Stories of Amazing Animals: Inspiring Tales of Animal Friendship & Four-Legged Heroes, Plus Crazy Animal Antics* by National Geographic Kids

• *Talking Tails: The Incredible Connection Between People and Their Pets* by Ann Love and Jane Drake ▬RI.4.10, RI.5.10

Performance Task

WRITE & PRESENT

1. Have small groups refer to the text to discuss an animal they would like as a pet, based on the recommendations and information contained in the article. Have them support their opinions with reasons from the article. ▬RI.4.8, RI.5.8

2. Ask students to each write an opinion paragraph in which they identify their favorite pet and provide reasons to support their opinion, based on the reasons provided in the article.
▬W.4.1, W.5.1

3. Partners share their paragraphs and edit their writing.
▬W.4.5, W.5.5

4. Have students present their final paragraphs to classmates.
▬SL.4.4, SL.5.4

5. Individual students turn in their final summaries to the teacher.

See Copying Masters, pp. 144–147.

STUDENT CHECKLIST

Writing

☑ Write an opinion paragraph.

☑ Support opinions with facts and details from the text.

☑ Use correct language conventions.

Speaking & Listening

☑ Engage effectively in collaborative conversations.

☑ Respond appropriately to questions and comments.

☑ Cite text evidence that supports opinions.

▶ **OBJECTIVES**

- Compare and contrast information
- Interpret information presented visually
- Give reasons to support points
- Analyze text using text evidence

"Ancient Mound Builders" is broken into three instructional segments.

Options for Reading

Independent Students read the article independently or with a partner and then answer questions posed by the teacher.

Supported Students read a segment and answer questions with teacher support.

"Ancient Mound Builders"

by E. Barrie Kavasch

SUMMARY This article from *Cobblestone* magazine presents information about the ancient peoples who lived in the southeastern parts of what is now the United States as long ago as 1000 B.C. and the mounds they built from soil. Some of the mounds were so large they were used as tombs, temples, and houses.

ABOUT THE AUTHOR E. Barrie Kavasch was born in 1942 in Springfield, Ohio. She has written many books on topics related to American Indians including *Zuni Children and Elders Talk Together, Native Harvests: Recipes and Botanicals of the American Indian,* and *A Student's Guide to Native American Genealogy.*

Discuss Genre and Set Purpose

INFORMATIONAL TEXT Look at the selection with students, and help them find and identify characteristics of informational text, including photographs, captions, and side notes.

SET PURPOSE Help students set a purpose for reading, such as to find information about who the mound builders were and what they did.

COMMON CORE Common Core Connection

RI.4.1 refer to details and examples when explaining what the text says explicitly and when drawing inferences; **RI.4.3** explain events/procedures/ideas/concepts in a text

RI.5.1 quote accurately when explaining what the text says explicitly and when drawing inferences; **RI.5.3** explain the relationships between individuals/events/ideas/concepts in a text

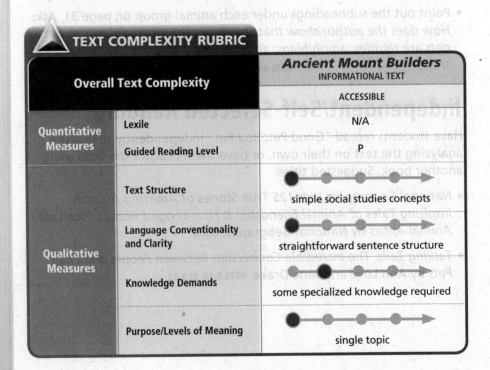

TEXT COMPLEXITY RUBRIC		*Ancient Mount Builders* INFORMATIONAL TEXT
Overall Text Complexity		ACCESSIBLE
Quantitative Measures	Lexile	N/A
	Guided Reading Level	P
Qualitative Measures	Text Structure	simple social studies concepts
	Language Conventionality and Clarity	straightforward sentence structure
	Knowledge Demands	some specialized knowledge required
	Purpose/Levels of Meaning	single topic

Academic Vocabulary

Read each word with students and discuss its meaning.

coordinated (p. 6) • organized

vehicle (p. 6) • a means of transportation such as a car or train

diverse (p. 6) • different; varied

latter (p. 7) • the second of two

depleted (p. 9) • robbed of nutrients

legacy (p. 9) • inheritance; something from the past

 ENGLISH LANGUAGE LEARNERS

Use Visuals

When discussing the highlighted vocabulary words, use pictures if available to show a *conical* shape, as well as *steatite* and *galena*. Paraphrase given definitions to help English learners understand the meanings. For example, say: *Steatite is a soft rock. Another name for steatite is soapstone.* Say and have students repeat *steatite*.

FIRST READ ## Think Through the Text

Have students use text evidence and draw inferences to answer questions.

p. 6, paragraph 1 • *Where did the ancient mound builders live?* today's southeastern U.S. **How do you know?** *The first sentence of the article identifies the mound builders as the ancestors of today's southeastern Indian people.* ▬ RI.4.1, RI.5.1

p. 6, paragraph 1 • *What does the text say the mounds were made of?* soil *What were they used for?* tombs, temples, and chiefs' houses ▬ RI.4.1

p. 6, paragraph 2 • *What does the text say were the three major mound building periods?* from 1000 B.C. to 100 B.C., from 200 B.C. to A.D. 500, and from 1000 to 1600 ▬ RI.4.1

RESPOND TO SEGMENT 1

 Classroom Collaboration

Have partners work together to create and present a summary, as well as raise questions that might be answered in the next segment.

SECOND READ ## Analyze the Text

• *What did steatite and galena have in common in ancient times?* Sample answer: *Both were raw materials the Indians at Poverty Point sought to trade. Both were used to make products such as cups and bowls.* ▬ RI.4.3, RI.5.3

• *How were the mounds built from 200 B.C. to A.D. 500 different than those built from 1000–1600? How were they alike?* Sample answer: *The earlier mounds were built for burials and were conical in shape. The later mounds had flat tops. They were both built by constructing piles of soil.* ▬ RI.4.3, RI.5.3

• *Why did the Indians of Poverty Point establish trading networks?* Sample answer: *They needed raw materials that came from faraway places to make things they needed such as cups, bowls, pipes, and beads.* ▬ RI.4.3, RI.5.3

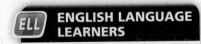
RESPOND TO SEGMENT 2

Classroom Collaboration

Have small groups work together to summarize what they have learned. Have them ask questions about what they don't understand.

COMMON CORE Connection

RI.4.3 explain events/procedures/ideas/concepts in a text; **RI.4.7** interpret information presented visually, orally, or quantitatively; **RI.4.8** explain how an author uses reasons and evidence to support points; **RI.4.10** read and comprehend informational texts; **W.4.2** write informative/explanatory texts to examine a topic and convey ideas and information clearly; **W.4.5** develop and strengthen writing by planning, revising, and editing; **SL.4.4** report on a topic or text, tell a story, or recount an experience/speak clearly at an understandable pace

RI.5.3 explain the relationships between individuals/events/ideas/concepts in a text; **RI.5.7** draw on information from print and digital sources to locate answers or solve problems; **RI.5.8** explain how an author uses reasons and evidence to support points; **RI.5.10** read and comprehend informational texts; **W.5.2** write informative/explanatory texts to examine a topic and convey ideas and information clearly; **W.5.5** develop and strengthen writing by planning, revising, editing, rewriting, or trying a new approach; **SL.5.4** report on a topic or text, tell a story, or recount an experience/speak clearly at an understandable pace

---

FIRST READ · # Think Through the Text

Have students use text evidence and draw inferences to answer questions.

p. 7 • *What does the author say the Poverty Point mounds look like?* They are in the shape of a giant bird and connected to three smaller mounds and six concentric low ridges arranged in a crescent shape. ◖ **RI.4.1, RI.5.1**

p. 8 • *How does the text define what Moundville was?* The text says that Moundville was a large ceremonial center. ◖ **RI.4.1, RI.5.1**

pp. 7–8 • *How are the locations of Poverty Point and Moundville alike? How are they different?* Sample answer: *Both are near rivers. Poverty Point is near the Mississippi River in Louisiana, and Moundville is near the Black Warrior River in Alabama.* ◖ **RI.4.3, RI.5.3**

SECOND READ · # Analyze the Text

- *What is the author's opinion of the Poverty Point Indians?* She admires them. *How do you know from the text?* The text says they were great craftsmen and engineers. *What reasons does she give to support this opinion?* They built a collection of mounds that formed a giant bird. They had to move millions of cubic feet of earth to build these mounds. ◖ **RI.4.8, RI.5.8**

- *How were the Mississippian mounds that were built for important people different from the burial mounds built by the Poverty Point Indians?* The Mississippian mounds were built as foundations for temples and houses of chiefs. When the chiefs died the mound-top houses were torn down and covered with earth, and then a new building was made for the new chief. The burial mounds built by the Poverty Point Indians were used as tombs for the dead and built one on top of the other. ◖ **RI.4.3, RI.5.3**

- Point out the photos and captions on the bottom of page 7 and top of page 8. Ask: *How are these photos and captions different? How are they alike?* Sample answer: *Both show and tell about places to visit today to see what mounds were like. Page 7 shows a museum that has exhibits about Moundville in Mississippi; page 8 shows a historic site that shows the actual mound built in Poverty Point in Louisiana.* ◖ **RI.4.7, RI.5.7**

FIRST READ ## Think Through the Text

Have students use text evidence and draw inferences to answer questions.

p. 9, paragraph 3 • *What does the text say is the reason the ancient peoples constructed these enormous mounds?* to honor their leaders and loved ones ▬RI.4.1

p. 9, paragraph 4 • *What evidence does the author provide to explain why many mounds were destroyed?* It was due to economic development and farming. ▬RI.4.8, RI.5.8

p. 9, paragraph 4 • *How are the mounds protected today?* They are protected as part of state and national parks. *What might you see at a mound site?* museums, reconstructed dwellings, and artifacts ▬RI.4.3, RI.5.3

SECOND READ ## Analyze the Text

• Guide students to think about what they learned about Moundville and Poverty Point. *How do these different ceremonial centers differ in location, time, and purpose?* Sample answer: *They were at different locations—Poverty Point in Louisiana and Moundville in Alabama. They were built during different time periods— Poverty Point, 1000 B.C.– 100 B.C and Moundville, 1000–1600. They were built for different purposes—Poverty Point mounds were built as tombs; Moundville mounds were built as foundations for temples and houses.* ▬RI.4.3, RI.5.3

• *Was trading important to Indian cultures?* yes *What evidence on this page supports your answer?* The text says that like the Poverty Point peoples, the Mississippians had trading systems in place that covered much of the eastern United States. ▬RI.4.1, RI.5.1

• *How does the photo on this page add to the reader's understanding of the article?* Sample answer: *It shows what a mound in Moundville looks like and helps the reader to understand how big the mounds actually were.* ▬RI.4.7, RI.5.7

Independent/Self-Selected Reading

Have students reread "Ancient Mound Builders" independently to practice analyzing the text on their own, or have them practice the skills using another book. Possible titles:

• *Cave Detectives* by David L. Harrison

• *Mesa Verde* by Mary Quigley ▬RI.4.10, RI.5.10

WRITE & PRESENT

1. Have partners refer to the text to discuss the similarities and differences between Poverty Point and Moundville and complete a Venn Diagram to show the similarities and differences. ▬RI.4.3, RI.5.3

2. Have students write a paragraph on their own comparing the two places. Encourage them to use words and phrases to link ideas that are the same or different. ▬W.4.2, W.5.2

3. Partners reconvene to share their paragraphs and edit their writing. ▬W.4.5, W.5.5

4. Individual students present their final paragraphs to classmates. ▬SL.4.4, SL.5.4

5. Individual students turn in their final summaries to the teacher.

See Copying Masters, pp. 144–147.

STUDENT CHECKLIST

Writing

☑ Write comparison/contrast paragraphs.

☑ Include appropriate linking words.

☑ Use correct language conventions.

Speaking & Listening

☑ Engage effectively in collaborative conversations.

☑ Respond appropriately to questions and comments.

☑ Cite text evidence that supports opinions.

- Explain the relationship between time and clocks
- Explain events, procedures, and concepts in a text
- Interpret information presented visually
- Analyze text using text evidence

About Time: A First Look at Time and Clocks is broken into three instructional segments.

SEGMENTS

Options for Reading

Independent Students read the book independently or with a partner and then answer questions posed by the teacher.

Supported Students read a segment and answer questions with teacher support.

COMMON CORE Connection

RI.4.1 refer to details and examples when explaining what the text says explicitly and when drawing inferences; **RI.4.3** explain events/procedures/ideas/concepts in a text; **RI.4.4** determine the meaning of general academic and domain-specific words and phrases; **RI.4.7** interpret information presented visually, orally, or quantitatively

RI.5.1 quote accurately when explaining what the text says explicitly and when drawing inferences; **RI.5.3** explain the relationships between individuals/events/ideas/concepts in a text; **RI.5.4** determine the meaning of general academic and domain-specific words and phrases; **RI.5.7** draw on information from print and digital sources to locate answers or solve problems

About Time
A First Look at Time and Clocks

by Bruce Koscielniak

SUMMARY This book defines the concept of time, gives a history of clocks, and explains the relationship between time and clocks. Illustrations and diagrams provide detailed descriptions of various types of clocks.

ABOUT THE AUTHOR Bruce Koscielniak has been writing and illustrating books for children for over twenty years. He researches extensively to provide accurate text and illustrations. His books include *Hear, Hear, Mr. Shakespeare*; *Johann Gutenberg and the Amazing Printing Press*; and *The Story of the Incredible Orchestra*.

Discuss Genre and Set Purpose

INFORMATIONAL TEXT Look at the selection with students, and help them find and identify characteristics of informational text, including diagrams, illustrations, and captions.

SET PURPOSE Help students set a purpose for reading, such as to find information about the history of clocks and the relationship between time and clocks.

▲ TEXT COMPLEXITY RUBRIC

Overall Text Complexity		About Time: A First Look at Time and Clocks INFORMATIONAL TEXT
		ACCESSIBLE
Quantitative Measures	Lexile	1070L
	Guided Reading Level	P
Qualitative Measures	Text Structure	more than one text structure
	Language Conventionality and Clarity	some academic language
	Knowledge Demands	some specialized knowledge required
	Purpose/Levels of Meaning	single topic

Academic Vocabulary

Read each word with students and discuss its meaning.

accuracy (p. 6) • correctness; exactness

monumental (p. 8) • huge; enormous

varied (p. 9) • different

complicated (p. 20) • having many parts

precision (p. 22) • accuracy

adjacent (p. 26) • next to

FIRST READ ## Think Through the Text

Have students use text evidence and draw inferences to answer questions.

p. 4 • *What is the author's definition of time?* Time is what is measured by a regular interval that is displayed on a clock. *What are some examples of intervals?* second, minute, hour RI.4.4, RI.5.4

pp. 6–7 • *How was keeping records of the natural divisions of time helpful to our ancient ancestors?* They were able to predict the coming of the seasons and have a more accurate understanding of the weather.
 RI.4.3, RI.5.3

pp. 8–9 • *What details in the text explain that the ancient Egyptians, Greeks, and Romans had similar approaches to timekeeping?* It says on page 9 that they all divided both the day and the night into twelve equal parts called hours. RI.4.1, RI.5.1

SECOND READ ## Analyze the Text

• Have students review pages 3–7. Ask: *How do the illustrations and captions help you understand the methods of timekeeping used by our ancient ancestors?* Sample answer: *The illustrations and captions show and tell about the movement of objects in the sky. Our ancestors studied the patterns of these objects' movement to create methods of timekeeping.* RI.4.7, RI.5.7

• Guide students to look back at pages 10–11. Ask: *What can you tell about early clocks by looking at the illustrations and captions?* Sample answer: *Some early clocks were hard to use and may not have been too accurate.* RI.4.7, RI.5.7

Domain Specific Vocabulary

interval (p. 4) • a time between two events

cycle (p. 6) • a series of events that are repeated in the same order

mechanical (p. 14) • operated by a machine

pulse (p. 25) • beat, rhythm

vibrations (p. 25) • movements back and forth

ELL ENGLISH LANGUAGE LEARNERS

Use Visuals and Sentence Frames

Point to and name each kind of clock in the illustrations. Have students repeat. Then help them complete sentence frames such as, *The <u>sundial</u> had to be used in the daylight. The water clock could keep time at <u>night</u> or on <u>cloudy</u> days. The <u>atomic</u> clock measures time in a very fast way.*

RESPOND TO SEGMENT 1

 Classroom Collaboration

Have partners work together to create and present a summary, as well as raise questions that might be answered in the next segment.

RESPOND TO SEGMENT 2

💬 **Classroom Collaboration**

Have small groups work together to summarize what they have learned. Have them ask questions about what they don't understand.

COMMON CORE **Common Core Connection**

RI.4.1 refer to details and examples when explaining what the text says explicitly and when drawing inferences; **RI.4.3** explain events/procedures/ideas/concepts in a text; **RI.4.7** interpret information presented visually, orally, or quantitatively; **RI.4.10** read and comprehend informational texts; **W.4.2** write informative/explanatory texts to examine a topic and convey ideas and information clearly; **W.4.5** develop and strengthen writing by planning, revising, and editing; **SL.4.4** report on a topic or text, tell a story, or recount an experience/speak clearly at an understandable pace

RI.5.1 quote accurately when explaining what the text says explicitly and when drawing inferences; **RI.5.3** explain the relationships between individuals/events/ideas/concepts in a text; **RI.5.7** draw on information from print and digital sources to locate answers or solve problems; **RI.5.10** read and comprehend informational texts; **W.5.2** write informative/explanatory texts to examine a topic and convey ideas and information clearly; **W.5.5** develop and strengthen writing by planning, revising, editing, rewriting, or trying a new approach; **SL.5.4** report on a topic or text, tell a story, or recount an experience/speak clearly at an understandable pace

FIRST READ **Think Through the Text**

Have students use text evidence and draw inferences to answer questions.

pp. 12–13 • *What kinds of clocks were used in ancient China and the Middle East?* water clocks *What other types of clocks were used in Europe in the Middle Ages?* candle clocks, lamp clocks, and sand-pouring clocks
🔲 RI.4.1

p. 14 • *Where and when was the all-mechanical clock invented?* in Europe around 1275 A.D. *How do you know?* The first paragraph on page 14 says that around 1275 A.D. a new type of clock was being used because someone had invented the all-mechanical clock. 🔲 RI.4.1, RI.5.1

pp. 16–17 • *What was the purpose of the public clock?* to unite the town or city 🔲 RI.4.3, RI.5.3

SECOND READ **Analyze the Text**

- Have students review page 12. Ask: *What does the word* elaborate *mean?* detailed or complicated *How can you tell from the illustration that the water clock is elaborate?* It has many parts and looks as if it would be hard to use. 🔲 RI.4.4, RI.5.4

- Point out the word *massive* on page 16. Ask: *What does the word* massive *mean?* huge, heavy *How can you tell that the gears in the illustration are massive?* The gears are in a large tower, and they look like they fill up most of the tower. 🔲 RI.4.4, RI.5.4

- Have students revisit pages 16–17. Say: *Think about how people depended on the public clock. Based on this information, what conclusion can you make about the relationship between time and clocks?* Sample answer: *People needed clocks to keep track of time and know when they should do certain tasks during the day, such as wake up, eat, work, and pray.* 🔲 RI.4.3, RI.5.3

- Guide students to reread the text on pages 18–19. Ask: *How did the flat spring change people's use of clocks?* Sample answer: *People could use the springs to make smaller, portable clocks. Once watches were made, people could carry them and keep track of time themselves.*
🔲 RI.4.3, RI.5.3

FIRST READ **Think Through the Text**

Have students use text evidence and draw inferences to answer questions.

pp. 20–21 • *How did different workers use their skills to make the parts of a clock?* Sample answer: *Founders melted and poured metal. Spring makers and screw makers made springs and screws. Gear cutters cut the gear teeth by hand. Engravers, guilders, and enamelers decorated the clocks.*
🔲 RI.4.1

pp. 22–23 • *What improvements to the clock did Christian Huygens make?* By using a pendulum in place of a foliot, he improved the accuracy of upright clocks. His invention of the balance spring helped to improve the accuracy of watches and portable clocks.* 🔲 RI.4.3, RI.5.3

pp. 26–27 • *What timekeeping problem came up in the modern age?* People needed to know the time in other parts of the world. *How was this problem solved?* An international conference in 1884 established twenty-four time zones for the world, each one hour apart.* 🔲 RI.4.3, RI.5.3

SECOND READ **Analyze the Text**

• Display pages 20–21. Ask: *Which workers are shown in the illustrations?* Page 20 shows a founder, and page 21 shows a gear cutter cutting gear teeth.* 🔲 RI.4.7, RI.5.7

• Have students look back on pages 24–25. Ask: *What is something new you learned about clocks from these pages?* Sample answers: *Line-current clocks plug into the wall. Atomic clocks can measure time down to trillionths of a second.* 🔲 RI.4.7, RI.5.7

• Guide students to review pages 28–30. Ask: *How do you know people have always been fascinated with the idea of time?* The author says on page 28 that time has always been a topic as mysterious and difficult to grasp as it is important in our lives.* 🔲 RI.4.1, RI.5.1

Independent/Self-Selected Reading

Have students reread *About Time: A First Look at Time and Clocks* independently to practice analyzing the text on their own, or have them practice the skills using another book, such as:

• *The Clock and How It Changed the World* by Michael Pollard

• *Clocks: Chronicling Time* by A. J. Brackin 🔲 RI.4.10, RI.5.10

Performance Task

WRITE & PRESENT

1. Have small groups refer to the text and illustrations to explain the relationship between time and clocks. Encourage students to take notes using specific information from the text that supports their ideas. 🔲 RI.4.3, RI.5.3

2. Have students write a paragraph that explains the relationship between time and clocks. 🔲 W.4.2, W.5.2

3. Students reconvene to share their paragraphs with partners and edit their writing. 🔲 W.4.5, W.5.5

4. Students present their final paragraphs to classmates. 🔲 SL.4.4, SL.5.4

5. Students turn in their final paragraphs to the teacher.

See Copying Masters, pp. 144–147.

STUDENT CHECKLIST

Writing

☑ Write in complete sentences.

☑ Explain the relationship between time and clocks.

☑ Provide reasons supported by facts and details.

☑ Use correct language conventions.

Speaking & Listening

☑ Engage effectively in collaborative conversations.

☑ Logically present claims and findings.

☑ Cite text evidence to support ideas.

England the Land is broken into three instructional segments.

Options for Reading

Independent Students read the selection independently or with a partner and then answer questions posed by the teacher.

Supported Students read a segment and answer questions with teacher support.

Common Core Connection

RI.4.1 refer to details and examples when explaining what the text says explicitly and when drawing inferences; **RI.4.2** determine the main idea and explain how it is supported by details/summarize; **RI.4.3** explain events/procedures/ideas/concepts in a text; **RI.4.7** interpret information presented visually, orally, or quantitatively

RI.5.1 quote accurately when explaining what the text says explicitly and when drawing inferences; **RI.5.2** determine two or more main ideas and explain how they are supported by details/summarize; **RI.5.3** explain the relationships between individuals/events/ideas/concepts in a text; **RI.5.7** draw on information from print and digital sources to locate answers or solve problems

England the Land
by Erinn Banting

SUMMARY This nonfiction book gives information about the land, people, and culture of England. A summary of the history and industry of England are included. Numerous photographs, maps, and sidebars provide additional information.

ABOUT THE AUTHOR Erinn Banting is the author of many nonfiction books for young people. She has contributed to book series on various topics, including countries, ecosystems, and inventions. In addition, she has written about the lives of famous women, such as Condoleezza Rice and Katie Couric.

Discuss Genre and Set Purpose

INFORMATIONAL TEXT Have students use the table of contents to predict what information they will learn about England. Then help students find and identify features of informational text, including photographs, maps, and sidebars.

SET PURPOSE Help students set a purpose for reading, such as to find out information about what life in England is like and to learn about the history and culture of England.

TEXT COMPLEXITY RUBRIC

Overall Text Complexity		*England the Land* INFORMATIONAL TEXT
		MORE COMPLEX
Quantitative Measures	Lexile	1160L
	Guided Reading Level	T
Qualitative Measures	Text Structure	complex social studies concepts
	Language Conventionality and Clarity	increased academic language
	Knowledge Demands	some specialized knowledge required
	Purpose/Levels of Meaning	multiple topics

Academic Vocabulary

Read each word with students and discuss its meaning.

fertile (p. 9) • having minerals that help produce farm crops

conquered (p. 14) • gained control with force

residence (p. 15) • the place where someone lives

upgrading (p. 29) • improving; making better

FIRST READ ## Think Through the Text

Have students use text evidence and draw inferences to answer questions.

p. 6 • *What effect did melting glaciers have on England?* *The waters around Great Britain rose and covered the land bridge that had connected England to Norway and Ireland.* RI.4.3, RI.5.3

p. 9 • *In the 1600s, why were sewers and windmills built in the Fens?* *They were built to drain and pump water from the area so people could farm in the fertile soil.* RI.4.3, RI.5.3

p. 11 • *What details does the author give to support the idea that England has a mild climate?* *Temperatures are about 68° in the summer and 36° in the winter. Any snow in the winter usually melts quickly. The Gulf Stream helps to create the mild climate.* RI.4.2, RI.5.2

SECOND READ ## Analyze the Text

• Have students look at the "Facts at a glance" box on page 4. Ask: *What is the purpose of this text feature?* *to provide the main facts about England in one place so that readers don't have to search for them* RI.4.7, RI.5.7

• Reread page 9 with students. Then point to the picture and caption of the Fens. Say: *We can connect information we read in the main text with the information in captions and sidebars.* Ask: *What would the Fens be like if they were returned to the way they were before farming?* *They would be marshes and scrubland, and there would be too much water to grow crops.* RI.4.7, RI.5.7

• Guide students to review page 10. Then ask: *Why are only five of the Isles of Scilly inhabited?* *The threat of tall waves and winds that blow in from the ocean makes the other islands uninhabitable.* RI.4.1, RI.5.1

Domain Specific Vocabulary

peat (p. 8) • soil from a wet area

 ENGLISH LANGUAGE LEARNERS

Use Visuals and Sentence Frames

Confirm that students comprehend the segment by discussing the photographs. Point to the image of traffic, name it, and have students repeat. Do the same for *cattle, lake, cliffs,* and *bogs.* Then have students use each word in a sentence. Provide frames, such as: *Many cars on the street make a lot of _____. traffic*

 RESPOND TO SEGMENT 1

Classroom Collaboration

Have small groups summarize what they have learned so far. Have them ask questions about what they don't understand.

RESPOND TO SEGMENT 2

💬 **Classroom Collaboration**

Have partners work together to create a summary. Ask them to raise questions that might be answered in the next segment.

COMMON CORE **Common Core Connection**

RI.4.1 refer to details and examples when explaining what the text says explicitly and when drawing inferences; **RI.4.2** determine the main idea and explain how it is supported by details/summarize; **RI.4.3** explain events/procedures/ideas/concepts in a text; **RI.4.10** read and comprehend informational texts; **W.4.2** write informative/explanatory texts to examine a topic and convey ideas and information clearly; **W.4.5** develop and strengthen writing by planning, revising, and editing; **SL.4.4** report on a topic or text, tell a story, or recount an experience/speak clearly at an understandable pace

RI.5.1 quote accurately when explaining what the text says explicitly and when drawing inferences; **RI.5.2** determine two or more main ideas and explain how they are supported by details/summarize; **RI.5.3** explain the relationships between individuals/events/ ideas/concepts in a text; **RI.5.10** read and comprehend informational texts; **W.5.2** write informative/explanatory texts to examine a topic and convey ideas and information clearly; **W.5.5** develop and strengthen writing by planning, revising, editing, rewriting, or trying a new approach; **SL.5.4** report on a topic or text, tell a story, or recount an experience/speak clearly at an understandable pace

---

FIRST READ # Think Through the Text

Have students use text evidence and draw inferences to answer questions.

pp. 12–13 • *What are some reasons why immigrants settled in England?* *People came to escape religious persecution, to escape famine, to escape war in their own countries, and to find work.* 🔲 **RI.4.2, RI.5.2**

p. 15 • *What is the job of the Queen today?* *The Queen is the country's head of state, or symbolic ruler, and she participates in important ceremonies and celebrations.* 🔲 **RI.4.1, RI.5.1**

p. 20 • *What were England's castles originally used for?* *They protected noble families from invaders.* *What are they used for today?* *Some are the homes of wealthy families; others are hotels and museums.* 🔲 **RI.4.3, RI.5.3**

SECOND READ # Analyze the Text

- Reread page 12 with students. Ask: *What effect have different people had on the regions of England?* *As different people settled in each region, they influenced the customs, traditions, and languages there.* 🔲 **RI.4.3, RI.5.3**

- Reread the first paragraph on page 14. Ask: *What was London like during Celtic times?* *It was a fort.* *What is it like today?* *It is the capital city and is divided into 33 sections.* 🔲 **RI.4.1**

- Review page 23. Ask: *How does the information in the sidebar about mad cow disease relate to the main text?* *The sidebar tells of sicknesses that affected cattle in the United Kingdom. It relates to the information in the main text, which tells how cattle are part of the United Kingdom's livestock industry.* 🔲 **RI.4.7, RI.5.7**

FIRST READ Think Through the Text

Have students use text evidence and draw inferences to answer questions.

p. 24 • *Between 1760 and 1830, what changed how goods were produced and how farmers worked?* the Industrial Revolution *How did it change manufacturing and farming?* New inventions made jobs like harvesting and spinning wool easier and quicker. ▭ RI.4.3, RI.5.3

p. 29 • *How has traveling across the English Channel changed?* For a long time, boats were the only way to cross the English Channel. Now high-speed trains run through an underwater tunnel, called the "Chunnel." ▭ RI.4.1, RI.5.1

p. 30 • *What is the government doing to save England's plants and animals?* The government is offering money to farmers if they turn land into forested conservation areas. Restrictions are placed on when hunters can hunt certain animals. Laws restrict the use of coal and pesticides. ▭ RI.4.2, RI.5.2

SECOND READ Analyze the Text

• Reread the section "Coal Mines" on page 24. Ask: *Why do you think cleaner, safer resources are starting to be used? Support your inference with specific details from the text.* Sample answer: *Cleaner resources are starting to be used because coal mines caused many illnesses and problems. Miners were killed in collapsed coal mines. People developed breathing problems and lung disease in cities where factories burned coal. Plants and animals were also killed by fog from coal smoke.* ▭ RI.4.3, RI.5.3

• Guide students to look back at page 25. Ask: *What effects did John Mercer and mercerized cotton have in England in the 1800s and 1900s?* The demand for this cotton grew, and England became the world's largest producer and exporter of both woolen and cotton textiles. ▭ RI.4.1, RI.5.1

• Review pages 26–27. Ask: *How has industry in England changed over time?* England now produces fewer texiles and machines than they once did. Today they manufacture more electronics, automobiles, and medicines. The majority of people work in service industries, such as education. ▭ RI.4.3, RI.5.3

Independent/Self-Selected Reading

Have students reread *England the Land* independently to practice analyzing the text on their own, or have them practice the skills using another book. Suggested titles:

• *Smokestacks and Spinning Jennys* by Sean Price

• *If the World Were a Village* by David J. Smith ▭ RI.4.10, RI.5.10

Performance Task

WRITE & PRESENT

1. Have small groups discuss the causes and effects the author uses to describe how England became a nation with many different kinds of people and industries. Have students create a cause-and-effect chart with one main idea, such as how England came to have many cultures. ▭ RI.4.3, RI.5.3

2. Have individual students write a paragraph about the main idea they described in their chart. Remind them to use words and phrases that show how the ideas are connected. ▭ W.4.2, W.5.2

3. Have students share their writing in small groups and then edit their writing. ▭ W.4.5, W.5.5

4. Have partners present their final explanations to their classmates. ▭ SL.4.4, SL.5.4

5. Individual students turn in their final summaries to the teacher.

See Copying Masters, pp.144–147.

STUDENT CHECKLIST

Writing

☑ Describe how the author uses causes and effects to present information about one aspect of England, such as its culture or industry.

☑ Write in complete sentences.

☑ Use correct language conventions.

Speaking & Listening

☑ Participate effectively in a collaborative discussion.

☑ Present information in a logical sequence.

☑ Cite specific text evidence that demonstrates causes and effects.

- State main ideas and supporting details
- Identify text structure
- Interpret information presented visually
- Analyze text using text evidence

A History of US: The First Americans is broken into three instructional segments.

Options for Reading

Independent Students read the book independently or with a partner and then answer questions posed by the teacher.

Supported Students read a segment and answer questions with teacher support.

Common Core Connection

RI.4.1 refer to details and examples when explaining what the text says explicitly and when drawing inferences; **RI.4.2** determine the main idea and explain how it is supported by details/summarize; **RI.4.3** explain events/procedures/ideas/concepts in a text; **RI.4.5** describe the overall structure of a text or part of a text; **RI.4.7** interpret information presented visually, orally, or quantitatively

RI.5.1 quote accurately when explaining what the text says explicitly and when drawing inferences; **RI.5.3** explain the relationships between individuals/events/ideas/concepts in a text; **RI.5.7** draw on information from print and digital sources to locate answers or solve problems; **RI.5.8** explain how an author uses reasons and evidence to support points

A History of US
The First Americans: Prehistory to 1600

by Joy Hakim

SUMMARY This book, the first volume of a 10-volume series, describes the early history of people in North America. It includes information about Stone Age inhabitants, Native American tribes, Columbus and other explorers, and the first English colony at Roanoke.

ABOUT THE AUTHOR Joy Hakim is a former teacher and newspaper reporter. The series *A History of US* won the James Michener Award in Writing. Hakim is now working on a *History of Science* series.

Discuss Genre and Set Purpose

INFORMATIONAL TEXT Page through the selection with students, and help them find and identify characteristics of informational text, including chapter titles, maps, illustrations, captions, sidebars, features, and the index. Ask them to describe the kinds of information they may learn from each text feature.

SET PURPOSE Help students set a purpose for reading, such as to find information about the early history of people in North America.

▲ TEXT COMPLEXITY RUBRIC

Overall Text Complexity		A History of US: The First Americans INFORMATIONAL TEXT
		MORE COMPLEX
Quantitative Measures	Lexile	820L
	Guided Reading Level	W
Qualitative Measures	Text Structure	multiple text structures
	Language Conventionality and Clarity	increased unfamiliar or academic words
	Knowledge Demands	some specialized knowledge required
	Purpose/Levels of Meaning	multiple topics

Academic Vocabulary

Read each word with students and discuss its meaning.

villains (p. 11) • people who do evil or nasty things

adjust (p. 20) • to get used to something

vast (p. 31) • very large in amount or size

leisure (p. 32) • free time to relax

pyramids (p. 46) • solid figures or buildings in the shape of a triangle

abundant (p. 48) • more than enough

Domain Specific Vocabulary

citizens (p. 12) • people who live in a country legally

domesticated (p. 15) • tamed by humans

continents (p. 16) • the large landmasses of the Earth

glacier (p. 16) • a large, slow-moving mass of ice

reservoir (p. 28) • a lake or tank that stores water for later use

conservation (p. 30) • protection of valuable things

FIRST READ ## Think Through the Text

Have students use text evidence and draw inferences to answer questions.

p. 12 • *What does the text say is the reason that history is especially important for Americans?* In many other nations, people share a common background, but in the United States that isn't true.
 RI.4.1, RI.5.8

pp. 31–33 • *How do you know what life was like for Native Americans in the Northwest?* The second paragraph on page 31 says the Indians of the Northwest were affluent. They caught and picked plenty of food in the wild, and they had plenty of wood for fires and houses. RI.4.1, RI.5.1

pp. 52–55 • *How did the Iroquois keep track of their history and records?* The chiefs and other leaders kept their history and records by using picture writing done with shell beads. RI.4.3, RI.5.3

SECOND READ ## Analyze the Text

- Review some of the text features in this book including the chapter titles and the sidebars. Then reread the quotes in the sidebars on pages 11–13. Ask: *Why did the author include this information?* Sample answer: *to share someone else's opinion about history* RI.4.5, RL.5.7

- Reread pages 14–15. Point out that the main idea may be directly stated, or students may have to make inferences about it. Ask: *What is the main idea of this segment?* Early people lived in Mongolia during the Stone Age. *What are some of the supporting details?* Sample answer: *The invention of the bone needle made it easy for people to sew better clothes. Hunters moved to follow the herds.* RI.4.2, RI.5.3

- Guide students to look at the map on pages 38–39. Say: *What did you learn about the first Americans by looking at this map?* Sample answer: *Most of the tribes lived along the East Coast. There were more tribes on the coasts than in the middle of the country.* RI.4.7, RI.5.7

ELL **ENGLISH LANGUAGE LEARNERS**

Use Visuals and Sentence Frames

Use the text illustrations to develop students' oral language. Say: *This illustration shows ____. Some details in the illustration are ____, ____, and ____.*

RESPOND TO SEGMENT 1

Classroom Collaboration

Have partners work together to create and present a summary, as well as raise questions that might be answered in the next segment.

RESPOND TO SEGMENT 2

 **Classroom
Collaboration**

Have partners summarize
the information. Encourage
them to ask questions.

Academic Vocabulary

Read each word with students and discuss its meaning.

terror (p. 56) • something that causes great fear

fierce (p. 56) • violent, destructive

efficient (p. 63) • well-organized

conquer (p. 69) • defeat or overcome by force

accomplishment (p. 79) • a success or achievement

FIRST READ ▶ **Think Through the Text**

Have students use text evidence and draw inferences to answer questions.

pp. 56–59 • *Who were the first Europeans to come to America?* the Vikings *Why did they come to America?* It was an accident; their ship went off course. *Did these people settle permanently in America?* no *Where did they go?* They moved back to Scandinavia. ▬RI.4.3, RI.5.3

p. 63 • *Why is Prince Henry the Navigator so important in the early history of America?* He was willing to send his sailors on voyages of discovery. His enthusiasm encouraged people from other countries to go on journeys, too. ▬RI.4.3, RI.5.3

pp. 72–73 • *What happened to the Spanish settlers on Hispaniola?* The Spaniards fought over gold and Indian women and killed some of their own men. The Indians killed most of the rest of the Spaniards. ▬RI.4.3, RI.5.3

SECOND READ ▶ **Analyze the Text**

• Have students reread Chapters 15 and 16. Say: *Summarize the main idea of each chapter and identify some supporting details.* Chapter 15: Christopher Columbus thought he could find a sea route from Europe to China. He believed the earth was small and that he was a superb sailor. Columbus took his ideas to one person after another. Chapter 16: Columbus thought he had reached China, but he had really reached the Indies. Soon he knew he was not in China; the island was small, but splendid with tall trees, gorgeous birds, a beautiful beach, and friendly people. ▬RI.4.2, RI.5.2

• Tell students to look at the maps on pages 65–66. Ask: *How do the maps help you understand Columbus's misunderstanding about the world?* Sample answer: *The first map shows landmasses much closer together than they really are and in incorrect sizes, so Columbus thought China would be easy to reach.* ▬RI.4.7, RI.5.7

• Have students reread page 71. Ask: *How does this excerpt help you to better understand Christopher Columbus?* Sample answer: *The letter describes what he thought about the natives and how he compared things he saw with familiar things from Spain.* ▬RI.4.3, RI.5.3

Performance
Task

Academic Vocabulary

Read each word with students and discuss its meaning.

brutality (p. 112) • extreme cruelty or violence

aghast (p.121) • shocked

revenge (p. 131) • payback

agog (p. 149) • curious

FIRST READ · Think Through the Text

Have students use text evidence and draw inferences to answer questions.

pp. 115–116 • *Where was the first permanent European settlement in the North American West?* Santa Fe, New Mexico **How do you know?** *The second paragraph on page 116 says that Santa Fe was the first permanent European settlement in the North American West.*
🔲 RI.4.1, RI.5.1

p. 121 • *How did the writings of de Las Casas influence the English explorers?* The English read about the evil things the Spaniards had done to the Indians and thought they had to protect the Indians. They said they would treat the Indians differently. 🔲 RI.4.3, RI.5.3

pp. 140–142 • *Why did Sir Walter Raleigh want to explore America?* He wanted to continue his brother's dream to find Utopia. **Where did Raleigh plan to establish a colony?** in Virginia 🔲 RI.4.3, RI.5.3

SECOND READ · Analyze the Text

• Reread pages 117–121. Ask: *What is the main idea?* At age 40, Las Casas realized that slavery was wrong and worked for the rest of his life to stop it. **What are some of the details that support the main idea?** Sample answer: He started a new, fair colony in Venezuela. He wrote books about freedom. 🔲 RI.4.2, RI.5.3

• Reread pages 150–151. Ask: *What is the main idea?* In 1600, life for the first Americans would change. **What are some of the details that support the main idea?** Sample answer: The English colony would be the cause of the change. 🔲 RI.4.2, RI.5.3

Independent/Self-Selected Reading

Have students reread *A History of US: The First Americans* independently to practice analyzing the text on their own, or have them practice the skills using another book. Suggested titles:

• *We Were There, Too!: Young People in U.S. History* by Phillip Hoose

• *The Complete Book of U.S. History* by American Education Publishing
🔲 RI.4.10, RI.5.10

WRITE & PRESENT

1. Have small groups refer to different chapters in the text to explain how the author uses the text structure of main idea and details to explain events in early U.S. history.
🔲 RI.4.2, RI.5.2

2. Have individual students choose one chapter from the book and write a paragraph that describes how the author uses the text structure of main idea and details to convey information. Have them cite text evidence to support their ideas.
🔲 W.4.2, W.5.2

3. Students reconvene to share their paragraphs with partners and edit their writing. 🔲 W.4.5, W.5.5

4. Students present their final paragraphs to classmates.
🔲 SL.4.4, SL.5.4

5. Students turn in their final paragraphs to the teacher.

See Copying Masters, pp. 144–147.

STUDENT CHECKLIST

Writing

☑ Write in complete sentences.

☑ Explain how the author uses main ideas and details to give information.

☑ Provide reasons supported by facts and details from the text.

☑ Use correct language conventions.

Speaking & Listening

☑ Engage effectively in collaborative conversations.

☑ Logically present claims and findings.

☑ Cite text evidence to support ideas.

▶ OBJECTIVES

- Identify and explain cause-and-effect relationships
- Determine how an author structures text
- Interpret information presented visually
- Analyze text using text evidence

My Librarian Is a Camel is broken into three instructional segments.

Options for Reading

Independent Students read the book independently or with a partner and then answer questions posed by the teacher.

Supported Students read a segment and answer questions with teacher support.

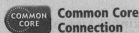 **Common Core Connection**

RI.4.1 refer to details and examples when explaining what the text says explicitly and when drawing inferences; **RI.4.3** explain events/procedures/ideas/concepts in a text;

RI.5.1 quote accurately when explaining what the text says explicitly and when drawing inferences; **RI.5.3** explain the relationships between individuals/events/ideas/concepts in a text.; **RI.5.10** read and comprehend informational texts

My Librarian Is a Camel

How Books Are Brought to Children Around the World

by Margriet Ruurs

SUMMARY This book describes mobile libraries that deliver books to children and their families living in remote places around the world.

ABOUT THE AUTHOR Margriet Ruurs travels the world, sharing her love of books with children. She has taught reading and writing in Pakistan, Indonesia, and Malaysia, and written more than twenty books.

Discuss Genre and Set Purpose

INFORMATIONAL TEXT Have students look through the selection to find and identify characteristics of informational text, including section headings, photographs and captions, and sidebars with maps and flags.

SET PURPOSE Help students set a purpose for reading, such as to find information about how books travel to remote places.

▲ TEXT COMPLEXITY RUBRIC

Overall Text Complexity		My Librarian Is a Camel INFORMATIONAL TEXT
		COMPLEX
Quantitative Measures	Lexile	980L
	Guided Reading Level	Q
Qualitative Measures	Text Structure	organization of main idea and details may be complex, but is clearly stated and generally sequential
	Language Conventionality and Clarity	some unfamiliar or academic words
	Knowledge Demands	some specialized knowledge required
	Purpose/Levels of Meaning	explicitly stated

Academic Vocabulary

Read each word with students and discuss its meaning.

remote (p. 5) • at a very far distance from towns or other human settlements

mobile (p. 5) • able to move or be moved easily from one place or position to another

inspire (p. 5) • to give someone the desire or courage to do something

isolated (p. 10) • apart from other people or things

access (p. 10) • the ability to enter, look at, or use something

avid (p. 27) • having an eager desire for

Domain Specific Vocabulary

solar-powered (p. 7) • powered by the sun

UPS (p. 7) • uninterrupted power supply

Southern Hemisphere (p. 7) • the half of the Earth that is south of the equator

aboriginal (p. 7) • native to an area

archipelago (p. 14) • a group of islands

FIRST READ ## Think Through the Text

Have students use text evidence and draw inferences to answer questions.

pp. 4–5 • *Which sentence on page 5 explains what the author wants you to think about after reading this book? Next time you borrow books, think of how lucky you are to be able to choose from all of those free books and to take home as many as you wish.*  RI.4.1, RI.5.1

pp. 6–9 • *How are the mobile libraries of Australia and Azerbaijan alike? They both use trucks to take books to children in remote places.*
RI.4.3, RI.5.3

SECOND READ ## Analyze the Text

• Guide students to look back at page 5. Ask: *What was the sequence of events that caused the author to write this book? First, she read an article about a camel in Kenya that took books to people in remote places. Next, she wondered about mobile libraries in other parts of the world and did research on them. Then, she assembled a scrapbook of mobile libraries from all over the world.* RI.4.3, RI.5.3

• *On page 5 the author says that she wants these stories of mobile libraries to inspire readers. What does she mean by this? Sample answer: The author wants these stories to give readers the desire to use their own libraries and appreciate how important they are.*
RI.4.1, RI.5.10

• *At the bottom of page 11, the author calls the Northwest Territories a remote corner of Canada's Arctic. What causes access to books to be especially important to the children who live there? Access to books is important to these children because they don't have local public libraries in their small towns, and it is too far to travel to other towns. The frigid weather there also makes children want to read because it is often too cold to do other activities.* RI.4.3, RI.5.3

ELL ENGLISH LANGUAGE LEARNERS

Use Visuals and Sentence Frames

Discuss with students the many ways children can get a library book. Have them point to and name ways using the visuals in the selection. Then help them complete sentence frames such as, *Children can get a library book from a library _____ or _____ or by _____ . building, truck, mail*

RESPOND TO SEGMENT 1

 Classroom Collaboration

Have partners work together to create and present a summary, as well as raise questions that might be answered in the next segment.

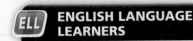

RESPOND TO SEGMENT 2

Classroom Collaboration

Have small groups work together to summarize what they have learned. Have them ask questions about what they don't understand.

Common Core Connection

RI.4.2 determine the main idea and explain how it is supported by details/summarize; **RI.4.4** determine the meaning of general academic and domain-specific words and phrases; **RI.4.7** interpret information presented visually, orally, or quantitatively; **RI.4.8** explain how an author uses reasons and evidence to support points; **RI.4.10** read and comprehend informational texts; **W.4.2** write informative/explanatory texts to examine a topic and convey ideas and information clearly; **W.4.5** develop and strengthen writing by planning, revising, and editing; **SL.4.4** report on a topic or text, tell a story, or recount an experience/speak clearly at an understandable pace

RI.5.2 determine two or more main ideas and explain how they are supported by details/summarize; **RI.5.4** determine the meaning of general academic and domain-specific words and phrases; **RI.5.7** draw on information from print and digital sources to locate answers or solve problems; **RI.5.8** explain how an author uses reasons and evidence to support points; **W.5.2** write informative/explanatory texts to examine a topic and convey ideas and information clearly; **W.5.5** develop and strengthen writing by planning, revising, editing, rewriting, or trying a new approach; **SL.5.4** report on a topic or text, tell a story, or recount an experience/speak clearly at an understandable pace

FIRST READ

Think Through the Text

Have students use text evidence and draw inferences to answer questions.

pp. 14–15 • *What evidence in the text supports the effect that if the book boat didn't come, the children in the Gulf of Finland might not be reading at all?* The author tells us that these are rocky islands and that only some of them are inhabited year round. Winters are so severe that the boat can only go out from May to October. In this harsh and remote landscape, children might not have any access to books without the book boat. ▬ RI.4.1, RI.5.1

pp. 18–19 • *How do the photographs help you understand what is being described on pages 18 and 19?* The photos show the camels, the children who receive the books, and the librarian. The photos show how the mats are placed on the camels' backs. ▬ RI.4.7, RI.5.7

pp. 20–21 • *What evidence does the author provide that books are treasured by the people of Mongolia, especially the children?* First, the author tells us that there is almost no illiteracy, or people who do not know how to read and write, in Mongolia. Second, the author tells us that the children think books are sweeter than candy. ▬ RI.4.8, RI.5.8

SECOND READ

Analyze the Text

- Guide students to look at the box with the map on page 13. *Photographs with captions and special features, such as sidebars, are visuals that include information that is not in the main text. Why do you think the author included a map and a flag from each country in the article? How do these features connect to the text?* Sample answer: The features provide information about the extreme climates and landscapes of each place. They help explain why people living there need a special way to deliver books to children. ▬ RI.4.7, RI.5.7

- Have students find the words *nomadic*, *steppe*, *livestock*, and *countryside* on pages 20–21. *How are these words related?* All the words tell about the lifestyle of the people in Mongolia that is described in the text. *How does this connect with the main topic of the book?* The topic is getting books to people in remote places. The words help explain why many children in Mongolia are so isolated. ▬ RI.4.4, RI.5.4

FIRST READ Think Through the Text

Have students use text evidence and draw inferences to answer questions.

pp. 24–25 • *What causes volunteers from Hope Worldwide to have to take long four-by-four truck trips followed by a four-hour hike through the jungle?* They want to get books and needed medicine to people who live in remote places. These places have no roads that lead there. RI.4.1

pp. 26–27 • *Name and describe three different programs for taking books to communities in Peru.* El Libro Compartido en Familia takes bags of twenty books each to families in Peru. Children and parents read the books together. They are written at four different reading levels. Aspaderuc is a program in which a reading promoter selects books for adults and children and lends them for three months at a time. Fe Y Alegría takes children's books directly by wagon to schools in rural areas. RI.4.1, RI.5.1

pp. 28–29 • *Which book-distribution efforts from other countries does the Books-by-Elephant program most resemble?* The elephants are a mobile library, much like the mini-bus in Mongolia, the camels in Kenya, and the donkeys in Peru. RI.4.1

SECOND READ Analyze the Text

• Guide students to review the sections on Papua New Guinea and Zimbabwe. *What else, in addition to books, do the mobile library programs take to remote areas of these countries?* medicines in Papua New Guinea and a TV, VCR, computer, and satellite dish in Zimbabwe *How do these things benefit more than just the children?* The medicines help people who get sick when there is no doctor or other health care; the TV and other electro-communications help people learn about and communicate with others who live in other parts of the world. RI.4.3, RI.5.3

• Say: *Think about all the mobile library programs that you read about in this book. What effect are they having on the children who receive the books?* Sample anwer: The mobile library programs increase literacy, or the ability to read and write, among children who don't have regular access to books. RI.4.2, RI.5.2

Independent/Self-Selected Reading

Have students reread *My Librarian Is a Camel* independently to practice analyzing the text on their own, or have them practice the skills using another book, such as:

• *My School in the Rain Forest* by Margriet Ruurs

• *A School Like Mine* by DK Publishing RI.4.10, RI.5.10

WRITE & PRESENT

1. Have small groups refer to the text to discuss ways the author uses cause and effect to describe different mobile libraries around the world. Encourage students to take notes. RI.4.8, RI.5.8

2. Have students work with a partner to select three countries they read about and create a detailed cause-and-effect chart that shows how the author presents information. Then partners use their chart to write a summary. W.4.2, W.5.2

3. Partners reconvene to share their summaries with other sets of partners and edit their writing. W.4.5, W.5.5

4. Partners present their final summaries to classmates. SL.4.4, SL.5.4

5. Individual students turn in their final summaries to the teacher.

See Copying Masters, pp. 144–147.

STUDENT CHECKLIST

Writing

☑ Write in complete sentences.

☑ Describe how the author presents the information, identifying both causes and their effects to describe mobile libraries in three different countries.

☑ Use correct language conventions.

Speaking & Listening

☑ Engage effectively in collaborative conversations.

☑ Logically present claims and findings.

☑ Cite text evidence demonstrating cause and effect.

- Identify and compare structures of books
- Identify main idea and supporting details
- Determine the meanings of words and phrases
- Analyze text using text evidence

Horses is broken into three instructional segments.

SEGMENTS

Options for Reading

Independent Students read the book independently or with a partner and then answer questions posed by the teacher.

Supported Students read a segment and answer questions with teacher support.

Common Core Connection

RI.4.2 determine the main idea and explain how it is supported by details/summarize; **RI.4.3** explain events/procedures/ideas/concepts in a text; **RI.4.5** describe the overall structure of a text or part of a text; **RI.4.7** interpret information presented visually, orally, or quantitatively; **RI.4.8** explain how an author uses reasons and evidence to support points

RI.5.1 quote accurately when explaining what the text says explicitly and when drawing inferences; **RI.5.2** determine two or more main ideas and explain how they are supported by details/summarize; **RI.5.3** explain the relationships between individuals/events/ideas/concepts in a text; **RI.5.5** compare and contrast the overall structure in two or more texts; **RI.5.8** explain how an author uses reasons and evidence to support points

Horses
by Seymour Simon

SUMMARY This book provides an overview of horses that includes information about different breeds, their bodies, and their communication with humans. The four ways that horses move—walk, trot, canter, and gallop—are described. The book also presents how horses have played important roles throughout United States history.

ABOUT THE AUTHOR **Seymour Simon** is a well-known author of more than 250 children's books about science topics. Before he became a writer, he was a science teacher for 23 years. Many of Simon's books have won science and literature awards.

Discuss Genre and Set Purpose

INFORMATIONAL TEXT Have students look at the cover and the photographs of horses. Guide them to make predictions about the types of information about horses the author may have included in the book.

SET PURPOSE Help students set a purpose for reading, such as to learn new facts about horses.

◢ TEXT COMPLEXITY RUBRIC

Overall Text Complexity		*Horses* INFORMATIONAL TEXT
		COMPLEX
Quantitative Measures	Lexile	930L
	Guided Reading Level	R
Qualitative Measures	Text Structure	somewhat complex science and social studies concepts
	Language Conventionality and Clarity	increased academic language
	Knowledge Demands	some specialized knowledge required
	Purpose/Levels of Meaning	multiple topics

Academic Vocabulary

Read each word with students and discuss its meaning.

chariots (p. 5) • two-wheeled carts pulled by horses in ancient times

medieval (p. 5) • of the time period between the 5th and 15th centuries in Europe

accurate (p. 8) • correct

sensitive (p. 11) • able to smell, hear, or feel things very well

Domain Specific Vocabulary

nuzzling (p. 14) • gentle rubbing with the nose

nickering (p. 14) • neighing

snorting (p. 14) • forcing air out of the nostrils

grooming (p. 14) • brushing and cleaning a horse

FIRST READ ## Think Through the Text

Have students use text evidence and draw inferences to answer questions.

pp. 4–5 • *The author says that horses have always been important to humans. How does he support that point?* He says that people tamed horses 5,000 years ago. People in ancient times used horses in wars. Knights used horses in battles. Cowboys and American Indians also used horses. RI.4.8, RI.5.8

p. 6 • *Compare and contrast the size of ancient horses to that of horses today.* Horses today are larger than ancient horses. The earliest ancestor of the horse was about as big as a small dog. After millions of years, horses were as big as large dogs. Ten million years ago, horses were as big as ponies. RI.4.3, RI.5.3

SECOND READ ## Analyze the Text

• Have students reread page 6. Ask: *What are the main ideas of this page?* Horses have changed over time. Horses have gotten larger. *How does the author support those ideas?* The author compares the sizes and diets of horses that lived at different times. RI.4.2, RI.5.2

• Revisit pages 8–9. Ask: *What text detail shows how horses use their teeth?* A horse's mouth is full of strong teeth used mostly for chewing and grinding grasses. *What does the photo show?* It shows the big, flat tooth surfaces that grind grasses. *How are foals' teeth similar to humans' baby teeth?* Foals have a set of milk teeth when they are nine months old. Then they lose their milk teeth and grow permanent teeth, like humans. RI.4.7, RI.5.1

• Help students note the structure of the ideas in the text and compare the organization with the structure of text in *Hurricanes* or another informational text they have read. *What is alike about the organization of the two books?* Sample answer: *Both tell about a certain subject. Both have photos to help readers understand the text.* RI.4.5, RI.5.5

ELL ENGLISH LANGUAGE LEARNERS

Use Gestures

Help students understand key ideas. Point to your eye and have students read about horses' eyes on page 11. Open your eye wide to reinforce the idea that horses have large eyes. Point to the sides of your head to show where a horse's eyes are. Then twist your head around as far as possible to demonstrate the idea that eyes on the side of the head can see all the way around. Check comprehension by asking questions, such as: *Where are a horse's eyes? What size are their eyes?*

RESPOND TO SEGMENT 1
Classroom Collaboration

Have partners work together to summarize what they have read and ask questions about what they don't understand.

Common Core Connection

RI.4.1 refer to details and examples when explaining what the text says explicitly and when drawing inferences; **RI.4.2** determine the main idea and explain how it is supported by details/summarize; **RI.4.4** determine the meaning of general academic and domain-specific words and phrases; **RI.4.5** describe the overall structure of a text or part of a text; **RI.4.10** read and comprehend informational texts; **W.4.2** write informative/explanatory texts to examine a topic and convey ideas and information clearly; **W.4.5** develop and strengthen writing by revising and editing; **SL.4.4** report on a topic or text, tell a story, or recount an experience/speak clearly at an understandable pace

RI.5.1 quote accurately when explaining what the text says explicitly and when drawing inferences; **RI.5.2** determine two or more main ideas and explain how they are supported by details/summarize; **RI.5.4** determine the meaning of general academic and domain-specific words and phrases; **RI.5.5** compare and contrast the overall structure in two or more texts; **RI.5.10** read and comprehend informational texts; **W.5.2** write informative/explanatory texts to examine a topic and convey ideas and information clearly; **W.5.5** develop and strengthen writing by planning, revising, editing, rewriting, or trying a new approach; **SL.5.4** report on a topic or text, tell a story, or recount an experience/speak clearly at an understandable pace

Academic Vocabulary

Read each word with students and discuss its meaning.

offspring (p. 21) • the young of an animal or person

specifically (p. 24) • for a certain reason or purpose

mallet (p. 24) • long-handled tool used in polo

FIRST READ ▸ ## Think Through the Text

Have students use text evidence and draw inferences to answer questions.

p. 17 • *What does the author say about different ways a horse walks?* *Horses move in four natural ways, called gaits or paces. They can walk, trot, canter, and gallop.* **How do walking and galloping differ?** *Walking is slowest and galloping is fastest.* ▬ RI.4.1, RI.5.1

p. 21, paragraph 1 • *Determine what the word* breed *means from text evidence.* *a certain kind or type of horse* ▬ RI.4.4, RI.5.4

p. 21, paragraph 4 • *What two breeds were crossed to create the Thoroughbred, the fastest and most expensive horse breed?* *the Arabians and native English breeds* ▬ RI.4.3, RI.5.3

SECOND READ ▸ ## Analyze the Text

- Have students reread pages 18–19. Ask: *How are horses usually described?* *by their coat colors and by the white markings on their bodies* *What does the author say about most horses that look white?* *The author says that most horses that look white are actually gray. Colorless, pure-white horses are called albinos and are rare.* ▬ RI.4.1, RI.5.1

- Review pages 21–25. Then ask: *What is steeplechasing?* *It is a type of horse racing during which riders on horses jump over obstacles.* *What clues in the text and photos helped you determine this meaning?* *The text says that horses and riders jump over barriers or obstacles. The photo on page 25 shows a rider and a horse jumping over a barrier in a race.* ▬ RI.4.4, RI.5.4

- Remind students that they have compared the organization of *Horses* with that of *Hurricanes* or another nonfiction book. Ask: *How does the organization of the books differ?* *Sample answer: Hurricanes has chapters with titles; Horses doesn't have chapters and covers each topic with a page of text and a photo. Also, Hurricanes has photos with captions, maps, and diagrams; Horses uses photos without captions.* ▬ RI.4.5, RI.5.5

Academic Vocabulary

Read each word with students and discuss its meaning.

barges (p. 32) • long boats that carry things on rivers or canals

shod (p. 34) • put a horseshoe on a horse's foot to protect the foot

FIRST READ Think Through the Text

Have students use text evidence and draw inferences to answer questions.

p. 27 • *How does the text say ponies and horses are different?* Ponies are smaller, have shorter legs, and have thick manes and tails. **RI.4.3, RI.5.3**

pp. 30–32 • *Summarize how horses got to America. Use supporting details to describe the role of horses in America from the 1500s through the 1800s.* Spanish explorers brought them for trade and fighting in the 1500s. American Indians and American cowboys rode horses in the 1600s. In the 1800s, horses were used to settle the West, plow fields, and run machines. **RI.4.2, RI.5.2**

SECOND READ Analyze the Text

• Reread pages 28–29 with students. Ask: *Why are Mustangs in the dry deserts of the American Southwest protected? Cite text evidence to support your answer.* They are protected so that they can continue to live wild. **RI.4.1, RI.5.1**

• Discuss with students how they have compared the structure of *Horses* with that of *Hurricanes* or another nonfiction book. Guide students to look at the material at the end of each book. Ask: *Do the authors put the same kind of information in the back? Explain.* The back of *Horses* has a dedication page and tells where the photos are from. The back of *Hurricanes* tells where the photos are from and has an index and an additional reading list. **RI.4.5, RI.5.5**

Independent/Self-Selected Reading

Have students reread *Horses* independently to practice analyzing the text on their own, or have them practice the skills using another book. Suggested titles:

• *Everything Horse; What Kids Really Want to Know About Horses* by Marty Crisp

• *The Kingfisher Illustrated Horse and Pony Encyclopedia* by Sandy Ransford **RI.4.10, RI.5.10**

Performance Task

WRITE & PRESENT

1. Have small groups create Venn diagrams. Label one circle *Horses* and the other circle *Hurricanes* or the title of another informational text students have read. Label the overlapping area *Both*. Have students record how the structures of the two texts are similar and different. **RI.4.5, RI.5.5**

2. Have individual students write a paragraph comparing the structures of the two books. Ask them to use text evidence and details from their Venn diagram. **W.4.2, W.5.2**

3. Students return to their small groups to share their writing and edit their paragraphs. **W.4.5, W.5.5**

4. Have individual students present their comparisons orally. **SL.4.4, SL.5.4**

5. Individual students turn in their final writing to the teacher.

See Copying Masters, pp. 144–147.

STUDENT CHECKLIST

Writing

☑ Complete a Venn diagram comparing the texts' structures.

☑ Include examples that illustrate similarities and differences.

☑ Use correct language conventions.

Speaking & Listening

☑ Present ideas on a topic.

☑ Compare ideas by different writers.

☑ Ask and answer questions about text details.

► **OBJECTIVES**

- State main ideas and supporting details
- Determine how an author structures text
- Interpret information presented visually
- Analyze text using text evidence

Quest for the Tree Kangaroo is broken into three instructional segments.

Options for Reading

Independent Students read the book independently or with a partner and then answer questions posed by the teacher.

Supported Students read a segment and answer questions with teacher support.

 Common Core Connection

RI.4.1 refer to details and examples when explaining what the text says explicitly and when drawing inferences; **RI.4.2** determine the main idea and explain how it is supported by details/summarize; **RI.4.3** explain events/procedures/ideas/concepts in a text; **RI.4.5** describe the overall structure of a text or part of a text

RI.5.1 quote accurately when explaining what the text says explicitly and when drawing inferences; **RI.5.2** determine two or more main ideas and explain how they are supported by details/summarize; **RI.5.3** explain the relationships between individuals/events/ideas/concepts in a text

Quest for the Tree Kangaroo

An Expedition to the Cloud Forest of New Guinea

by Sy Montgomery

SUMMARY This book describes the journey of a scientist, a writer, and a photographer to find tree kangaroos in their native surroundings of New Guinea. Photographs and their captions provide an up-close look at the tree kangaroos and the nearby bush people.

ABOUT THE AUTHOR Sy Montgomery travels the world and encounters many interesting animals to research for her books. Her book *Quest for the Tree Kangaroo* received the Robert F. Sibert Honor Informational Book Award.

Discuss Genre and Set Purpose

INFORMATIONAL TEXT Look at the selection with students, and help them identify characteristics of informational text, including chapter titles, maps, photographs, captions, and the index.

SET PURPOSE Help students set a purpose for reading, such as to learn information about the tree kangaroo.

▲ TEXT COMPLEXITY RUBRIC

Overall Text Complexity		Quest for the Tree Kangaroo INFORMATIONAL TEXT
		COMPLEX
Quantitative Measures	Lexile	830L
	Guided Reading Level	U
Qualitative Measures	Text Structure	somewhat complex science concepts
	Language Conventionality and Clarity	more complex sentence structure
	Knowledge Demands	specialized knowledge required
	Purpose/Levels of Meaning	multiple purposes

Academic Vocabulary

Read each word with students and discuss its meaning.

quest (p. 1) • search

rarest (p. 8) • not often seen or found

survive (p. 8) • live; stay alive

expeditions (p. 9) • long trips made for specific purposes

track (p. 13) • to follow

coordinator (p. 15) • someone who plans events

Domain Specific Vocabulary

conservationists (p. 12) • people who take care of the environment

marsupial (p. 23) • animal with a pouch

ENGLISH LANGUAGE LEARNERS

Use Visuals and Sentence Frames

Point to and name items in the photograph on page 6. Then help students complete sentence frames. Say: *The _____ is on the ground. moss The_____ are almost as tall as the trees. ferns The _____ hang down from the trees. vines* Then invite students to describe other photographs from the book in their own words.

FIRST READ ## Think Through the Text

Have students use text evidence and draw inferences to answer questions.

pp. 7–8 • *Who is Lisa Dabek? What animal is she studying in New Guinea? Dabek is a scientist and the leader of the research team. She wants to learn more about tree kangaroos.* RI.4.1

pp. 11–13 • *What is the team going to do with the tree kangaroos? They are going to capture them, put radio collars on them, release them, and track them.* RI.4.3, RI.5.3

p. 17 • *Where and when did the author meet Lisa? when she was director of conservation and research at the Roger Williams Park Zoo in Providence, Rhode Island, in the year 2000* RI.4.1, RI.5.1

SECOND READ ## Analyze the Text

- Guide students to reread pages 7–13. Ask: *Which text structure does the author primarily use to give information in this book? The author uses a main idea and detail structure. How can you tell when the topic in the chapter changes? There is a white space with three green dots across it between sections.* RI.4.5

- Have students reread page 17. Ask: *What is the point of view in this book? first person Who is telling the story? The author, Sy Montgomery, is telling the story.* RI.4.3, RI.5.3

- Have students think about the main ideas in this segment. Then reread pages 14–17. Ask: *What is the main idea of this section? The first sentence says that the team members have come from all over the world to join Lisa's tree kangaroo expedition. What are some of the details? Sample answer: The team includes a veterinarian, two field scientists, an artist, a photographer, and the writer.* RI.4.2, RI.5.2

RESPOND TO SEGMENT 1

 Classroom Collaboration

Have partners work together to create and present a summary, as well as raise questions that might be answered in the next segment.

Use Peer Supported Learning

Organize students into mixed-proficiency small groups. Have each group draw a web with the words *Tree Kangaroo* in the center. Tell students to pass the web around the group so each student can write something learned from the text. Then ask groups to share their webs orally.

RESPOND TO SEGMENT 2

Classroom Collaboration

Have small groups work together to summarize what they have learned. Have them ask questions about what they don't understand.

COMMON CORE **Common Core Connection**

RI.4.4 determine the meaning of general academic and domain-specific words and phrases; **RI.4.7** interpret information presented visually, orally, or quantitatively; **RI.4.10** read and comprehend informational texts; **W.4.2** write informative/explanatory texts to examine a topic and convey ideas and information clearly; **W.4.5** develop and strengthen writing by planning, revising, and editing; **SL.4.4** report on a topic or text, tell a story, or recount an experience/speak clearly at an understandable pace

RI.5.4 determine the meaning of general academic and domain-specific words and phrases; **RI.5.7** draw on information from print and digital sources to locate answers or solve problems; **RI.5.10** read and comprehend informational texts; **W.5.2** write informative/ explanatory texts to examine a topic and convey ideas and information clearly; **W.5.5** develop and strengthen writing by planning, revising, editing, rewriting, or trying a new approach; **SL.5.4** report on a topic or text, tell a story, or recount an experience/speak clearly at an understandable pace

Academic Vocabulary

Read each word with students and discuss its meaning.

venom (p. 33) • poison produced by some snakes and spiders

endurance (p. 33) • the ability to do something difficult for a long time

slopes (p. 33) • the sides of a hill or mountain

hazards (p. 35) • something that can cause danger

solar (p. 47) • having to do with the sun

FIRST READ ## Think Through the Text

Have students use text evidence and draw inferences to answer questions.

pp. 33–34 • *How do you know from the text that the first three hours of climbing are the worst?* Sample answer: *Oxygen gets thinner the higher you climb. There are many bugs and stinging plants. The trail is slippery and muddy.* **RI.4.1, RI.5.1**

pp. 37–39 • *Is this Lisa, Joel, and Gabriel's first expedition?* no *How do you know?* Page 38 says that Lisa, Joel, and Gabriel became the first scientists ever to radio-collar and track wild Matschie's tree kangaroos the year before this expedition. **RI.4.1, RI.5.1**

pp. 52–53 • *Are the scientists able to learn everything about the tree kangaroos, Jessie and Shelby?* no *How do you know?* The text says that even with the radio collars, the tree kangaroos keep many secrets. **RI.4.1, RI.5.1**

SECOND READ ## Analyze the Text

• Have students reread pages 42–44. Ask: *What is the main idea on page 42?* The hunters have captured a tree kangaroo. *What are some of the details that support the main idea?* Sample answer: *It is a healthy, young male. Its name is Ombom. It weighs eighteen pounds. It landed on its back. They put it in a burlap bag.* **RI.4.2, RI.5.3**

• Have students reread the text on page 45 and look at the photograph. Ask: *How does the photograph help you understand the text about the cloud forest?* Sample answer: *The photograph shows how tall and how close together the trees are. It shows what the mist looks like.* **RI.4.7, RI.5.7**

• Have students reread the first paragraph on page 53. Ask: *What does the word* pierced *mean?* put a hole in *Which words in the text are clues to the meaning?* curved beak and sharp claws **RI.4.4, RI.5.4**

Academic Vocabulary

Read each word with students and discuss its meaning.

caked (p. 65) • covered, coated

ambassadors (p. 74) • people who represent a larger group

endangered (p. 75) • threatened by the danger of dying out

FIRST READ ## Think Through the Text

Have students use text evidence and draw inferences to answer questions.

pp. 55–56 • *What does the text say about how the explorers record the tree kangaroos?* *The text says that they photograph and videotape the animals in the trees.* **RI.4.1**

pp. 69–71 • *What did the trackers find?* *a mother and her nearly grown son* *What does the text say is important about the young male?* *He is nearly old enough to leave his mother. He may be the first young male tree kangaroo in history ever to be tracked during this phase of life.* **RI.4.1, RI.5.1**

pp. 74–75 • *What happened to Ombom?* *He died.* *How do you know that the scientists are sad?* *The bottom paragraph on page 74 says that, to everyone's sorrow and despite the best care we could give, he died just before Lisa had to leave.* **RI.4.1, RI.5.1**

SECOND READ ## Analyze the Text

- Have students reread page 55. Say: *The first paragraph tells us the main idea for the chapter. What is it?* *The team has captured two tree kangaroos.* *What are some supporting details?* Sample answer: *The animals are in trees eighty feet above them. They think one of the tree kangaroos is a baby.* **RI.4.2, RI.5.2**

- Have students reread the text on pages 72–73. Ask: *How does the photograph help you understand the text about the surgical site?* Sample answer: *The photograph shows all of the equipment, so you can tell what the vet needs. You can see how the vet and his assistants work with the tree kangaroo.* **RI.4.7, RI.5.7**

Independent/Self-Selected Reading

Have students reread *Quest for the Tree Kangaroo* independently to practice analyzing the text on their own, or have them practice the skills using another book. Suggested titles:

- *Tree-Kangaroos Of Australia and New Guinea* by Roger Martin

- *Tree Kangaroos* by Chuck Miller **RI.4.10, RI.5.10**

WRITE & PRESENT

1. Have groups of students refer to the text and photographs to discuss how the author uses a main idea and supporting details structure to describe the search for the tree kangaroo. Have them refer to specific sections and encourage them to take notes. **RI.4.2, RI.5.2**

2. Have individual students choose one section from the book and write a paragraph that describes how the author uses a main idea and supporting details structure to convey information. Have them cite specific information from the text that supports their ideas. **W.4.2, W.5.2**

3. Students reconvene to share their paragraphs with partners and edit their writing. **W.4.5, W.5.5**

4. Students present their final paragraphs to classmates. **SL.4.4, SL.5.4**

See Copying Masters, pp. 144–147.

STUDENT CHECKLIST

Writing

☑ Write in complete sentences.

☑ Explain how the author uses main ideas and details to give information.

☑ Provide reasons supported by facts and details from the text.

☑ Use correct language conventions.

Speaking & Listening

☑ Engage effectively in collaborative conversations.

☑ Logically present claims and findings.

☑ Cite text evidence to support ideas.

- Determine the meanings of words and phrases
- Identify main ideas and supporting details
- Analyze text using text evidence

Volcanoes is broken into three instructional segments.

Options for Reading

Independent Students read the selection independently or with a partner and then answer questions posed by the teacher.

Supported Students read a segment and answer questions with teacher support.

COMMON CORE **Common Core Connection**

RI.4.1 refer to details and examples when explaining what the text says explicitly and when drawing inferences; **RI.4.2** determine the main idea and explain how it is supported by details/ summarize; **RI.4.4** determine the meaning of general academic and domain-specific words and phrases; **RI.4.7** interpret information presented visually, orally, or quantitatively; **RI.4.8** explain how an author uses reasons and evidence to support points

RI.5.1 quote accurately when explaining what the text says explicitly and when drawing inferences; **RI.5.2** determine two or more main ideas and explain how they are supported by details/summarize; **RI.5.4** determine the meaning of general academic and domain-specific words and phrases; **RI.5.7** draw on information from print and digital sources to locate answers or solve problems; **RI.5.8** explain how an author uses reasons and evidence to support points

Volcanoes
by Seymour Simon

SUMMARY This book explores volcanoes around the world and discusses their history and the important roles they play in nature. The book's maps and photographs display the locations of volcanoes, volcanic eruptions, and damage volcanoes have caused.

ABOUT THE AUTHOR Seymour Simon worked as a science teacher for 23 years. He uses his teaching experience to create books that make science exciting for children. He has written over 200 books, and in 1992 he received the Lifetime Achievement Commendation from the National Forum on Children's Science Books.

Discuss Genre and Set Purpose

INFORMATIONAL TEXT Have students look at the volcano on the book's cover and then page through the text. Ask students to identify features of informational text, including facts, photographs, and maps.

SET PURPOSE Help students set a purpose for reading, such as to find out what causes volcanoes.

▲ TEXT COMPLEXITY RUBRIC		*Volcanoes* INFORMATIONAL TEXT
Overall Text Complexity		COMPLEX
Quantitative Measures	Lexile	920L
	Guided Reading Level	O
Qualitative Measures	Text Structure	more difficult science concepts
	Language Conventionality and Clarity	increased unfamiliar or academic words
	Knowledge Demands	some specialized knowledge required
	Purpose/Levels of Meaning	single topic

Academic Vocabulary

Read each word with students and discuss its meaning.

spouted (p. 6) • shot up with force, like a fountain

destructive (p. 12) • causing great damage

advancing (p. 17) • approaching or getting closer

billow (p. 21) • rise and swell

weathered (p. 21) • changed as a result of the weather

Domain Specific Vocabulary

crust (p. 6) • Earth's top layers of solid rock

magma (p. 6) • melted rock

lava (p. 6) • liquid rock that pours out of a volcano

crater (p.13) • hollow area that looks like a bowl

FIRST READ ## Think Through the Text

Have students use text evidence and draw inferences to answer questions.

p. 6 • *How are volcanoes formed?* *Volcanoes are formed by cracks or holes that poke through the earth's crust.* 🔲 **RI.4.1, RI.5.1**

pp. 10–11 • *What evidence does the author give to show that Mount St. Helens erupted with incredible force?* *The eruption released energy equal to ten million tons of dynamite.* 🔲 **RI.4.8, RI.5.8**

p. 12 • *What is the main idea of this paragraph?* *The main idea is that the eruption of Mount St. Helens was the most destructive in United States history.* **What details support this idea?** *Sample answer: hundreds of houses were destroyed; miles of highways were damaged* 🔲 **RI.4.2, RI.5.2**

SECOND READ ## Analyze the Text

• Point to the word *magma* on page 6. *How are the words* magma *and* lava *related?* *Magma is melted or molten rock. Lava is magma that pours onto the surface.* 🔲 **RI.4.4, RI.5.4**

• Have students reread page 10. Ask: *Do you think the eruption on May 18 was expected?* *no* *Which sentence helps you know this?* *sentence 7* 🔲 **RI.4.1, RI.5.1**

• Guide students to look back at page 13. Ask: *How was Mount St. Helens different after the eruption? Give evidence from the text and the photographs.* *Sample answer: The text says that the top of the mountain was blown away. The photograph of the mountain from after the eruption shows a giant crater where the pointed peak used to be.* 🔲 **RI.4.7, RI.5.7**

ELL **ENGLISH LANGUAGE LEARNERS**

Use Visuals

Point to a photograph of Mount St. Helens, name it, and have students repeat. Repeat for *lava, mountain,* and *erupted.* Have students look at the photographs and complete a sentence frame for each word, such as *The volcano _____. erupted*

RESPOND TO SEGMENT 1

Classroom Collaboration

Have small groups summarize what they have read so far. Have them ask questions about what they still don't understand.

Domain Specific Vocabulary

cinder (p. 27) • something that burns continuously

caldera (p. 31) • huge crater formed by a volcano

ENGLISH LANGUAGE LEARNERS

Use Visuals

Point to the photographs. Have students orally describe the volcanoes in the images. Then have students write a complete sentence about a photograph.

RESPOND TO SEGMENT 2

Classroom Collaboration

Have small groups work together to summarize this segment and ask questions that may be answered in the next section.

COMMON CORE Common Core Connection

RI.4.3 explain events/procedures/ideas/concepts in a text; **RI.4.10** read and comprehend informational texts; **W.4.2** write informative/explanatory texts to examine a topic and convey ideas and information clearly; **W.4.5** develop and strengthen writing by planning, revising, and editing; **SL.4.4** report on a topic or text, tell a story, or recount an experience/speak clearly at an understandable pace

RI.5.3 explain the relationships between individuals/events/ideas/concepts in a text; **RI.5.10** read and comprehend informational texts; **W.5.2** write informative/explanatory texts to examine a topic and convey ideas and information clearly; **W.5.5** develop and strengthen writing by planning, revising, editing, rewriting, or trying a new approach; **SL.5.4** report on a topic or text, tell a story, or recount an experience/speak clearly at an understandable pace

---

FIRST READ ## Think Through the Text

Have students use text evidence and draw inferences to answer questions.

pp. 14–15 • *What has caused a chain of underwater volcanoes to form down the middle of the North Atlantic Ocean?* Two plates are moving apart and hot magma pushes up between them. 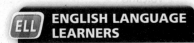 **RI.4.3, RI.5.3**

p. 18 • *How are the volcanoes in the Hawaiian Islands different from most volcanoes?* They are in the middle of the Pacific plate rather than along the edges. **RI.4.3, RI.5.3**

pp. 24–25 • *How do the photographs help you understand what is being described?* The photos show the two different kinds of rocks formed by aa and pahoehoe. **RI.4.7, RI.5.7**

SECOND READ ## Analyze the Text

- Have students reread page 14. Ask: *How are the words* crust *and* plates *related?* Plates *are pieces of the earth's* crust. *How are these words related to the topic of volcanoes?* Almost all the volcanoes in the world erupt in places where two plates meet. **RI.4.4, RI.5.4**

- Review page 18 with students. Ask: *How can volcanoes form islands?* As underwater volcanoes erupt over time, layers of lava build up and harden on top of each other. Thousands of eruptions are needed to build mountains that reach above the sea and appear as islands. **RI.4.3, RI.5.3**

- Guide students to look back at pages 24–25. Ask: *How are* aa *and* pahoehoe *alike?* They are both kinds of lava. They both have Hawaiian names. *How are they different?* Aa is thick and slow moving; it hardens into sharp rocks. Pahoehoe is thin, quick-moving lava; it hardens into a smooth, billowy surface. **RI.4.3, RI.5.3**

FIRST READ ## Think Through the Text

Have students use text evidence and draw inferences to answer questions.

p. 28 • *What forms strato-volcanoes?* *Strato-volcanoes are formed by the lava, cinders, and ashes of an eruption.* RI.4.1, RI.5.1

p. 31 • *Why are some volcanoes called extinct?* *They no longer erupt.* RI.4.4, RI.5.4

p. 32 • *What happens in the months after a volcano erupts?* *At first, everything is buried under lava or ashes. But then, life begins to return. Plants grow in the cracks, and insects and other animals return to the area.* RI.4.3, RI.5.3

SECOND READ ## Analyze the Text

- *Name and describe the four groups of volcanoes.* *Shield volcanoes have broad, gentle slopes. Cinder cone volcanoes erupt explosively, blowing out burning ashes and cinders. The most common volcanoes, strato-volcanoes, are formed by the lava, cinders, and ashes of eruptions. Dome volcanoes have thick, slow-moving lava that forms a steep-sided dome shape.* RI.4.1, RI.5.1

- Guide students to make text connections. Ask: *If you wanted to see a shield volcano, where could you go?* *Hawaii* *Why?* *The text says that Mauna Loa is a shield volcano. I read in the previous segment that Mauna Loa is the highest volcano in Hawaii.* RI.4.3, RI.5.3

- Point to the word *caldera* on page 31. Then ask: *What words help you figure out what* caldera *means?* *a huge crater* *Is a caldera at the top or the bottom of a volcano?* *the top* RI.4.4, RI.5.4

- Reread page 32 with students. Then ask: *What is one detail that supports the main idea that volcanoes do not just destroy?* *Sample answer: They bring new mountains to the land.* RI.4.2, RI.5.2

Independent/Self-Selected Reading

If students have already demonstrated comprehension of *Volcanoes*, have them practice skills using another book. Suggested titles:

- *Hottest Coldest Highest Deepest* by Steve Jenkins
- *Volcanoes* by Franklyn M. Branley RI.4.10, RI.5.10

WRITE & PRESENT

1. Have small groups discuss how the author uses domain-specific words to give information about volcanoes. Then have students create a flow chart that shows how volcanoes form. RI.4.2, RI.5.2

2. Have individual students write a paragraph explaining how volcanoes form. Tell them to use domain-specific words, such as *magma, lava, plates,* and *crust.* W.4.2, W.5.2

3. Have students share their writing in small groups and edit their writing. W.4.5, W.5.5

4. Have students present their final explanations to their classmates. SL.4.4, SL.5.4

5. Individual students hand in their final paragraphs to the teacher.

See Copying Masters, pp. 144–147.

STUDENT CHECKLIST

Writing

☑ Write in complete sentences.

☑ Use domain-specific words in an explanation of how volcanoes form.

☑ Use correct language conventions.

Speaking & Listening

☑ Participate effectively in a collaborative discussion.

☑ Present information in a logical sequence.

☑ Use language that is appropriate for the purpose.

- Identify main ideas and supporting details
- Compare and contrast perspectives
- Analyze text using text evidence

We Are the Ship is broken into three instructional segments.

SEGMENTS

Options for Reading

Independent Students read the book independently or with a partner and then answer questions posed by the teacher.

Supported Students read a segment and answer questions with teacher support.

We Are the Ship
The Story of Negro League Baseball

by Kadir Nelson

SUMMARY *We Are the Ship* traces the history of the Negro League from its beginnings in 1920 to its eventual ending after Jackie Robinson broke the color barrier of major league baseball.

ABOUT THE AUTHOR **Kadir Nelson** is an artist, illustrator, and author who focuses on African-American culture and history. His artwork has been featured in major publications and museums, including the National Baseball Hall of Fame. *We Are the Ship*, which was his first book, won the Coretta Scott King Award in 2009.

Discuss Genre and Set Purpose

INFORMATIONAL TEXT Have students skim through the book to examine the text and the accompanying illustrations. Discuss with students how they can tell that this book is informational.

SET PURPOSE Help students set a purpose for reading, such as to learn about the Negro Leagues and African-American baseball players.

COMMON CORE Connection

RI.4.1 refer to details and examples when explaining what the text says explicitly and when drawing inferences; **RI.4.2** determine the main idea and explain how it is supported by details/summarize; **RI.4.3** explain events/procedures/ideas/concepts in a text; **RI.4.6** compare and contrast a firsthand and secondhand account of the same event or topic

RI.5.1 quote accurately when explaining what the text says explicitly and when drawing inferences; **RI.5.2** determine two or more main ideas and explain how they are supported by details/summarize; **RI.5.3** explain the relationships between individuals/events/ideas/ concepts in a text; **RI.5.6** analyze multiple accounts of the same event or topic

TEXT COMPLEXITY RUBRIC

Overall Text Complexity		*We Are the Ship* INFORMATIONAL TEXT
		COMPLEX
Quantitative Measures	Lexile	900L
	Guided Reading Level	U
Qualitative Measures	Text Structure	organization of main ideas and details is complex
	Language Conventionality and Clarity	complex and varied sentence structure
	Knowledge Demands	somewhat unfamiliar perspective
	Purpose/Levels of Meaning	multiple purposes

Academic Vocabulary

Read each word with students and discuss its meaning.

prohibited (p. 2) • forbade

integrate (p. 9) • to open to people of all races

rival (p. 9) • competing or opposing

consistent (p. 21) • having a regular pattern

Domain Specific Vocabulary

bunt (p. 17) • to hit a baseball softly so it lands close by

segregated (p. 24) • separated by race

barnstorming (p. 26) • traveling through rural areas to play games

FIRST READ ## Think Through the Text

Have students use text evidence and draw inferences to answer questions.

pp. 1–3 • *Why did African Americans start their own professional baseball teams? Give specific details from the text.* White baseball team owners decided to do away with African Americans in professional baseball. African Americans needed to form their own leagues.

RI.4.2, RI.5.2

p. 9 • *What did Rube Foster decide to do?* He decided to organize the Negro League. *Why?* He wanted African-American players to be ready when professional baseball was integrated. **RI.4.1, RI.5.1**

pp. 23–24 • *What made life in the Negro Leagues difficult?* Segregation made life difficult for the players. They often couldn't find restaurants, restrooms, or hotels they could go to. **RI.4.3, RI.5.3**

SECOND READ ## Analyze the Text

• Review page 1 with students. Explain that this story is told by a narrator who represents the voices of all the Negro League players. Point out that the author of this text is giving a secondhand account because he did not actually play in the Negro Leagues. Then ask: *What are some words that show that the point of view represents more than one voice?* we; ours **RI.4.6, RI.5.6**

• Guide students to look back at page 9. Ask: *Why do you think the author called this book* We Are the Ship? *Rube Foster said, "We are the ship; all else the sea" when he organized the Negro League.* **RI.4.1, RI.5.1**

• Have students reread page 17. Ask: *According to the narrator, how was Negro League baseball different from the majors?* Sample answer: *He says that Negro League baseball was fast, flashy, and daring and always exciting to watch.* **RI.4.1, RI.5.1**

 ENGLISH LANGUAGE LEARNERS

Use Visuals and Sentence Frames

Discuss the sport of baseball with students. Have them describe the sport using the illustrations in this segment. Then help them complete sentence frames, such as *Baseball players swing a ___.* bat

RESPOND TO SEGMENT 1

Classroom Collaboration

Have partners summarize what they have read so far. Have them ask questions about what they don't understand.

Domain Specific Vocabulary

commissioner (p. 58) • leader of a baseball league

draft (p. 63) • required military duty

plantation (p. 78) • large farm in the U.S. South

 ENGLISH LANGUAGE LEARNERS

Use Visuals

Use illustrations to develop students' language skills. Have partners look at the pictures and guide them to name domain-specific words. Then have them give sentences to describe the illustrations.

RESPOND TO SEGMENT 2

 Classroom Collaboration

Have small groups work together to create a summary and raise questions that may be answered in the next segment.

 Common Core Connection

RI.4.4 determine the meaning of general academic and domain-specific words and phrases; **W.4.2** write informative/explanatory texts to examine a topic and convey ideas and information clearly; **W.4.5** develop and strengthen writing by planning, revising, and editing; **SL.4.4** report on a topic or text, tell a story, or recount an experience/speak clearly at an understandable pace

RI.5.4 determine the meaning of general academic and domain-specific words and phrases; **W.5.2** write informative/explanatory texts to examine a topic and convey ideas and information clearly; **W.5.5** develop and strengthen writing by planning, revising, editing, rewriting, or trying a new approach; **SL.5.4** report on a topic or text, tell a story, or recount an experience/speak clearly at an understandable pace

Academic Vocabulary

Read each word with students and discuss its meaning.

stance (p. 41) • way of standing

legendary (p. 47) • renowned or famous

barrier (p. 55) • something that stands in the way of communication

FIRST READ # Think Through the Text

Have students use text evidence and draw inferences to answer questions.

p. 31 • *How did the Great Depression affect Negro League baseball?* Business collapsed. Banks closed. People spent the money they had on food and heat. Most teams disappeared. **RI.4.3, RI.5.3**

p. 38 • *How did night baseball change everything?* People who worked during the day could see games at night. It was tough on the players, who had to play three or four games a day instead of two. **RI.4.3, RI.5.3**

pp. 41–51 • *What is the main idea of these pages?* The Negro League was full of great players that many people never got to see play. *What is one detail that supports this main idea?* Sample answer: Satchel Paige was one of their finest pitchers, but they had other guys who threw just as hard, and even harder. **RI.4.2, RI.5.2**

SECOND READ # Analyze the Text

• Have students reread page 34. Say: *Compare and contrast the Negro Leagues and the major leagues.* Negro League teams had fifteen or sixteen players, and major league teams had about twenty-five.. Negro League players got between $500-$800 a month and major league players got about $7,000 per month during the 1940s. **RI.4.3, RI.5.3**

• Review page 51 with students. Ask: *What is the author's point of view about Negro League players?* He says that unfortunately, most of them will never receive the recognition they deserve. **RI.4.1, RI.5.1**

• Reread page 53. Ask: *Why did Negro League players like playing in Latin America?* There was no segregation. They could stay at any hotel and eat at any restaurant. Good players were treated like kings. **RI.4.2, RI.5.2**

Academic Vocabulary

Read each word with students and discuss its meaning.

ammunition (p. 63) • Objects used as projectiles in offense or defense.

eloquent (p. 74) • well-spoken; using words well

FIRST READ ## Think Through the Text

Have students use text evidence and draw inferences to answer questions.

p. 58 • *How did the players in the Negro Leagues know they were good enough to play in the major leagues?* *At the end of the season, the major leaguers would barnstorm against the Negro League players. The Negro Leagues won about 60 percent of the games.* ▬RI.4.3, RI.5.3

p. 75 • *Summarize what Jackie Robinson did that made people proud.* *He brought the Negro League style of play to the major leagues. He helped bring the rest of the country closer to seeing black people as equals.* ▬RI.4.2, RI.5.2

SECOND READ ## Analyze the Text

• *On page 66, the narrator says that the almighty dollar has a way of changing folks' minds. What does he mean?* *When major league owners saw how much money the Negro League players could bring in, they started to think about integrating baseball.* ▬RI.4.4, RI.5.4

• Review pages 72–74. Ask: *How was Jackie Robinson different from the other players?* *He was eloquent and impressed Branch Rickey.* *What did Rickey think about Robinson?* *Rickey felt that Robinson could handle the pressure without fighting back.* ▬RI.4.3, RI.5.3

• Have students reread pages 77–78. Ask: *Why weren't most players in the Negro Leagues bitter when they couldn't play in the major leagues?* *They still got paid for doing what they loved, and they paved the way for men like Jackie Robinson.* ▬RI.4.2, RI.5.2

Independent/Self-Selected Reading

Have students reread *We Are the Ship* and compare this secondhand account with a firsthand account of the treatment of the players, such as the following texts. Ask students to attend to the focus of each account and the information provided by each one.

• *Catching Dreams: My Life in the Negro Baseball Leagues* by Frazier "Slow" Robinson and Paul Bauer

• *I Was Right on Time* by Buck O'Neil ▬RI.4.6, RI.5.6

Performance Task

WRITE & PRESENT

1. Have small groups discuss the similarities and differences between the Negro Leagues and the major leagues. Then have students complete a Venn diagram with details from the text. ▬RI.4.3, RI.5.3

2. Have individual students write a paragraph comparing and contrasting the Negro Leagues and the major leagues. Tell them to use the main ideas and details from their Venn diagram. ▬W.4.2, W.5.2

3. Have students share their writing in small groups and edit their writing. ▬W.4.5, W.5.5

4. Have students present their final parahraphs to their classmates. ▬SL.4.4, SL.5.4

5. Have individual students hand in their final paragraphs.

See Copying Masters, pp. 144–147.

STUDENT CHECKLIST

Writing

☑ Analyze the author's comparison of the Negro leagues and the major leagues.

☑ Write in complete sentences.

☑ Use correct language conventions.

Speaking & Listening

☑ Participate effectively in a collaborative discussion.

☑ Ask and answer questions.

☑ Use language that is appropriate for the purpose.

"Kenya's Long Dry Season"

by Nellie Gonzalez Cutler

SUMMARY This *Time for Kids* article explains the cause and effects of a long drought in Kenya. Photographs and a map add details.

ABOUT THE AUTHOR **Nellie Gonzalez Cutler** is a journalist who writes for *Time for Kids* magazine. Her articles include "State of the Union" and "Egypt's President Resigns."

Discuss Genre and Set Purpose

INFORMATIONAL TEXT Have students look through the selection, and help them find and identify characteristics of an informational text, including sidebars, a map, photographs, and captions.

SET PURPOSE Help students set a purpose for reading, such as to find information about the drought in Kenya.

TEXT COMPLEXITY RUBRIC		"Kenya's Long Dry Season" INFORMATIONAL TEXT
Overall Text Complexity		ACCESSIBLE
Quantitative Measures	Lexile	830L
	Guided Reading Level	R
Qualitative Measures	Text Structure	implicit cause/effect text structure
	Language Conventionality and Clarity	clear, direct language
	Knowledge Demands	some specialized knowledge required
	Purpose/Levels of Meaning	single level of simple meaning

FIRST READ **Think Through the Text**

Have students use text evidence and draw inferences to answer questions.

paragraph 1 • *For how long has the drought been going on?* three seasons *How do you know?* The first sentence says that rain has not come to Kenya for the past three seasons. **RI.4.1, RI.5.1**

paragraph 2 • *What does the text say are some of the effects of the drought?* The grasslands are dried out, watering holes are dry, cattle are dying, and crops are shriveling. Food prices are rising. **RI.4.3, RI.5.3**

paragraph 3 • *What will the WFP do to help?* provide emergency food aid to 3.8 million people **RI.4.3, RI.5.3**

paragraph 5 • *How does the drought affect children in school?* Many children get pulled out of school to go to work. **RI.4.3, RI.5.3**

SECOND READ **Analyze the Text**

- Review basic text structures with students, including sequence, cause and effect, problem and solution, and main idea and details. Ask: *Which text structure does the author primarily use in this article?* cause and effect Have students name some examples discussed in the article. Sample answer: *cause–drought, effect–severe food crisis* **RI.4.5**

- Have students look at the photographs and read the captions. Ask: *What information do you get from the photographs?* Many bags of food are needed. If the watering hole dries up, the hippo may die. **RI.4.7, RI.5.7**

- Have students reread the section "Keeping Kids in School." Ask: *What reason is given to explain why the dropout rate is lower in some areas?* In areas where school meals are provided, students are more likely to stay in school. **RI.4.1, RI.5.1**

Independent/Self-Selected Reading

Have students reread "Kenya's Long Dry Season" independently to practice analyzing the text on their own, or have them practice the skills using another book, such as:

- *Kenya (Countries of the World)* by Michael Dahl

- *Kenya* by Barbara Saffer **RI.4.10, RI.5.10**

WRITE & PRESENT

1. Have small groups ask and answer questions about the text and photographs. Then ask them to share their own opinions about the article, supporting their opinions with details and and facts from the text. **RI.4.1, RI.5.1**

2. Have individual students write opinion paragraphs that tell what they learned from this article and what they think about it. Tell them to include facts and details from the text that support their opinions. **W.4.1, W.5.1**

3. Students meet with partners to share their paragraphs and edit their writing. **W.4.5, W.5.5**

4. Students present their final paragraphs to classmates. **SL.4.4, SL.5.4**

5. Students turn in their final paragraphs to the teacher.

See Copying Masters, pp. 144–147.

STUDENT CHECKLIST

Writing

☑ Write in complete sentences.

☑ Explain facts from the article and express opinions about it.

☑ Support opinions with facts and details from the text.

☑ Use correct language conventions.

Speaking & Listening

☑ Engage effectively in collaborative conversations.

☑ Logically present claims and findings.

☑ Cite text evidence to support ideas.

- Quote accurately from the text to support inferences
- Describe the sequence of events in a process
- Explain how sight works
- Analyze text using text evidence

"Seeing Eye to Eye" is broken into three instructional segments.

SEGMENTS

SEGMENT 1...paragraphs 1–14
SEGMENT 2...paragraphs 15–26
SEGMENT 3...paragraphs 27–37

Options for Reading

Independent Students read the selection independently or with a partner and then answer questions posed by the teacher.

Supported Students read a segment and answer questions with teacher support.

COMMON CORE   Common Core Connection

RI.4.1 refer to details and examples when explaining what the text says explicitly and when drawing inferences; **RI.4.3** explain events/procedures/ideas/concepts in a text

RI.5.1 quote accurately when explaining what the text says explicitly and when drawing inferences; **RI.5.3** explain the relationships between individuals/events/ideas/concepts in a text

"Seeing Eye to Eye"
by Leslie Hall

SUMMARY This Pathfinder edition article from *National Geographic Explorer* gives information about light and how our eyes work. Although human eyes come in many colors, shapes, and sizes, all eyes do the same job—catch light so that we can see. In the article, the author explains how our eyes turn light into images.

ABOUT THE AUTHOR Leslie Hall was an associate editor for a children's educational publisher before she began writing articles, poems, and stories for young people. She has also written nonfiction articles for *National Geographic Explorer*.

Discuss Genre and Set Purpose

INFORMATIONAL TEXT Have students look at the selection to find and identify features of informational text, including section headings and images. Guide them to use these features to make predictions about the information the article will present.

SET PURPOSE Help students set a purpose for reading, such as to find out how light and sight are connected.

▲ TEXT COMPLEXITY RUBRIC		"Seeing Eye to Eye" INFORMATIONAL TEXT
Overall Text Complexity		COMPLEX
Quantitative Measures	Lexile	570L
	Guided Reading Level	O
Qualitative Measures	Text Structure	somewhat complex science concepts
	Language Conventionality and Clarity	some unfamiliar or academic words
	Knowledge Demands	some specialized knowledge required
	Purpose/Levels of Meaning	multiple topics

Academic Vocabulary

Read each word with students and discuss its meaning.

beady (paragraph 1) • small and round
artificial (paragraph 6) • not from nature; made by humans
scatters (paragraph 9) • spreads out; projects
image (paragraph 13) • a picture formed in a lens or mirror

FIRST READ **Think Through the Text**

Have students use text evidence and draw inferences to answer questions.

paragraphs 1–5 • *What do all eyes have in common? They all catch light. They all turn light into sight, with help from the brain.* RI.4.3, RI.5.3

paragraphs 6–8 • *What rules does light always follow? It reflects off objects. and also refracts, or bends. It can be absorbed by objects.*
RI.4.3, RI.5.3

paragraphs 12–14 • *What happens after light passes through the cornea? It enters the pupil and passes through your lens.* RI.4.3, RI.5.3

SECOND READ **Analyze the Text**

• *Does the shape, size, or color of the eye affect what it does? Give evidence from the text to support your inference. The text says that they do the same job, that they all catch light. This tells me that eyes all do the same thing no matter what they look like.* RI.4.1, RI.5.1

• *Would you be able to see without light? What evidence from the text helps you know? The text says that objects become visible when light bounces off them. From this, I can infer that I would not be able to see without light.* RI.4.1, RI.5.1

• *Why is the brain an important part of vision? When images appear on the retina, they are upside down. Our brain flips the images so we can see them correctly.* RI.4.3, RI.5.3

Domain Specific Vocabulary

retina (paragraph 14) • the part of the eye at the back of the eyeball

ELL **ENGLISH LANGUAGE LEARNERS**

Use Gestures

Use simplified language and gestures to restate complex terms. For example, restate *refracted* as *bent*. Hold your arm out straight and demonstrate bending it as you say *refracted*. Have students complete sentence frames such as the following: *The cornea ____ light. refracts, bends*

RESPOND TO SEGMENT 1
Classroom Collaboration

Have small groups summarize what they have learned about sight. Invite them to share their summaries. Have them ask questions about what they don't understand.

FIRST READ # Think Through the Text

Have students use text evidence and draw inferences to answer questions.

paragraphs 15–18 • *What is the colored ring around your pupil called?* the iris *What does it do?* changes the size of your pupil ▬ RI.4.4, RI.5.4

paragraphs 19–22 • *Why do leaves look green?* They reflect more green light than any other color. ▬ RI.4.1

paragraphs 23–26 • *Explain the sequence of events when light waves hit the cones.* Light waves create a reaction when they hit the cones. The cones send messages about the colors to the brain, and then the brain mixes the colors together. This allows us to many different colors. ▬ RI.4.3, RI.5.3

SECOND READ # Analyze the Text

- Have students reread the section "Night Sight." Then ask: *Would you expect your rods to work better at noon or at midnight? How do you know?* Guide students to support their inference by quoting accurately from the text. *Rods would work better at midnight. I know this because the text says that rods work best in dim light.* ▬ RI.4.1, RI.5.1

- *Why might nocturnal animals have extra big eyes for the size of their heads?* They might have extra big eyes for the size of their heads to help their eyes collect more light. *Why would nocturnal animals need this feature?* They are active at night and need to be able to see in darkness. ▬ RI.4.3, RI.5.3

- Explain that students can use what they read in "The Colors of Light" to help them understand what they read in "Color Vision." Ask: *Why do you think squids don't have cones?* Sample answer: Cones are used for seeing colors and it takes bright light to see many colors. Since squids live in the dark ocean, they would not be able to see many colors and therefore, do not need cones. ▬ RI.4.3, RI.5.3

FIRST READ # Think Through the Text

Have students use text evidence and draw inferences to answer questions.

paragraphs 27–29 • *Why are animal eyes different? Animals have eyes with features that best help them catch the light they need to survive.*
RI.4.1, RI.5.1

paragraphs 27–32 • *How is monocular vision different from binocular vision? In monocular vision, the eyes are on the sides of the head and each eye sees a different view. In binocular vision, the eyes are on the front of the head and see much of the same view.* RI.4.3, RI.5.3

paragraphs 33–35 • *What is a compound eye? an eye with many lenses*
RI.4.4, RI.5.4

SECOND READ # Analyze the Text

• *Based on what you read, do you think people have binocular vision or monocular vision?* Sample answer: *Humans have binocular vision. Their eyes are on the front of their heads, face forward, and see the same view. The text says that in binocular vision, both eyes see much of the same view.* RI.4.1, RI.5.1

• Have students review "A Bug's Eye View." Ask: *Why does the author compare putting together the images from a compound eye to putting together a puzzle?* Sample answer: *The separate images are put together to form one image, just like all the pieces of a puzzle form one image.* RI.4.3, RI.5.3

• Reread "A Bright Future" with students. Ask: *What does the author mean when she says that eyes just might help us see a better, brighter future?* Sample answer: *She means that scientists and engineers are using what they learn from studying eyes to design and build new inventions that may help us live and see better.* RI.4.1, RI.5.1

Independent/Self-Selected Reading

Have students reread "Seeing Eye to Eye" independently to practice analyzing the text on their own, or have them practice the skills using another book. Suggested titles:

• *The Secrets of Animal Flight* by Nic Bishop

• *Cold Light: Creatures, Discoveries, and Inventions that Glow* by Anita Sitarski RI.4.10, RI.5.10

Performance Task

WRITE & PRESENT

1. Have small groups refer to the text to discuss inferences they made while reading "Seeing Eye to Eye." Guide them to support the inferences with text evidence. RI.4.1, RI.5.1

2. Have individual students write an explanation of one inference they made about sight or light. Tell them to quote accurately and explicitly from the text to explain their inference. W.4.2, W.5.2

3. Have students share their writing in small groups and then edit their writing. W.4.5, W.5.5

4. Have students present their final explanations to their classmates. SL.4.4, SL.5.4

5. Have individual students turn in their final explanations to the teacher.

See Copying Masters, pp. 144–147.

STUDENT CHECKLIST

Writing

☑ Quote accurately and explicitly from the text to explain an idea they inferred from the article.

☑ Use precise language and domain-specific vocabulary.

☑ Write in complete sentences.

Speaking & Listening

☑ Participate effectively in a collaborative discussion.

☑ Speak clearly and at an understandable pace.

☑ Use language that is appropriate for the purpose.

- Compare and contrast main ideas
- Summarize main ideas and supporting details
- Determine the meaning of domain-specific words
- Analyze text using text evidence

"Telescopes" is broken into three instructional segments.

SEGMENTS

SEGMENT 1
paragraphs 1–17

SEGMENT 2
paragraphs 18–22

SEGMENT 3
paragraphs 23–29

Options for Reading

Independent Students read the selection independently or with a partner and then answer questions posed by the teacher.

Supported Students read a segment and answer questions with teacher support.

 Common Core Connection

RI.4.1 refer to details and examples when explaining what the text says explicitly and when drawing inferences; **RI.4.2** determine the main idea and explain how it is supported by details/summarize; **RI.4.3** explain events/procedures/ideas/concepts in a text; **RI.4.4** determine the meaning of general academic and domain-specific words and phrases
RI.5.1 quote accurately when explaining what the text says explicitly and when drawing inferences; **RI.5.2** determine two or more main ideas and explain how they are supported by details/summarize; **RI.5.3** explain the relationships between individuals/events/ideas/concepts in a text; **RI.5.4** determine the meaning of general academic and domain-specific words and phrases

"Telescopes"
by Colin A. Ronan

SUMMARY This article describes many kinds of telescopes and how they work. Telescopes use different lenses, mirrors, and electronic detectors to focus on objects far away. Modern technology today helps scientists see clearer images than in the past.

ABOUT THE AUTHOR Colin A. Ronan was a British author of over 40 books on astronomy and a specialist in the history of science. He also founded the Ronan Picture Library, which includes many scientific and historical illustrations and pictures.

Discuss Genre and Set Purpose

INFORMATIONAL TEXT Have students look at the article and find and identify features of informational text, including bold print words and section headings.

SET PURPOSE Help students set a purpose for reading, such as to find out about different kinds of telescopes.

TEXT COMPLEXITY RUBRIC		"Telescopes" INFORMATIONAL TEXT
Overall Text Complexity		COMPLEX
Quantitative Measures	Lexile	1030L
	Guided Reading Level	S
Qualitative Measures	Text Structure	complex science concepts
	Language Conventionality and Clarity	general academic and domain-specific language
	Knowledge Demands	some specialized knowledge required
	Purpose/Levels of Meaning	single topic

Academic Vocabulary

Read each word with students and discuss its meaning.

emitted (paragraph 2) • sent something out, such as light or heat

celestial (paragraph 6) • of outer space

composition (paragraph 7) • makeup of an object

tedious (paragraph 13) • boring; tiresome

minute (paragraph 23) • very tiny

vital (paragraph 25) • very important

Domain Specific Vocabulary

diameter (paragraph 8) • a line that passes through the center of a circle and touches the circumference at each end

concave (paragraph 9) • curled inward like the inside of a bowl

parallel (paragraph 20) • going in the same direction

perpendicular (paragraph 24) • at a right angle

FIRST READ ## Think Through the Text

Have students use text evidence and draw inferences to answer questions.

paragraphs 1–2 • *How does the article define* telescope? *The text says a* telescope *is an instrument used to produce magnified images of distant objects.* ▬RI.4.1, RI.5.1

paragraphs 3–5 • *What are the three main types of optical telescopes?* refracting, reflecting, and catadioptric *What does the text say that these three telescopes do?* *They gather and focus light in different ways.*
▬RI.4.1, RI.5.1

paragraphs 6–8 • *Summarize what happens when light strikes the lenses of a refracting telescope. Give details that support the main idea. Light is bent and brought to a focus within the tube. This forms an image of a distant object. The eyepiece magnifies the image.* ▬RI.4.2, RI.5.2

SECOND READ ## Analyze the Text

• Have students reread paragraph 5. Then ask: *What does the word* objective *mean?* the main lens or mirror in an optical telescope *How does the author show readers that this is an important word?* *It is in bold print.* ▬RI.4.4, RI.5.4

• *What key details tell the differences between the three types of optical telescopes?* *Refracting telescopes use lenses, reflecting telescopes use mirrors, and catadioptrics use both lenses and mirrors.* ▬RI.4.3, RI.5.3

• *What details support why the world's largest optical telescopes are reflectors?* *It is easier and less expensive to create the mirror for a reflector than it is to create the lens for a refractor. A mirror doesn't bend under its own weight because the back can be supported, whereas a lens can only be supported around its edges.* ▬RI.4.1, RI.5.1

ELL **ENGLISH LANGUAGE LEARNERS**

Use Gestures and Sentence Frames

Use gestures and simplified language to restate key terms and the main ideas. For example, restate *magnified* as "made bigger." Use your hands to show something growing bigger. Check students' comprehension by giving them sentence frames, such as "Telescopes make objects look ____." *bigger*

RESPOND TO SEGMENT 1

 Classroom Collaboration

Have small groups summarize what they have learned about optical telescopes. Invite them to share their summaries. Have them ask questions about what they don't understand.

ENGLISH LANGUAGE LEARNERS

Use Comprehensible Input and Gestures

Guide students to recognize the difference between optical and non-optical telescopes. Say: *Optical telescopes collect light we can see. Non-optical telescopes collect radiation, or energy, that we can't see.* Have students use words and hand gestures, such as covering their eyes, to explain the differences.

RESPOND TO SEGMENT 2

Classroom Collaboration

Have partners work together to summarize what they have learned. Tell them to ask questions about anything they don't understand.

Common Core Connection

FIRST READ Think Through the Text

Have students use text evidence and draw inferences to answer questions.

paragraph 18 • *What does the text say that non-optical telescopes do?* The text says that non-optical telescopes collect forms of electromagnetic radiation that are invisible to the eye. **RI.4.1, RI.5.1**

paragraph 20 • *What are some of the different types of non-optical telescopes mentioned in the text?* radio telescopes, microwave telescopes, infrared telescopes, ultraviolet telescopes, and x-ray telescopes *How are infrared telescopes, ultraviolet telescopes, and x-ray telescopes alike?* They all use mirrors to collect forms of electromagnetic radiation. **RI.4.3, RI.5.3**

paragraphs 21–22 • *What is an* interferometer? a group of two or more telescopes with the observing power of one large telescope *What is the advantage of interferometers?* They provide a greater degree of detail than any of the individual telescopes alone. **RI.4.4, RI.5.4**

SECOND READ Analyze the Text

- Have students reread paragraph 18 and think about the details that support the main idea about non-optical telescopes. Then ask: *What can the radiation used in non-optical telescopes do?* The forms of radiation can give us information about objects or regions of space otherwise hidden from sight. **RI.4.1, RI.5.1**

- Review paragraph 19. Then ask: *What key details show how a radio telescope is different from a reflector telescope?* A radio telescope lacks a mirror; instead, it has a bowl-shaped metal structure that is covered with netting or metal. The structure collects radio waves instead of light and focuses them on a receiver. **RI.4.2, RI.5.2**

- Reread paragraphs 21–22. Then ask: *How are non-optical interferometers and optical interferometers alike?* They both are groups of two or more telescopes. They both use the light-collecting capabilities of the individual telescopes. The observational abilities are equivalent to one large telescope. *What word does the author use to signal that he is making a comparison?* the word similarly **RI.4.3, RI.5.3**

FIRST READ **Think Through the Text**

Have students use text evidence and draw inferences to answer questions.

paragraph 23 • *What does the text say are the two most common telescope mounts?* altazimuth and equatorial RI.4.1, RI.5.1

paragraph 25 • *Which sentence states the main idea about telescopes and computers?* the first sentence in the paragraph *What key details support the main idea?* Sample answer: They can be programmed with the precise positions of thousands of celestial objects. RI.4.2, RI.5.2

paragraph 29 • *Summarize how Galileo used the telescope. Cite details from the text.* Galileo was the first to use a telescope to look at the heavens. He built his own telescope, and used it to discover craters and plains on the moon, four moons in orbit around Jupiter, and the rings of Saturn. He also discovered that Venus goes through phases as it orbits the sun and that the Milky Way has seemingly countless stars. RI.4.2, RI.5.2

SECOND READ **Analyze the Text**

• Have students reread paragraphs 23–24 about telescope mounts. Then ask: *What is the difference between altazimuth mounts and equatorial mounts?* Altazimuth mounts move the telescope up and down and side to side. Equatorial mounts allow the telescope to track objects as they move across the sky due to the Earth's rotation. RI.4.2, RI.5.2

• Review paragraphs 25–27 with students. Then say: *Summarize how computers are used in telescopic observations.* Sample answer: Computers can help viewers find objects in the sky. They are also used to record and analyze the data that telescopes collect. RI.4.2, RI.5.2

• Tell students to think about how modern technology affects science. Then ask: *Do scientists have to be right in front of a telescope to use it?* no *How do you know?* Remote observing allows astronomers to use computers to access, control, and view images from telescopes that are miles—or even continents—away. RI.4.1, RI.5.1

Independent/Self-Selected Reading

Have students reread "Telescopes" independently to practice analyzing the text on their own, or have them practice the skills using another book. Suggested titles:

• *Telescopes* by Lionel Bender

• *Space, Stars, and the Beginning of Time: What the Hubble Telescope Saw* by Elaine Scott RI.4.10, RI.5.10

Performance Task

WRITE & PRESENT

1. Have small groups discuss the overall main idea of "Telescopes" and the details that support the main idea. Ask students to think about the distinctions that the author makes between the different types of telescopes. RI.4.2, RI.5.2

2. Have individual students create a summary of "Telescopes." Tell them to include key details about the different types of microscopes. W.4.2, W.5.2

3. Students reconvene in their small groups to share and edit their writing. W.4.5, W.5.5

4. Individual students present their final summaries to their classmates. SL.4.4, SL.5.4

5. Individual students turn in their summaries to the teacher.

See Copying Masters, pp. 144–147.

STUDENT CHECKLIST

Writing

☑ Compare and contrast telescopes.

☑ Use details from the text that describe differences between the types of telescopes.

☑ Write in complete sentences.

☑ Use correct language conventions.

Speaking & Listening

☑ Participate effectively in a collaborative discussion.

☑ Speak clearly at an understandable pace.

☑ Use language that is appropriate for the purpose.

- Identify main ideas and details
- Identify causes and effects
- Determine how an author structures text
- Analyze text using text evidence

"The Underground Railroad" is broken into three instructional segments.

SEGMENTS

SEGMENT 1 . . . paragraphs 1–3
SEGMENT 2 . . . paragraphs 4–8
SEGMENT 3 . . paragraphs 9–13

Options for Reading

Independent Students read the article independently or with a partner and then answer questions posed by the teacher.

Supported Students read a segment and answer questions with teacher support.

 Common Core Connection

RI.4.1 refer to details and examples when explaining what the text says explicitly and when drawing inferences; **RI.4.2** determine the main idea and explain how it is supported by details/summarize; **RI.4.3** explain events/procedures/ideas/concepts in a text; **RI.4.4** determine the meaning of general academic and domain-specific words and phrases; **RI.4.5** describe the overall structure of a text or part of a text

RI.5.1 quote accurately when explaining what the text says explicitly and when drawing inferences; **RI.5.3** explain the relationships between individuals/events/ideas/concepts in a text; **RI.5.4** determine the meaning of general academic and domain-specific words and phrases

"Underground Railroad"
by Henrietta Buckmaster

SUMMARY This article explains the origin of the Underground Railroad and describes its purpose. Through the Underground Railroad, black and white Americans helped slaves reach freedom. People took many risks by participating in the Underground Railroad, and these risks contributed to many important changes in the United States.

ABOUT THE AUTHOR Henrietta Buckmaster was a historian and magazine editor. She wrote many children's books and historical novels for adults. Her books for children include *Flight to Freedom: The Story of the Underground Railroad* and *All About Sir Walter Raleigh*.

Discuss Genre and Set Purpose

INFORMATIONAL TEXT Have students look at the article and identify characteristics of informational text, including section headings.

SET PURPOSE Help students set a purpose for reading, such as to find out about the Underground Railroad and the results of its use in the United States.

TEXT COMPLEXITY RUBRIC		"Underground Railroad"
Overall Text Complexity		INFORMATIONAL TEXT
		COMPLEX
Quantitative Measures	Lexile	990L
	Guided Reading Level	S
Qualitative Measures	Text Structure	somewhat complex social studies concepts
	Language Conventionality and Clarity	increased unfamiliar or academic language
	Knowledge Demands	specialized knowledge required
	Purpose/Levels of Meaning	multiple purposes

Academic Vocabulary

Read each word with students and discuss its meaning.

authorities (paragraph 2) • people who work for the government

vanished (paragraph 4) • disappeared suddenly

pursuers (paragraph 4) • people who follow others to try to catch them

precautions (paragraph 5) • something done beforehand to prevent danger

hostile (paragraph 6) • angry and aggressive

infuriated (paragraph 6) • made someone very angry

cunning (paragraph 7) • skill or craftiness

Domain Specific Vocabulary

refuge stations (paragraph 1) • places where the slaves could stop or rest safely

abolitionists (paragraph 1) • people who supported ending slavery before the Civil War

bondage (paragraph 1) • slavery

fugitives (paragraph 2) • runaway slaves

auctioned (paragraph 3) • sold to the person who paid the most money

FIRST READ ## Think Through the Text

Have students use text evidence and draw inferences to answer questions.

paragraph 1 • *How is the Underground Railroad defined in the text?* *a secret network of refuge stations in the United States* **RI.4.1, RI.5.1**

paragraph 2 • *Why did some slaves escape to Canada, Mexico, and the Caribbean?* *Fugitives were safe in these places. Officials in Canada refused to take the fugitives to the authorities in the United States. In both Mexico and the Caribbean, slavery had been abolished.* **RI.4.3, RI.5.3**

paragraph 3 • *What did slave traders do in Maryland and Virginia?* *They bought slaves in Maryland and Virginia. Then the men sold the slaves in the South.* **RI.4.3, RI.5.3**

SECOND READ ## Analyze the Text

• Review basic text structures, including sequence, cause and effect, problem and solution, and main idea and details. Ask: *Which two text structures does the author use in this segment?* *The author uses a main idea and details structure to tell about the Underground Railroad. She also uses a cause and effect structure to explain how key events occurred.* **RI.4.5, RI.5.3**

• *What is the main idea of the second paragraph?* *Rescuers helped more than 40,000 slaves North to freedom.* *What details support the main idea?* *Sample answer: Fugitives used the Mississippi and Ohio Rivers as escape routes.* **RI.4.2, RI.5.1**

• *What does the word* domestic *mean?* *within a country* *Which words and phrases are clues to the meaning of* domestic? *illegal to import from Africa; already in the United States* **RI.4.4, RI.5.4**

ELL ## ENGLISH LANGUAGE LEARNERS

Use Peer Supported Learning

Organize students into small groups. Have each group draw a web with the words *Underground Railroad* in the center. Tell students to pass the web from student to student, and have each student add a word or phrase related to the Underground Railroad. Then call on groups to share their completed webs. Suggest that groups add information from other groups to their own webs.

RESPOND TO SEGMENT 1

 Classroom Collaboration

Have partners work together to create and present a summary. Encourage them to raise questions that may be answered in the next segment.

FIRST READ ## Think Through the Text

Have students use text evidence and draw inferences to answer questions.

paragraph 6 • *What law did Congress pass in 1850?* the Fugitive Slave Law *How was the work of abolitionists more dangerous after 1850?* The Fugitive Slave Law said that anyone who helped a slave could be fined or go to prison. ▬ RI.4.3, RI.5.3

paragraphs 7–8 • *When did fugitives usually travel?* at night *What were some of the ways that fugitives used to escape?* Some hid at the bottoms of farm wagons underneath vegetables and other produce. Some hid in closed carriages during funeral processions. One slave even had someone ship him in a box to the North. ▬ RI.4.3, RI.5.3

SECOND READ ## Analyze the Text

- Have students reread paragraphs 4–6. Then ask: *What is the main idea of paragraph 5?* The main idea of paragraph 5 is that abolitionists used railroad terms as a code. *What are some of the details given in the text?* Hiding places were called stations or depots. *Fugitives were called* freight. ▬ RI.4.2, RI.5.1

- Tell students to think about the risks that people took to help slaves escape to freedom. Then say: *Describe how sheltering fugitive slaves was dangerous. Include text evidence for support.* Neighbors could report them. Slave catchers could shoot them. Abolitionists could be fined or imprisoned for their work. ▬ RI.4.1, RI.5.1

- Review paragraphs 7–8 with students. Then ask: *What does the word* concealment *mean?* hiding *Which words and phrases in paragraph 8 provide clues to the meaning of* concealment? *The phrases* hide the slave, provided perfect disguises, *and* nail him into a box *all provide clues that the word* concealment *means* hiding. ▬ RI.4.4, RI.5.4

COMMON CORE

FIRST READ **Think Through the Text**

Have students use text evidence and draw inferences to answer questions.

paragraph 9 • *What was the purpose of Vigilance Committees?* *They gave protection to fugitives and raised money for clothing, food, and shelter.* *Which group was known for its humanitarianism?* *the Religious Society of Friends, or Quakers* **RI.4.1, RI.5.1**

paragraph 13 • *How were the techniques of the Underground Railroad used during the Civil War?* *Southern blacks and pro-Union whites helped Union prisoners escape back to the North. They used means of travel and disguises similar to those that fugitive slaves had used before the war.* **RI.4.3, RI.5.3**

SECOND READ **Analyze the Text**

• Have students reread paragraph 11. Then ask: *What is the main idea of this paragraph?* *The main idea is that some blacks who had already escaped slavery through the Underground Railroad went back to the South to rescue others.* *What are some of the details that support the main idea?* *Sample answer: One detail is that Harriet Tubman returned 19 times and brought out 300 fugitives on the underground line.* **RI.4.2, RI.5.1**

• Review paragraph 12. Then ask: *What did white Northerners and some white Southern abolitionists do to spread the word of the Underground Railroad?* *Northerners used disguises to hide their identities. They casually dropped the word of escape in black churches or while gossiping over a fence with workers in a field. Some Southerners risked going to prison to help fugitives.* **RI.4.1, RI.5.1**

Independent/Self-Selected Reading

Have students reread "Underground Railroad" independently to practice analyzing the text on their own, or have them practice the skills using another book. Suggested titles:

• *The Underground Railroad* by Ann Heinrichs

• *The Underground Railroad for Kids: From Slavery to Freedom* by Mary Kay Carson **RI.4.10, RI.5.10**

Performance Task

WRITE & PRESENT

1. Have small groups refer to the text to explain the way the author uses a main idea and details to explain the work of the Underground Railroad. **RI.4.2, RI.5.1**

2. Have individual students write a paragraph about one main idea in the article. Tell them to cite details and specific information from the text that support the main idea. **W.4.2, W.5.2**

3. Have students share their paragraphs in small groups and then edit their writing. **W.4.5, W.5.5**

4. Have individual students present their paragraphs to classmates. **SL.4.4, SL.5.4**

5. Students turn in their final paragraphs to the teacher.

See Copying Masters, pp. 144–147.

STUDENT CHECKLIST

Writing

☑ Explain how the author uses main ideas and details to give information.

☑ Provide reasons supported by facts and details from the text.

☑ Write in complete sentences.

☑ Use correct language conventions.

Speaking & Listening

☑ Engage effectively in collaborative conversations.

☑ Logically present claims and findings.

"The Echoing Green"

by William Blake (1789)

The Sun does arise,
And make happy the skies.
The merry bells ring,
To welcome the Spring.
The skylark and thrush,
The birds of the bush,
Sing louder around,
To the bells' cheerful sound,
While our sports shall be seen
On the Echoing Green.

Old John with white hair
Does laugh away care,
Sitting under the oak,
Among the old folk.
They laugh at our play,
And soon they all say,
"Such, such were the joys,
When we all girls and boys,
In our youth-time were seen
On the Echoing Green."

Till the little ones weary
No more can be merry;
The sun does descend,
And our sports have an end.
Round the laps of their mothers,
Many sisters and brothers,
Like birds in their nest,
Are ready for rest,
And sport no more seen
On the darkening Green.

"The New Colossus"

by Emma Lazarus (1883)

Not like the brazen giant of Greek fame,
With conquering limbs astride from land to land;
Here at our sea-washed, sunset gates shall stand
A mighty woman with a torch, whose flame
Is the imprisoned lightning, and her name
Mother of Exiles. From her beacon-hand
Glows world-wide welcome; her mild eyes command
The air-bridged harbor that twin cities frame.
"Keep, ancient lands, your storied pomp!" cries she
With silent lips. "Give me your tired, your poor,
Your huddled masses yearning to breathe free,
The wretched refuse of your teeming shore.
Send these, the homeless, tempest-tost to me,
I lift my lamp beside the golden door!"

"Casey at the Bat"

by Ernest Lawrence Thayer (1888)

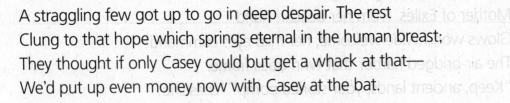

The outlook wasn't brilliant for the Mudville nine that day;
The score stood four to two with but one inning more to play.
And then when Cooney died at first, and Barrows did the same,
A sickly silence fell upon the patrons of the game.

A straggling few got up to go in deep despair. The rest
Clung to that hope which springs eternal in the human breast;
They thought if only Casey could but get a whack at that—
We'd put up even money now with Casey at the bat.

But Flynn preceded Casey, as did also Jimmy Blake,
And the former was a lulu and the later was a cake;
So upon that stricken multitude grim melancholy sat,
For there seemed but little chance of Casey's getting to the bat.

But Flynn let drive a single, to the wonderment of all,
And Blake, the much despised, tore the cover off the ball;
And when the dust had lifted, and the men saw what had occurred,
There was Johnnie safe at second and Flynn a-hugging third.

 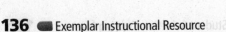

Then from 5,000 throats and more there rose a lusty yell;
It rumbled through the valley, it rattled in the dell;
It knocked upon the mountain and recoiled upon the flat,
For Casey, mighty Casey, was advancing to the bat.

There was ease in Casey's manner as he stepped into his place;
There was pride in Casey's bearing and a smile on Casey's face.
And when, responding to the cheers, he lightly doffed his hat,
No stranger in the crowd could doubt 'twas Casey at the bat.

Ten thousand eyes were on him as he rubbed his hands with dirt;
Five thousand tongues applauded when he wiped them on his shirt.
Then while the writhing pitcher ground the ball into his hip,
Defiance gleamed in Casey's eye, a sneer curled Casey's lip.

And now the leather-covered sphere came hurtling through the air,
And Casey stood a-watching it in haughty grandeur there.
Close by the sturdy batsman the ball unheeded sped—
"That ain't my style," said Casey. "Strike one," the umpire said.

From the benches, black with people, there went up a muffled roar,
Like the beating of the storm-waves on a stern and distant shore.
"Kill him! Kill the umpire!" shouted some one on the stand;
And it's likely they'd have killed him had not Casey raised his hand.

With a smile of Christian charity great Casey's visage shone;
He stilled the rising tumult: he bade the game go on;
He signaled to the pitcher, and once more the spheroid flew;
But Casey still ignored it, and the umpire said, "Strike two."

"Fraud," cried the maddened thousands, and echo answered fraud;
But one scornful look from Casey and the audience was awed.
They saw his face grown stern and cold, they saw his muscles strain,
And they knew that Casey wouldn't let that ball go by again.

The sneer is gone from Casey's lip, his teeth are clinched in hate;
He pounds with cruel violence his bat upon the plate.
And now the pitcher holds the ball, and now he lets it go,
And now the air is shattered by the force of Casey's blow.

Oh, somewhere in this favored land the sun is shining bright;
The band is playing somewhere, and somewhere hearts are light,
And somewhere men are laughing and somewhere children shout;
But there is no joy in Mudville—mighty Casey has struck out.

"A Bird Came Down the Walk"

by Emily Dickinson (1891)

A bird came down the walk:
He did not know I saw;
He bit an angle-worm in halves
And ate the fellow, raw.

And then he drank a dew
From a convenient grass,
And then hopped sidewise to the wall
To let a beetle pass.

He glanced with rapid eyes
That hurried all abroad,—
They looked like frightened beads, I thought;
He stirred his velvet head

Like one in danger; cautious,
I offered him a crumb,
And he unrolled his feathers
And rowed him softer home

Than oars divide the ocean,
Too silver for a seam,
Or butterflies, off banks of noon,
Leap, plashless, as they swim.

Academic Vocabulary

Alice's Adventures in Wonderland
blacking
coaxing
diligently
executed
hastily
hoarse
ignorant
impertinent
indignantly
languid
livery
melancholy
pity
quiver
spectacles
treacle

The Secret Garden
cautious
concealed
contrary
crooked
fantastically
ferociously
gnarled
indignantly
inquiringly
languid
peering
persevered
shrewd
smothering
triumphant
tyrannical

The Black Stallion
brusquely
clamored
contrary
crest
incredulous
inert
jarred
lurched
query
skeptical
slackened
surveyed
temperamental
tutelage

The Little Prince
abashed
abyss
asteroid
baobab
boa constrictor
dejection
encounters
essential
fragile
isolated
monarch
monotony
moralist
muzzle
naïve
resolute

Tuck Everlasting
blacksmith
bridle
brooch
constable
cross
dismay
flapjacks
gallows
haunted
marionette
melancholy
mingled
ordeal
pry
resentful
soothing

"Zlateh the Goat"
astonished
bored
chaos
exuded
imp
penetrated

M.C. Higgins, the Great
altered
anxious
contact
dread
festering
furtively
intense
lured
predicament
ravine
ripple
sensation
strutting
urgent

The Birchbark House

admonished
betrayed
bewilderment
dismay
envy
ferocious
ferocity
haughty
indignation
isolated
nimble
smallpox
surge
treaties

Bud, Not Buddy

bawling
commence
conscience
devoured
dignity
festering
insinuating
lavatory
paltry
provoked
resourceful
shunned
stricken
suspicious

Where the Mountain Meets the Moon

chagrined
daunting
engrossed
flourished
hospitality
immortals
implored
impulsive
intricate
malevolence
manipulation
subdued
vaguely

"The Echoing Green"

echoing
green
sports

"Casey at the Bat"

tumult
unheeded
visage

"A Bird Came Down the Walk"

angle-worm
plashless

"Fog"

harbor
haunches

"Dust of Snow"

hemlock
rued

"Little Red Riding Hood and the Wolf"

decent
leer
knickers

Discovering Mars: The Amazing Story of the Red Planet

bombarded
broadcast
conquest
fanciful
immense
mammoth
menace

Let's Investigate Marvelously Meaningful Maps

accurately
ancestors
cargoes
dimensions
foreign
loot
lot
mule
reproduced
rival
satellites

Hurricanes: Earth's Mightiest Storms

ablaze
barreling
bucked
bulge
eerie
equator
evacuate
looters
migrant
mooring
rotation
seized
suburbs
trend
wreckage

The Kid's Guide to Money: Earning It, Saving It, Spending It, Growing It, Sharing It

boutiques
charities
counterfeit
debt
inventory
matures
mechanized
phony
privileges
reap
technique
vault
walloping

Toys!: Amazing Stories Behind Some Great Inventions

converted
decay
devices
engineer
evolved
flop
inspiration
ironically
novelty
patented
standard
strategy
synthetic
tokens
trivial
versions

"Good Pet, Bad Pet"

affectionate
allergic
captivity
sprawl
unpredictable
vet

"Ancient Mound Builders"

coordinated
depleted
diverse
latter
legacy
vehicle

About Time: A First Look at Time and Clocks

accuracy
adjacent
complicated
monumental
precision
varied

England the Land

conquered
fertile
residence
upgrading

A History of US: The First Americans

abundant
accomplishment
adjust
aghast
agog
brutality
conquer
efficient
fierce
leisure
pyramids
revenge
terror
vast
villains

My Librarian Is a Camel: How Books Are Brought to Children Around the World

access
avid
inspire
isolated
mobile
remote

Horses
accurate
barges
chariots
mallet
medieval
offspring
sensitive
shod
specifically

Quest for the Tree Kangaroo: An Expedition to the Cloud Forest of New Guinea
ambassadors
caked
coordinator
endangered
endurance
expeditions
hazards
quest
rarest
slopes
solar
survive
track
venom

Volcanoes
advancing
billow
destructive
spouted
weathered

We Are the Ship: The Story of Negro League Baseball
ammunition
barrier
consistent
eloquent
integrate
legendary
prohibited
rival
stance

"Kenya's Long Dry Season"
crisis
shrivel
toll

"Seeing Eye to Eye"
artificial
beady
image
scatters

"Telescopes"
celestial
composition
emitted
minute
tedious
vital

"Underground Railroad"
authorities
cunning
hostile
infuriated
precautions
pursuers
vanished

Grade 4 Writing Checklist

Name _____

In my writing, did I . . .

Opinion	Informative	Narrative
☐ introduce my topic or book?	☐ clearly introduce my topic?	☐ tell about a real or imagined experience?
☐ state my opinion with reasons?	☐ group information logically and use headings, illustrations, and multimedia, if useful?	☐ use clear sequence and effective technique, including a conclusion or ending?
☐ organize information into a structure that makes sense?	☐ develop my topic with facts, definitions, and other details, examples, and information?	☐ include a situation or problem and introduce a narrator and characters?
☐ link my opinion and reasons with words and phrases?	☐ use clear language, linking words, and domain-specific vocabulary?	☐ include descriptive details and dialogue?
☐ write a concluding sentence or section?	☐ include a closing statement or section?	☐ use transitional words to show sequence?
☐ use correct grammar, spelling, and punctuation?	☐ use correct grammar, spelling, and punctuation?	☐ use correct grammar, spelling, and punctuation?

Other
☐
☐
☐
☐

Name _____

Grade 4 Speaking and Listening Checklist

In my speaking, did I . . .

- ☐ come to discussions prepared?
- ☐ use my preparation to explore ideas?
- ☐ explain my ideas as they relate to the discussion?
- ☐ make comments that link to the remarks of others?
- ☐ report on a topic or book, tell a story, or recount an experience with facts and details?
- ☐ speak so others could understand me?
- ☐ add recordings and visual displays when appropriate?
- ☐ use formal or informal English as appropriate to the task and situation?

In my listening, did I . . .

- ☐ follow rules for discussions?
- ☐ listen to others?
- ☐ pose and respond to questions to clarify or follow up?
- ☐ paraphrase a text read aloud or information presented in different media?
- ☐ identify reasons and evidence speakers provide to support their points?

Other

- ☐
- ☐
- ☐

Name _____

Grade 5 Writing Checklist

In my writing, did I . . .

Opinion	Informative	Narrative
☐ introduce my topic or book?	☐ clearly introduce my topic?	☐ tell about a real or imagined experience?
☐ state my opinion with reasons?	☐ group information logically and use formatting, illustrations, and multimedia, if useful?	☐ use clear sequence and effective technique, including a conclusion or ending?
☐ organize information into a structure that makes sense?	☐ develop my topic with facts, definitions, and other details, quotations, and information?	☐ include a situation or problem and introduce a narrator and characters?
☐ link my opinion and reasons with words, phrases, and clauses?	☐ use clear language, linking words, and domain-specific vocabulary?	☐ include descriptive details and dialogue?
☐ write a concluding sentence or section?	☐ include a closing statement or section?	☐ use transitional words to show sequence?
☐ use correct grammar, spelling, and punctuation?	☐ use correct grammar, spelling, and punctuation?	☐ use correct grammar, spelling, and punctuation?

Other
☐
☐
☐

Name _____

Grade 5 Speaking and Listening Checklist

In my speaking, did I . . .

☐	come to discussions prepared?
☐	use my preparation to explore ideas?
☐	make comments that contribute to the discussion?
☐	draw conclusions from the discussions?
☐	report on a topic or text or present an opinion, sequencing ideas and using facts and details?
☐	speak so others could understand me?
☐	add multimedia components and visuals when appropriate?
☐	adapt my speech to the task and situation, using formal English as appropriate?

In my listening, did I . . .

☐	follow rules for discussions?
☐	pose and respond to questions by making comments?
☐	summarize a text read aloud?
☐	summarize the points a speaker makes?
☐	identify reasons and evidence speakers provide to support their points?

Other

☐	
☐	
☐	

Performance Rubric

Use this rubric to evaluate writing and performance tasks.

	Focus and Support	**Organization and Structure**
Score 6	**6** The writing is focused and supported by facts or details.	**6** The writing has a clear introduction and conclusion (or beginning and ending). Ideas are clearly organized.
Score 5	**5** The writing is mostly focused and supported by facts or details.	**5** The writing has an introduction and a conclusion. Ideas are mostly organized.
Score 4	**4** The writing is mostly focused and supported by some facts or details.	**4** The writing has an introduction and a conclusion. Most ideas are organized.
Score 3	**3** Some of the writing is focused and supported by some facts or details.	**3** The writing has an introduction or a conclusion but might be missing one. Some ideas are organized.
Score 2	**2** The writing is not focused and is supported by few facts or details.	**2** The writing might not have an introduction or a conclusion. Few ideas are organized.
Score 1	**1** The writing is not focused or supported by facts or details.	**1** The writing is missing an introduction and a conclusion. Few or no ideas are organized.

Word Choice and Voice	Language Conventions
6 Ideas are linked with words, phrases, and clauses. Words are specific. The voice connects with the reader in a unique way.	**6** The writing has no errors in spelling, grammar, capitalization, or punctuation. There is a variety of sentences.
5 Most ideas are linked with words, phrases, and clauses. Words are specific. The voice connects with the reader.	**5** The writing has few errors in spelling, grammar, capitalization, or punctuation. There is some variety of sentences.
4 Some ideas are linked with words, phrases, and clauses. Some words are specific. The voice connects with the reader.	**4** The writing has some errors in spelling, grammar, capitalization, or punctuation. There is some variety of sentences.
3 Some ideas are linked with words, phrases, or clauses. Few words are specific. The voice may connect with the reader.	**3** The writing has some errors in spelling, grammar, capitalization, or punctuation. There is little variety of sentences.
2 Ideas may be linked with words, phrases, or clauses. Few words are specific. The voice may connect with the reader.	**2** The writing has many errors in spelling, grammar, capitalization, or punctuation. There is little variety of sentences. Some sentences are incomplete.
1 Ideas may not be linked with words, phrases, or clauses. No words are specific. The voice does not connect with the reader.	**1** The writing has many errors in spelling, grammar, capitalization, or punctuation. There is no variety of sentences. Sentences are incomplete.

Bibliography

Babbitt, Natalie. *Tuck Everlasting.* New York: Sunburst, 1975

Banting, Erinn. *England the Land.* St. Catherines, ON: Crabtree, 2012

Berger, Melvin. *Discovering Mars: The Amazing Story of the Red Planet.* Illustrated by Joan Holub. New York: Scholastic, 1992

Blake, William. "The Echoing Green." *Wider than the Sky: Poems to Grow Up With.* Collected and edited by Scott Elledge. New York: HarperCollins, 1990

Buckmaster, Henrietta. "Underground Railroad." Reviewed by Megan McClard. *The New Book of Knowledge.* Grolier Online http://nbk.grolier.com/ncpage?tn=encyc/article.html&id=a2030230-h&type=0ta

Burnett, Frances Hodgson. *The Secret Garden.* Illustrated by Tasha Tudor. New York: HarperCollins, 1938 (1911)

Carlisle, Madelyn Wood. *Let's Investigate Marvelously Meaningful Maps.* Illustrated by Yvette Santiago Banek. Happauge, NY: Barron's, 1992

Carroll, Lewis. *Alice's Adventures in Wonderland.* Illustrated by John Tenniel. New York: William Morrow, 1992 (1866)

Curtis, Christopher Paul. *Bud, Not Buddy.* New York: Delacorte, 1999

Cutler, Nellie Gonzalez. "Kenya's Long Dry Season." *Time for Kids.* September 25, 2009: 6

Dahl, Roald. "Little Red Riding Hood and the Wolf." *Roald Dahl's Revolting Rhymes.* Illustrated by Quentin Blake. New York: Knopf, 1982

Dickinson, Emily. "A Bird Came Down the Walk." *Poems for Youth.* Edited by Alfred Leete Hampson. Illustrated by Thomas B. Allen. Boston: Little, Brown, 1934 (1918)

Erdich, Louise. *The Birchbark House.* New York: Hyperion, 1999

Farley, Walter. *The Black Stallion.* New York: Bullseye, 1969 (1941)

Frost, Robert. "Dust of Snow." *Julie Andrews' Collection of Poems, Songs, and Lullabies.* Selected by Julie Andrews and Emma Walton Hamilton. Paintings by James McMullan. New York: Little, Brown, 2009

Hakim, Joy. *A History of US: The First Americans (Book One).* New York: Oxford University Press, 1993

Hall, Leslie. "Seeing Eye to Eye." *National Geographic Explorer.* September 2009. http://magma.nationalgeographic.com/ngexplorer/0909/articles/mainarticle.html

Hamilton, Virginia. *M. C. Higgins, the Great.* New York: Macmillan, 1974

Kavash, E. Barrie. "Ancient Mount Builders" in *Discover American History*, ed. Meg Chorlian (Peru, IL: Cobblestone, October 2003), 6

Koscielniak, Bruce. *About Time: A First Look at Time and Clocks.* Boston: Houghton Mifflin, 2004

Lauber, Patricia. *Hurricanes: Earth's Mightiest Storms.* New York: Scholastic, 1996

Lazarus, Emma. "The New Colossus." *Favorite Poems: Old and New.* Selected by Helen Ferris. Illustrated by Leonard Weisgard. New York: Doubleday, 1957

Lin, Grace. *Where the Mountain Meets the Moon.* New York: Little, Brown, 2009

Montgomery, Sy. *Quest for the Tree Kangaroo: An Expedition to the Cloud Forest of New Guinea.* Photographs by Nic Bishop. Boston: Sandpiper, 2006

Mora, Pat. "Words Free As Confetti." *Confetti: Poems for Children.* Illustrated by Enrique O. Sanchez. New York: Lee & Low, 1996

Nelson, Kadir. *We Are the Ship: The Story of Negro League Baseball.* New York: Jump at the Sun, 2008

Nichols, Grace. "They Were My People." *Come on into My Tropical Garden: Poems for Children.* Illustrations by Caroline Binch. New York: Lippincott, 1988

Otfinoski, Steve. *The Kid's Guide to Money: Earning It, Saving It, Spending It, Growing It, Sharing It.* Illustrated by Kelly Kennedy. New York: Scholastic, 1996

Ronan, Colin A. "Telescopes." Reviewed by William A. Gutsch. *The New Book of Knowledge*. Grolier Online http://nbk.grolier.com/ncpage?tn=encyc/article.html&id=a2028880-h&type=0ta

Ruurs, Margriet. *My Librarian Is a Camel: How Books Are Brought to Children Around the World*. Honesdale, PA: Boyds Mills, 2005

Saint-Exupéry, Antoine de. *The Little Prince*. San Diego: Harcourt Brace Jovanovich, 1961 (1943)

Sandburg, Carl. "Fog." *The Complete Poems of Carl Sandburg*. New York: Harcourt Brace, 1970

Schleichert, Elizabeth. "Good Pet, Bad Pet" *Ranger Rick*. June, 2002. 27-31

Simon, Seymour. *Horses*. New York: HarperCollins, 2006

Simon, Seymour. *Volcanoes*. New York: Morrow Junior Books, 1988

Singer, Isaac Bashevis. "Zlateh the Goat" in *Zlateh the Goat and Other Stories*, Pictures by Maurice Sendak (New York: HarperCollins, 1994 (1966), 79

Thayer, Ernest Lawrence. "Casey at the Bat." Illustrated by C. F. Payne. New York: Simon & Schuster, 2003 (1888)

Wulffson, Don. *Toys!: Amazing Stories Behind Some Great Inventions*. Illustrated by Laurie Keller. New York: Henry Holt, 2000

Internet Resources

Use the following websites to locate additional resources for teaching the exemplar texts. Check the website for your state's department of education for specific information on the implementation of the Common Core State Standards.

http://aasl.jesandco.org/

http://www.achieve.org/achieving-common-core

http://www.achievethecore.org/

http://www.ascd.org/common-core-state-standards/common-core.aspx

http://www.ccsso.org/documents/2012/common_core_resources.pdf

http://www.corestandards.org/

http://www.engagingeducators.com/

http://www.ncte.org/standards/commoncore

http://www.ode.state.or.us/wma/teachlearn/commoncore/ela-publishers-criteria.pdf

http://www.parcconline.org/

http://www.reading.org/Resources/ResourcesByTopic/CommonCore-resourcetype/CommonCore-rt-resources.aspx

http://www.smarterbalanced.org/

https://www.teachingchannel.org/videos?categories=topics_common-core